KARL MARX AND THE CLASSICS

Karl Marx and the Classics
An Essay on Value, Crises and the Capitalist Mode of Production

John Milios

Dimitri Dimoulis

George Economakis

LONDON AND NEW YORK

First published 2002 by Ashgate Publishing

Reissued 2018 by Routledge
2 Park Square, Milton Park, Abingdon, Oxon OX14 4RN
711 Third Avenue, New York, NY 10017, USA

Routledge is an imprint of the Taylor & Francis Group, an informa business

Copyright © John Milios, Dimitri Dimoulis and George Economakis 2002

All rights reserved. No part of this book may be reprinted or reproduced or utilised in any form or by any electronic, mechanical, or other means, now known or hereafter invented, including photocopying and recording, or in any information storage or retrieval system, without permission in writing from the publishers.

Notice:
Product or corporate names may be trademarks or registered trademarks, and are used only for identification and explanation without intent to infringe.

Publisher's Note
The publisher has gone to great lengths to ensure the quality of this reprint but points out that some imperfections in the original copies may be apparent.

Disclaimer
The publisher has made every effort to trace copyright holders and welcomes correspondence from those they have been unable to contact.

A Library of Congress record exists under LC control number: 2001095433

ISBN 13: 978-1-138-72593-5 (hbk)
ISBN 13: 978-1-138-72590-4 (pbk)
ISBN 13: 978-1-315-19165-2 (ebk)

Contents

Preface vii

PART I: VALUE AND MONEY

1 Introduction: On the Object of Marx's "Critique of Political Economy"   3

2 Marx Versus Ricardo (Marx's Theory of Value)   13

3 Money and Capital (Marx's Theory of Money and the Circuit of Capital)   36

PART II: THEORY OF VALUE AND IDEOLOGY

4 The Question of "Commodity Fetishism"   67

PART III: THEORY OF VALUE AND PRICES: MARX'S AMBIVALENCE TOWARDS CLASSICAL POLITICAL ECONOMY

5 Social Capital and the General Rate of Profit   111

6 Theory of Value and Ground Rent (Smith-Ricardo-Marx: Converges and Disputes)   131

PART IV: THE CIRCUIT OF SOCIAL CAPITAL, THE PROFIT RATE AND THE ECONOMIC CRISES

7   The "Law of the Falling Tendency in the Rate of Profit"   145

8   The Historic Marxist Controversy on Economic Crises and its Theoretical Significance   158

9   Defining a Marxist Theory of "Overaccumulation Crises"   190

10   Epilogue: On the Character of Marxian Theory, "Ricardian Marxism" and the Role of F. Engels   206

   Bibliography   215

   Index   226

Preface

Marx developed his economic theory, under the rubric of *A Critique of Political Economy*, mainly in the period 1857-67. It is a well-defined system, structured as a logical array of original concepts and analyses based on Marx's notions of *value* and *surplus-value*. Marxian economics emerged from Marx's earlier historic-sociological analyses and is formulated along with a new methodological approach.

However, from the moment of Marx's death, it had already become apparent that Marxist theory and Marxist economic analysis would accommodate not only one interpretation, and do not evolve on the basis of a single, and unique, theoretical direction. On the contrary, the existence of Marxism is always interwoven with the formation of various Marxist trends or schools, which as a rule are constructed at the base of contradictory and opposed theoretical principles, positions and deductions. This phenomenon is universal, and has taken place in all of the countries where Marxism was developed.

The contradictory picture of Marxist theory can be partly interpreted by its conflictual and revolutionary character, i.e. by the fact that it is constituted as a critique to the established economic and social order and the ruling forms of ideology that aim to consolidate it. In its struggle with the ruling theoretical disciplines, Marxist theory often intertwines with it, in the means that certain bourgeoisie ideological forms are being reproduced within Marxist analysis. At the same time, the development of Marxist theory is affected by the political conjuncture, as Marxism, besides a theoretical discipline becomes also a mass ideology of the Left, influencing the modes in which theory develops.

The above mean, on the one hand, that Marxist theory acquires the form of a necessarily conflicting and schismatic science, and on the other, that the Marxist economist, social scientist or researcher should take a position in the conflict, the object of which is Marxist theory itself.

However, universal is the belief among Marxists that there is only one authentic interpretation of Marx's writings, the one shared by the person (or school) stating the argument.

The authors of the present book share the opinion that the schismatic character of Marxist theory shall also be attributed to the contradictory character of Marx's mature economic writings themselves, as Marx did not remain consistent to his own theoretical system of the *Critique of Political Economy*, i.e. to his *rupture* with the Ricardian value theory of "labour expended", but often slipped back to the Ricardian system of thought.

Marx's *Critique of Political Economy* constitutes not a "correction" of Classical Political Economy's "mistakes" or "misunderstandings", but the formation of a new theoretical domain, shaping thus a new theoretical object of analysis and a new theoretical "paradigm" of argumentation. Unlike the Ricardian, Marx's theory of value is a *monetary theory*. The value of a commodity cannot be determined as such, but only through its *form of appearance*; it cannot be determined in isolation but only in relation with all other commodities in the *exchange process*. This exchange-value relation is materialised by *money*. In Marx's system, no other "material embodiment" of (abstract) labour and no other quantitatively defined form of appearance (or measure) of value can exist. As money comprises the only *form of appearance* of value, both quantities do not belong to the same level of abstraction. In other words, they are *incommensurable*, and consequently they cannot be the subject of quantitative comparisons and mathematical calculations. In Marx's system, value does not belong to the world of empirically detectable (and measurable) quantities; only money does.

Marx formulated the arguments of his theoretical rupture with the Ricardian theory of value mainly in the *Manuscripts 1857-58*, (first published in 1939-41 as *Grundrisse, Foundations of the Critique of Political Economy*), in his *A Contribution to the Critique of Political Economy* (first published 1859) and in Volume 1 of *Capital* (first published 1867). The same arguments are also to be found in his other works of the period (the *Manuscript 1861-63*, a part of which was first published during the period 1905-10 under the title *Theories of Surplus Value*, and the *Manuscript 1863-65*, containing all drafts of Volumes 2 and 3 of *Capital* which were edited and first published by Engels in 1885 and 1894 respectively).

However, he used a highly abstract and mainly philosophical mode of presentation, which makes the comprehension of his theory rather difficult.

More important, in his writings of the period 1861-65, Marx becomes ambivalent towards Classical Political Economy. He repeatedly retreats to the Ricardian theory of value, thus abandoning his own theoretical system of the *Critique of Political Economy*.

Summarizing our argument we may say that Marx's economic writings comprise two different *discourses*:

a) The theoretical system of the *Critique of Political Economy*, which is mainly developed (albeit in a "philosophical" way of presentation, which makes its understanding not easy) in the first part of Volume 1 of *Capital*, in the 1859 *Contribution to the Critique of Political Economy*, in the *Grundrisse* and is repeated in his other works; and,

b) a sophisticated version of the Ricardian Political Economy of value as "labour expended", which is to be found mainly in sections of Volume 3 of *Capital*, such as the "Transformation of Commodity Values into Prices of Production" or the theory of "Absolute Ground-Rent" and at other parts of his 1861-65 writings. This second discourse seems to have influenced most contemporary approaches to Marxist value theory.

In *Part I* of the present Book (*Value and Money*) we reconstruct what we consider to be the first discourse, i.e. the tenets of Marx's theoretical system of the *Critique of Political Economy*, which was formed on the basis of a rupture with Ricardian Political Economy.

In *Part II* (*Theory of Value and Ideology*) we illustrate the conceptual problems arising with respect to ideology and the capitalist power relations from Marx's way of presentation of his value theory, and more specifically from the way that he introduces the concept of capital and the capitalist mode of production.

In *Part III* (*Theory of Value and Prices. Marx's Ambivalence towards Classical Political Economy*) we critically illustrate what we consider to be the second discourse in Marx's writings, which adheres to the Classical tradition of Political Economy.

Finally, in *Part IV* of the book (*The Circuit of Social Capital, the Profit Rate and Economic Crises*) we make use of our theoretical conclusions from the previous Parts, to focus on subjects such as crisis theory, instability, and the Circuit of Social Capital, which are related, on the one hand, to the present economic conjuncture, and on the other, to modern debates on value and Marxian economic theory.

Dimitri Dimoulis would like to thank the Universidade Bandeirante (São Paulo, Brazil) for supporting and funding a Research Project on *Law and the Economy*. All authors express their thanks to Howard Engelskirchen, Spyros Lapatsioras and Dimitris Sotiropoulos who have read and commented on this book. The errors that might remain are of course theirs.

John Milios
Dimitri Dimoulis
George Economakis.

PART I:
VALUE AND MONEY

1 Introduction: On the Object of Marx's "Critique of Political Economy"

1. Marx's Mature Economic Writings

The aim of this introductory chapter is to compendiously illustrate the position that Marx's mature economic writings acquire in the author's overall theoretical work, in order then to posit the questions, which this book will try to investigate: the relation of Marx's theoretical analysis to Classical economic theory on the one hand, and its significance as a tool for gaining an insight into contemporary capitalist economies on the other.

As stated in the Preface, Marx's mature economic writings contain the following works: the *Manuscripts 1857-58*, (*Grundrisse, Foundations of the Critique of Political Economy* – Marx 1993, MEGA II, 1.1); the book *A Contribution to the Critique of Political Economy* (Marx 1971, MEGA II, 1.2); the *Manuscript 1861-63* (comprising nearly 2,500 printed pages – MEGA II, 3.1-3.6, a part of which was published as the *Theories of Surplus Value* – Marx 1971); the *Manuscripts 1863-67* (containing all drafts of the three volumes of *Capital. A Critique of Political Economy* –MEGA II, 4.1 and 4.2); and Volume one of *Capital* (first published in 1867 –MEGA II, 5). In the second (1872-73) edition of Volume one of *Capital* (Marx 1990), Marx revised Part one of the book, entitled "Commodities and Money". Volumes two and three of *Capital* were edited and published by Engels in 1885 (Marx 1992) and 1894 (Marx 1991) respectively.

2. The Theoretical Background: Marx's Theory of History (Class Struggle and the Modes of Production)

The economic theory of Marx is firmly embedded in his theory of History as the *theory of class struggles*, which he had formulated and developed jointly with Frederick Engels since the mid 1840s.

Starting from his *Theses on Feurbach* (1845), Marx rejects the entire tradition of theoretical-philosophical humanism (the conception that the individual or human nature determines the form and the evolution pattern of societies). He wrote: "Feuerbach resolves the religious essence into the human essence. But the human essence is no abstraction inherent in each single individual. In its reality it is the ensemble of the social relations" (6th Thesis on Feuerbach). On this basis Marx formulated his concept of class struggle as the motive force of social evolution: "The history of all hitherto existing society is the history of class struggles" (*The Communist Manifesto*, Marx-Engels 1985: 79).

This approach creates certain relations of theoretical rupture but also continuity between Marx's analyses and Classical Political Economy:

On the one hand, Marx draws away from all forms of humanist-anthropological foundation of Political Economy, which comprehend commodity exchange and the social division of labour as the outcome of human nature;[1] on the other hand, however, he adopts the definition of classes introduced by Classical Political Economy, as a point of departure for the formulation of his own class-theory:[2] The specific position that each "individual" acquires in the social relations of production constitutes the initial condition which determines their class integration.

Marx, however, is not restricted to this position. He identifies, isolates, and develops the "relationist element" which contains the position of the Classical Economists, and in this way, he formulates *a new theory of social relations*, and of classes as the main element of these relations. Marx developed the position of the Classical Political Economists in two directions (see also Milios 2000):

a) He demonstrated the element of class antagonism, of the conflicting interests between the main classes of capitalist society and particularly between the capitalists and wage-labourers. Even further, he grasped the unity between the competing classes of society, the unity and coherence of society, in terms of social-class power:

Power no longer constitutes the "right of the sovereign," or the "power of the state" in relation to (equal and free) citizens, but a specific form of *class* domination. Power is always class power, the power of one class, (or a coalition of classes), of the ruling class, over the other, the dominated classes of society. This power, which stabilises on the basis of dominant social structures, is reproduced within class antagonism, within the struggle of the classes. The specific unity of society is, therefore, inseparable from the unity of the specific class power, which is insured within the class struggle.[3]

The Marxist theory of History thus constitutes a theory of class power within class struggle. The classes are defined exclusively on the field of class struggle (Poulantzas 1973 and 1973-a). This means that the classes shall be perceived mainly as *social relations and practices* and not as "groups of individuals". Class practices have therefore, according to Marxist theory, an objective dimension, independently of whether or not there is the capacity (in each circumstance) to acquire consciousness of their common social interests, of those who are part of classes that are oppressed and subject to exploitation. In fact, a crucial element of class power is its capacity to avert the realisation of common class interests by those who belong to classes that are being dominated or are sustaining economic exploitation (Dimoulis 1994).[4]

b) Parallel to the construction of the theory of class power, within the context of class struggle, Marx perceives that specific societies consist of a mosaic of social - class relations, which do not all belong to the same type of social coherence (the same type of class power). They constitute, rather, the specific historical result of the evolution of society, which, as a rule allows the "survival" of elements with roots to previous types of social organisation, to previous historical systems of class power (e.g. feudalism).

Marx seeks and isolates, in this way, those elements of social relations which: 1) Comprise the specific difference of capitalism, and discerns this from the corresponding elements of other types of class domination (and of the corresponding social organisation). 2) Constitute the permanent, "unaltered" nucleus of the capitalist system of class domination, independently from the particular evolution of each specifically studied (capitalist) society. This means that to each specific type of economic domination and exploitation corresponds to a *specific type* of organisation of political power and the domination of a *specific type* of ideological forms.[5]

Thus a new theoretical object emerges: the (capitalist) *mode of production*. On the basis of the theoretical analysis of the mode of production, each particular class society can thus be studied in depth (each particular class social formation).

3. The Capitalist Mode of Production as the Keystone of Marx's Analysis of the Capitalist Economy and Society

The notion of the capitalist mode of production refers to the causal *nucleus* of the *totality* of capitalist power relations, the fundamental social-class interdependencies which define a system of social power (a society) as a capitalist system.

It is established in the *capital-relation* initially on the level of production: in the separation of the worker from the means of production (who is thus transformed into a wage-labourer, possessor only of his labour-force) and in the full ownership of the production means by the capitalist: the capitalist has both the power to place into operation the means of production (which was not the case in pre-capitalist modes of production) as well as the power to acquire the final surplus product.

The (capitalist) mode of production does not, however, constitute exclusively an economic relation but refers to all of the social levels (instances). In this is also contained the core of (capitalist) political and ideological relations of power. In it, there is thus articulated the particular structure of the capitalist state. Consequently, it is revealed that the capitalist class possesses not only the economic, but also the *political power;* not because the capitalists man the highest political offices of the state, but because the structure of the political element in capitalist societies, and more especially of the capitalist state (its hierarchical - bureaucratic organisation, its "classless" function on the basis of the rule of Law etc.) corresponds to and insures the preservation and reproduction of the entire capitalist class domination. Similarly it becomes apparent that the structure of the dominant bourgeoisie *ideology* (the ideology of individual rights and equal rights, of national unity and of the common interest, etc.) corresponds to the perpetuation and the reproduction of the capitalist social order and of the long-term interests of the capitalist class. The dominant ideology thus constitutes a process of consolidation of capitalist class interests, precisely through its materialisation as a "modus vivendi," as a "way of life" not only of the ruling, but in an altered form, of the ruled classes as well.[6]

In order that the labourer is transformed into a wage-earner, the "ruler" must give way to the modern constitutional state and his "subjects" must be transformed, on the judicial-political level, into free citizens:

> This worker must be free in the double sense that as a free individual he can dispose of his labour-power as his own commodity, and that, on the other

hand, he has no other commodity for sale, i.e. he is rid of them, he is free of all the objects needed for the realisation of his labour-power (Marx 1990: 272-73).

In pre-capitalist modes of production, in contrast, the ownership of the means of production on the ruling class was never complete. The ruling class had under its *property* the means of production, i.e. it acquired the surplus product, but the working-ruled classes still maintained the "real appropriation" (Poulantzas 1973: 26) of the means of production (the power to put them into operation). This fact is connected to significant corresponding characteristics in the structure of the political and ideological social levels as well. Economic exploitation, that is the extraction of the surplus product from the labourer had as its complementary element *direct political coercion*: the relations of political dependence between the dominant and the dominated, and their ideological (as rule, religious) articulation,[7] which results in shaping certain forms of consensus of those subjected to exploitation towards the existing social order, thus reducing the use of direct violence by those possessing power.

The mode of production, therefore, describes the *specific difference* of a system of class domination and class exploitation. In a given society there may exist more modes (and forms) of production, and therefore a complex class configuration. The articulation of different modes of production is contradictory and is always accomplished under the domination of one particular mode of production.[8] The domination of one mode of production (and particularly of the capitalist mode of production) is connected to the tendency toward the dissolution of all the other *competing* modes of production.

The question posited by Marxist analysis is under what conditions pre-capitalist social structures are replaced by the capitalist mode of production, or to what extent they may constitute an impediment to capitalist development. Many authors have portrayed Marx as an advocate of a "linear evolutionism", according to which all countries will inevitably go through the same stages of economic and social evolution, from pre-capitalist forms to developed capitalism, culminating in socialism. Although such formulations can be found in the work of Marx and Engels, the "linear evolutionism" does not prevail in the economic writings of Marx's maturity. Marx recognises mainly the *possibility of capitalism* emerging as a *consequence of class struggle* and he outlined the prerequisites for such a historical development. The final domination or the deflection of this tendency is not a given a priori; its outcome is always determined by existing social relations of power. In most cases, the break-up of the pre-capitalist modes of production takes the form of agricultural reform, precisely since it involves modes of production, which are mainly based on pre-capitalist property relations in the land (Milios 1989).[9]

4. The Question of Value Theory

As argued above, the socio-economic concept of the (capitalist) mode of production modifies the Classical theory of economy and social classes, and constitutes the basis of Marx's unique theory of History (as the history of class struggles). Furthermore, it is formulated, from the first moment of its introduction, on the view that the economy forms the basis, in the last instance, of the whole class society – with property relations vis-à-vis the means of production the keystone of class identity: "Capital [is] that kind of property which exploits wage labour, and which cannot increase except upon conditions of begetting a new supply of wage labour for fresh exploitation" (Marx-Engels 1985: 96-7).

This explains why Marx always considered economic theory to be the foundation of his whole theoretical edifice. In this framework, Marx needed to formulate a *value theory* in order to vindicate his theory of class exploitation and his key-notion, the capitalist mode of production. However, until 1857 Marx had not yet developed his own value theory. His whole analysis of class struggle, class exploitation and the capitalist mode of production was thus initially derived from the Ricardian theory of value. In 1847 he wrote:

> Ricardo expounded scientifically (...) the theory of present-day society, of bourgeois society (...) Ricardo shows us the real movement of bourgeois production, which constitutes value. (...) The determination of value by labour time, is, for Ricardo, the law of exchange value (...) Ricardo establishes the truth of his formula by deriving it from all economic relations, and by explaining in this way all phenomena, even those like ground rent, accumulation of capital and the relation of wages to profits, which at first sight seems to contradict it; it is precisely that which makes his doctrine a scientific system (Marx-internet, *The Poverty of Philosophy*, Chapter 1: A scientific discovery).

Introduction: On the Object of Marx's "Critique of Political Economy" 9

Marx's rupture with the humanist-anthropological premises of Classical Political Economy seemed to merge well with the Classical (Ricardian) value theory. According to the main postulate of the Classical (Ricardian) theory of value as "labour expended", commodities are exchanged with each other at relative quantities reflecting the relative quantities of labour necessary for their production. Consequently, the value of each commodity corresponds to the quantity of labour bestowed on its production.

However, even at that time, this Classical (Ricardian) value theory had been theoretically destabilised by an unsolved internal contradiction: Its inability to cope with the empirical fact of the existence of a uniform general rate of profit in the capitalist economy, given the fact that individual enterprises in different production sectors generally comprise different value compositions (i.e. equal quantities of labour set into motion unequal quantities of capital, see Chapter 4 of this book).

As we will try to elucidate in Chapters 2 and 3 of this book, Marx overturned after 1857 this Classical value theory (value being identified with "labour expended") not only in his effort to overcome its internal theoretical contradictions, but mainly as a result of the fact that he conceived value (and the capitalist mode of production) in a non empiricist way, as the causal determinations ("laws") which regulate the empirically detectable phenomena. These causal determinations (the "law of value") do not belong to the level of tangible reality, in the same way that the law of gravity will never "appear" as such, but will always become valid through its effects on the motion of material bodies, functioning as a cause which can be scientifically identified and thus used for the explanation of physical phenomena.

5. The Object of Marx's Critique of Political Economy: Preliminary Remarks

Like every theoretical system of thought, Political Economy is constituted in relation to a *theoretical object of analysis*, which is different from the corresponding non-theoretical terms or notions, by means of which the empirically specific objects of investigation may be approached.[10]

The theoretical object of analysis is either a *complex notion*, as is the case in mathematical and physical sciences, or an *abstraction* that isolates what is considered to be the significant element of observable reality. The theoretical object of Political Economy is not (and cannot be) "the economy in general", but that specific notion which is considered to build the *specific difference* of (capitalist) economic relations. In this sense, the object of analysis is also a *theoretical tool* for the interpretation of all further aspects of economic reality. The formation of a theoretical object of analysis is thus the constitutive act of the formulation of (each) theory.

It is clear then from the schismatic character of social sciences in general and of Political Economy in particular (see Preface), that each different theoretical stream of thought must formulate its own theoretical object of analysis: In the case of the Classical School of Political Economy the theoretical object of analysis is *labour value*, which for Ricardo is identified with "labour expended". The contestation of the tenets of Classical (Ricardian) Political Economy by Neoclassical economics led to a change in the object of theoretical analysis: *marginal utility* (as the determinant factor in the formation of prices and the "market economy") emerged as the "new" theoretical object of analysis.

The Neoclassical constitutive notion of *marginal utility* does not derive from any form of social theory, either economic or sociological. It only constructs a (supposed) relationship between the individual and useful objects (i.e. use-values). In this sense, the isolated individual is supposed to represent the whole society. Society, as a theoretical notion, is absorbed by *the* individual, whose "nature" is considered to be nothing more than the "principle of utility".[11]

The authors of the present book share the opinion that Marx's *Critique* of Political Economy did not as well preserve the tenets and the theoretical object of Ricardian value theory, despite the contrary belief of many economists, or the ambiguities of Marx himself. However, the crashing modifications introduced by Marx in the theoretical object of Classical Political Economy were in an opposite direction as compared to those introduced by Neoclassical economics: The Marxian notion of value is a new *complex theoretical concept*, which replaces the Ricardian semi-empirical category of "labour expended" and introduces a theory of *social homogenisation of labour under capitalism* (whose manifestation is the general exchangeability, through money, of commodities on the market). This approach can explain why it is not only the products of labour ("labour expended"), but also all forms of claims on (future) production that acquire a price; it also comprehends the non-neutrality of money. Unlike the Ricardian (and the Neoclassical), the Marxian theory of value is a *monetary theory*.

Introduction: On the Object of Marx's "Critique of Political Economy" 11

Notes

1. Adam Smith considers the individual's "general disposition to truck, barter, and exchange" (Smith 1981: I.ii.5) to be the foundation on which the market economy and the whole division of labour is based. He therefore concludes that, guided by this inner nature of his, "every man lives by exchanging, or becomes in some measure a merchant, and the society itself grows to be what is properly a commercial society" (Smith 1981: I.iv.1).
2. In the unfinished 52nd chapter of the 3rd Volume of *Capital*, Marx notes, following the Classical scheme: "The owners of mere labour-power, the owners of capital and the land-owners, whose respective sources of income are wages, profit and ground-rent – in other words wage-laborers, capitalists and land-owners – form the three great classes of modern society based on the capitalist mode of production". This definition follows Ricardo's famous formulation: "The produce of the earth –all that is derived from its surface by the united application of labour, machinery, and capital, is divided among three classes of the community, namely, the proprietor of the land, the owner of the stock or capital for its cultivation, and the labourers by whose industry it is cultivated" (Ricardo 1992: 3). However, Marx hurries to note immediately that the criterion of income form does not close the theory of classes and posits the question: "What makes wage-labourers, capitalists and land-owners the formative elements of the three great social classes?" (Marx 1991: 1025-26).
3. "That which connects social groups and individuals is not a higher common interest, or a legal order, but a clash in continuous development" (Balibar 1988: 217). The non - class relations which exist in a society, such as e.g. the relations between adults and minors, the relations between the two sexes, the various "races" or the various religious groups are always determined and shaped in correspondence to the main aspect of social relations, the class relations of power. For the substantiation of this Marxist position, see Dimoulis 1994: 47-51. Also the very penetrating analysis of Wallerstein 1988 on the concepts "race" and "prestige group - formations", in which the conclusion is also substantiated that "prestige group - formations (such as parties) constitute confused collective representations of the classes" (Wallerstein 1988: 270).
4. For the critique of the opposite theoretical approach, according to which "a class exists as such only from the moment when it possesses a class consciousness of its own", see Poulantzas 1973: 78 ff. Also see Ste. Croix (1984: 102): "If ancient slaves are indeed to be regarded as a class, then neither class consciousness nor political activity in common (...) can possibly have the right to be considered *necessary* elements in class". For the tenets of a Marxist theory of classes see Carchedi (1977) and also Resnick and Wolff (1982).
5. "It is in each case the direct relationship of the owners of the conditions of production to the immediate producers (...) in which we find the innermost secret, the hidden basis of the entire social edifice, and hence also the political form of the relationship of sovereignty and dependence" (Marx 1991: 927). As Ste. Croix (1984: 100) correctly observes, according to Marxist theory "class (...) is the collective social expression of

the fact of exploitation, the way in which exploitation is embodied in a *social structure*" (emphasis added).
6. "It is not enough that the conditions of labour are concentrated at one pole of society in the shape of capital, while at the other pole are grouped masses of men who have nothing to sell but their labour-power. Nor it is enough that they are compelled to sell themselves voluntarily. The advance of capitalist production develops a working class which by education, tradition and habit looks upon the requirements of that mode of production as self-evident natural laws" (Marx 1990: 899).
7. See also Marx 1991: 927.
8. See analytically Milios (1988). Productive processes which do not lead to relations of exploitation (production and detachment of the surplus-product) as is the case with the self-employed producer, (simple commodity production), do not constitute a mode of production, but a *form of production* (Poulantzas 1973).
9. In a 1881 letter to the Russian socialist Vera Zasulitch Marx wrote: "I have shown in *Capital* that the transformation of feudal production into capitalist production has as its starting point the expropriation of producers, which mainly means that the expropriation of the peasants is the basis of this whole process. (...) Surely, if capitalist production is to establish its domination in Russia, then the great majority of the peasants must be transformed into wage-earners. But the precedent of the West will prove here absolutely nothing" (MEW, Vol. 19: 396-400). Only in the event of the capitalist mode of production becoming through class struggle fully dominant in a social formation is capitalist development established as an inherent tendency of social evolution: "But this inherent tendency to capitalist production does not become adequately realised –it does not become indispensable, and that also means technologically indispensable– until the specific mode of capitalist production and hence the real subsumption of labour under capital has become a reality" (Marx 1990: 1037).
10. "Matter", as the theoretical object of Molecular Physics, for example, has nothing to do with the empirical meaning of matter, as being conceived by the senses, or with the philosophical, religious etc. concept of it, as it is being confronted to the respective concepts of the "spirit" or the "mind". It is related with a series of sub-notions such as the forces of cohesion, the nucleus and the electrons, the orbits etc., not all of which have an empirical-experimental reflection (e.g. the "tunnel effect").
11. In the words of Jeremy Bentham, the philosopher who devoted his life to the theoretical foundation of the "principle of utility," "individual interests are the only real interests" (Bentham 1931: 144). This principle of substitution of society by the individual constitutes thus the major premise of Neoclassical theory: "A true theory of economy can only be attained by going back to the great springs of human action – the feelings of pleasure and pain. (...) A second part of the theory proceeds from feelings to the useful objects or utilities by which pleasurable feeling is increased or pain removed" (Jevons 1866).

2 Marx versus Ricardo (Marx's Theory of Value)

1. Introduction

As mentioned in Chapter 1, the point of departure for Marx's theoretical system, called by him *A Critique of Political Economy*, was his theory of History, which discarded the humanist underpinnings of Political Economy (that is to say the approaches which attempt to extrapolate the structural characteristics of the economy from what they define in self-validating fashion as "human nature" – "truck, barter and exchange" [Adam Smith], the "principle of utility" [Neoclassical school]).

On the basis of that theoretical premise he first of all approached the concept of value, formulating after 1857 a new labour theory of value. He placed particular emphasis on the question of the commensurability of "economic goods" which take the form of commodities. He preceded to construct around that idea of value the entirety of his theoretical system as a logically consistent chain of analyses and concepts.

Nevertheless, the Marxist concept of value is very frequently equated, whether explicitly or merely tacitly, by Marxist and non-Marxist economists, with the corresponding Ricardian: explicitly when it is stated that Marx as an economist was a Ricardian –this is the position usually taken by non-Marxist economists studying the history of economic theory– implicitly when the Marxist theory of value is confined to theses (and their grounding) encompassed by or derived directly from the Classical School of Political Economy, and it is also the view taken by many Marxist economists.[1]

In the present chapter referring to Marx's theory of value we will place particular emphasis on what distinguishes it from the Classical theory of value. From this starting point we can go on to present other significant developments in Marxist economic theory, which touch on issues such as the profit rate and role of technological innovation, economic crises and the

14 *Karl Marx and the Classics*

role of the money and credit in the process of expanded reproduction of the capitalist system.

2. The "Classical" Reading of Marx

Marx began to occupy himself systematically with Political Economy (see Chapter 1) just at the time that the Classical School had completed its historic cycle, that is to say when on the one hand its basic analyses (Smith, Ricardo) had been formulated, and on the other the Classical theory of value had begun to be disputed from a theoretical standpoint (as it appeared incompatible with the existence of a uniform rate of profit in the capitalist economy), but also for political and other reasons (Rubin 1989).

In accordance with the line of argument so far developed, the concept of value in its Smithian version of "labour expended" (on the production of a commodity), or in its relevant Ricardian version, can be summarised in the following theses:

> A commodity comprises use value and exchange value. What is interesting from an economic viewpoint is exchange value, which is determined independently of use value. Exchange value as a relation of commodity exchange expresses the value inherent in commodities (*Thesis 1*). *The value of a commodity (as a characteristic or property of the "economic good") derives from labour and (quantitatively) is proportional to the labour time which has been expended for its production. (Thesis 2)*.

Theses 1 and 2 are necessary conclusions from an analysis which holds that value is inherent in commodities (giving rise to Smith and Ricardo's notion of the inherent value of money[2] which is taken to be a commodity that simply facilitates the exchange of all other commodities). It is therefore considered that value is a *property* of all commodities (a qualitative feature of them), which derives from the fact that they are the products of labour. Consequently (following Thesis 2), *labour secures commensurability between commodities: their common quality is that they are the products of labour.*[3]

The following two *theses are logical consequences of Thesis 1 and 2*:

> The relative values, as *relations of exchange* between commodities derive from their (inherent) values, as the ratio of (the quotient of) their values (*Thesis 3*).[4] The incomes of the capitalist and the landowner derive from the

value of the totality of commodities produced by the labourer in a certain period of time. Otherwise formulated, *the possessing classes appropriate a part of the value produced by the labourer (Thesis 4)*.[5]

Those who maintain that Marx is an exponent of the Classical theoretical system consider that the four above mentioned Classical theses are also a distillation of the Marxist theory of value. According to these conceptions Marx "appended" to the abovementioned four theses a) the observation that these theses apply only in the context of certain historical epochs, b) the statement (which was in any case shared by the British socialists of the first half of the 19th century) that the incomes of the possessing classes (Thesis 4) derive from a relation of exploitation which will be abolished by socialism, c) the qualification that (for Thesis 4 to apply) the worker's wage (and that which the worker sells on the labour market) cannot entail (or in other words be) "labour" but must be the capacity to work or labour power.[6]

If this were indeed the case, then we would be obliged to agree with Schumpeter, who maintained: "Marx must be considered a 'classic' economist and more specifically a member of the Ricardian group" (Schumpeter 1994: 390).[7]

Before answering the question of how far Marx shares the assumptions of the four theses of the Classical School we have summarised above, we should perhaps mention another attempt at extrication from the theoretical crisis of the Classical School that was undertaken before the crystallisation of the Marxist outlook: the perception of value as a mere *relation* of exchange *between commodities*.

3. Value as Relation of Exchange

One response to the position of Smith (in the conception of labour "expended") and Ricardo on value as an inherent *content* or *property* of commodities (from which exchange relations *emerge* or *derive*) was put forward in 1828 by Samuel Bailey, who maintained that value cannot be understood as a property of the commodity but simply as a *relation between commodities:*

> Value is the exchange relation of commodities and consequently is not anything different from this relation. (...) Value denotes nothing positive and

intrinsic, but merely the relation in which two objects stand to each other as exchangeable commodities.[8]

Bailey argues that exchange value is not a property because it is a relation, and specifically a relation of exchange. However, even according to the Classical School value exists as an exchange relation (exchange value), with the difference that this relation emerges as a *consequence* of the common property of commodities, i.e. that they are products of labour, each of which has a different exchange value because different quantities of labour have been expended in producing it. What Bailey is essentially arguing is that the empirically observed relation (exchange value) should not be reduced to an inherent property, in labour and the value deriving therefrom, i.e. as an intrinsic quality of commodities. He is arguing that exchange value does not constitute the *derivative* of a property (value) but a *property in itself*, which exists simply as a relation of exchange. This last proposition is also espoused by contemporary (Neoclassical) economists.[9]

Thus the conception of value as exchange relation (bringing to mind its Smithian variant: "labour purchased"),[10] sidelines the issue of the commensurability of commodities, that is to say does not pose the question of *what prices are* or how (on the strength of what property and by means of what relation) commodities come to be constituted as commensurable quantities and as such exchangeable. It is used by detractors of the "Marxist concept" of value, which is however in their minds identified with the corresponding Classical concept, and above all with Thesis 2 and Thesis 3 (against which –addressing his criticism to Ricardo, not to the then 10-year-old Marx– Bailey had also reacted).

It seems, then, that the Neoclassical economists do not take very seriously the disquisitions of the founders of their School, like Jevons and Walras, according to which Bentham's conception of utility is the intrinsic property (the measure) from which stems exchange value. Explicitly or otherwise, they thus tend towards a Baileyan view in terms of which the value (of a commodity) is to be identified with the exchange relation as such of that commodity with other commodities or with money. This is admittedly true of the later Neoclassical (and Keynesian) economists while Pareto and the economists of his generation were still attempting to ground value as a relationship (exchange value) in the concept of *ordinal* utility.[11]

It becomes clear that *value as a relation*, (whether in the variant of Bailey or that of Pareto, see note 11), presupposes the consideration of exchange relations as relations of *exchange in kind* (barter), in which money plays merely an ancillary role. In accordance with this conception, for a person to be able to purchase something he/she must first sell, or more precisely *purchase by selling* (the aim being the attainment of the maximum subjective utility). A similar outlook of purchase by selling was adopted by Classical Political Economy (see note 2 of the present chapter).

4. The Structure of the Marxian Argument

In the great self-published work, Volume 1 of *Capital*, Marx devotes Part One, which is 120 pages long (Penguin edition) to an analysis of value. Of these the first seven (Marx 1990: 125-31) are devoted to formulating and clarifying Theses 1-3. The following six pages (Marx 1990: 132-37) are devoted to a formulation of the concept of *abstract labour*. Thesis 4 is not examined in this section of *Capital*, but is introduced, in the context of what has already been analysed, in Part Two of the work. The 107 pages which follow the analysis of abstract labour (Marx 1990: 138-244) are concerned with exchange value, that is to say with value as a *relation* of exchange, and in this framework (i.e. not that of Theses 1-3) they arrive at the question of money.

If we wish to take Marx seriously, we must therefore see what is said in these 6 + 107 pages beyond the Theses 1-3 of the first seven pages. To put the question another way, what is involved is how the Classical concepts of Theses 1 - 3 *are theoretically recast* by the 6 + 107 pages which follow. Because if Marx were a Classical (Ricardian) economist, if he had no wish to assign a different meaning to the Classical Theses 1 - 3, he would have had no reason to append so many additional pages to the crystal-clear formulations of these Theses in the first seven pages of his work. Crystal-clear formulations such as the following:

> If then we disregard the use-value of commodities, only one property remains, that of being products of labour. (...) The common factor in the exchange relation, or in the exchange value of the commodity, is therefore its value. (...) How, then, is the magnitude of this value to be measured? By means of the quantity of the 'value-forming substance', the labour, contained in the article (Marx 1990: 128-9).[12]

5. Abstract Labour

That "wealth", that is to say everything that is useful, is mostly a product of labour applies not only to capitalism but to every mode of production.

Every mode of production presupposes the *worker-producer* and his (her) particular relationship with the *means of production*, from which can be deciphered the particular structural characteristics of the community in which that mode of production is predominant.[13] However, as stressed by Marx on the very first page of *Capital*, it is only in "those societies in which the capitalist mode of production prevails", that wealth "presents itself as 'an immense accumulation of commodities'" (Marx 1990: 125).[14] It is thus obvious that it is not because it is a product of labour that wealth is a commodity, but because that labour is carried out within the framework of the capitalist mode of production and so is subjected to the standardisation and uniformity that is inherent in that mode of production. To put it another way, *value* is a manifestation of the structural characteristics of the capitalist mode of production and not a manifestation of labour in general.

It is therefore clear that Marx conceived of value as a historically specific *social relation*: Value is the "property" that products of labour acquire in capitalism, a property which acquires material substance, that is actualised, in the market, through the exchangeability of any product of labour with any other, i.e. through their character as commodities bearing a specific (monetary) price on the market. From the first text in the period under examination, the *Grundrisse* (1857-8),[15] to *Capital* (1867),[16] Marx insisted that value is an expression of relations exclusively characteristic of the capitalist mode of production. Thus, wherever in his work he introduces the concept of "generalised commodity production" (such as for example in the first section of the first volume of *Capital*) so as to comprehend value, in reality he is shaping a preliminary intellectual construct (which to some extent corresponds to the superficial "visible reality" of the capitalist economy[17]), which will help him to come to grips with capitalist production, and subsequently construct his concept of it (Murray 2000). In no way does he describe a (pre-capitalist) community of simple commodity production, as many Marxists have imagined: "Had we gone further, and inquired under what circumstances all, or even the majority of products take the form of commodities, we should have found that this only happens on the basis of one particular mode of production, the capitalist one" (Marx 1990: 273).

Value is thus not an "essence" infused by the individual worker always and everywhere, i.e. under any imaginable historical conditions, into the products of his labour.[18]

Marx approaches the problem by way of the question of commensurability. If under non-capitalist modes of production the "market economy" is absent and the *products of labour* are not exposed to relations of equivalence-for-exchange, then it is pointless arguing that under capitalism they become economically commensurable because they are products of labour. Put in another way, where Classical Political Economy believed that it was giving a conclusive answer (qualitatively different objects –use values– are rendered economically commensurate – exchangeable– because they are all products of labour), Marx simply sees a question which has to be answered: How and why can qualitatively different kinds of labour be made equivalents?

> Let us suppose that one ounce of gold, one ton of iron, one quarter of wheat and twenty yards of silk are exchange-values of equal magnitude. (...) But digging gold, mining iron, cultivating wheat and weaving silk are qualitatively different kinds of labour. In fact, what appears objectively as diversity of the use-values, appears, when looked at dynamically, as diversity of the activities which produce those use-values (Marx 1981: 29).

For the riddle of the equivalence of different kinds of labour to be solved, what must be comprehended is the *social character of labour under capitalism*: The capitalist organisation of production and the resultant social division of labour is underpinned by the direct (institutional) independence of each individual producer (capitalist) from all the others. Nevertheless, all these individual productive procedures are linked indirectly between themselves through the mechanism of the market, since each of them produces not for himself or for the "community" but for exchange on the market, for the rest of society, whose economic encounter with him takes place only in the market-place. This procedure imposes an increasing social (capitalistic) uniformity on all individual productive activities precisely through generalised commodity exchange and competition between individual commodity producers (capitalists).

Marx defines this procedure of social homogenisation of individual labour procedures and productive processes through introduction of the term *abstract labour*. Labour has a dual nature in the capitalist mode of production – on the one hand it is concrete labour (labour which produces a concrete use value, as in any mode of production) and on the other it is at the same time abstract labour (labour in general), *labour which is from the social viewpoint qualitatively identical*. From this stem the overall commensurability and exchangeability of the products of labour, i.e. that they are constituted (produced) as commodities: "The labour contained in exchange-value is abstract universal social labour, which is brought about by the universal alienation of individual labour" (Marx 1981: 56-7). This means that "every commodity is *the* commodity which, as a result of the alienation of its particular use-value, must appear as the direct materialisation of universal labour-time" (Marx 1981: 45). The expenditure in abstract labour (labour in general) or general labour time, thus regulates the magnitude of the value in the commodities.[19]

In Vol. 1 of *Capital* the analysis of abstract labour takes up no more than seven pages (Marx 1990: 131-37), in part because Marx had placed emphasis on that issue in *A Contribution to the Critique of Political Economy*. Nevertheless, he hastens to declare that he is proud of the formulation of this concept (which in the course of outlining his theory in *Capital* represents his first substantial differentiation from the Ricardian system), a declaration the like of which we would probably find no more than once or twice in all the rest of his writings: "I was the first to point out and examine critically this twofold nature of the labour contained in commodities" (Marx 1990: 132).

Abstract labour does not "emerge" from the concrete: it is the historically specific property of *all* labour under capitalism. Thus it is not the mechanisation of production and the de-specialisation of the worker that transform useful labour into abstract labour, as certain Marxists maintain. This assertion arises from a category confusion (from the inadmissible conjunction of the two sides of the semantic gap between concrete and abstract labour), because concrete-natural labour as a distinct concept can in no way be reduced to abstract labour or constitute the content of exchange value: Abstract labour is a "property" of *every (concrete) act of labour under the capitalist mode of production*, i.e. an expression of the particular form of social arrangement that characterises that (and only that) specific mode of production, irrespective of whether the work in question is simple or more complex and requiring a high degree of specialisation.[20]

The problem of social homogenisation of labour to which one is referred by the concept of abstract labour is also different from the problem of "quantitative correspondence" of work of differing degrees of intensity, specialisation and productivity. For one hour of the work of an engineer to be able to correspond (quantitatively) to n hours of the work of an unskilled labourer, the two types of work must already constitute "qualitatively similar" (i.e. *abstract*) labour. This is something that empiricism (even in its Marxist variants, see Howard/King 1985, Rosdolsky 1969) will never perceive.

In conclusion: The products of labour are commodities, hence values and exchange values, not simply because they are products of labour but

Marx Versus Ricardo 21

because they are products of abstract labour, i.e. "capitalist labour" (labour which is performed under capitalist conditions, within the framework of the capitalist mode of production). Abstract labour produces the value of commodities, which constitutes their common measure (securing the relationship of commensurability), since value lacks every predicate beyond that of size.[21]

Here it is worth noting two points (Heinrich 1999: 208 ff.):

a) Abstract labour (and consequently "abstract labour time") is not a straightforward (empirically verifiable) property of labour but an "abstraction", i.e. a non-empirical reality, a concept which renders comprehensible the process of social homogenisation of labour *under the capitalist mode of production*: "Universal labour-time itself is an abstraction which, as such, does not exist for commodities" (Marx 1981: 45). That which empirically exists is merely the specific commodities which are bought and sold on the market.

b) Abstract labour, as the concept which conveys the specifically social (capitalist) character of the labour process, does not have to do with each separate productive procedure but with the *social interrelation of all the separate, institutionally unrelated, capitalist productive processes*, as this interrelation reveals itself in the market-place: "Social labour-time exists in these commodities in a latent state, so to speak, and becomes evident only in the course of their exchange. (...) Universal social labour is consequently not a ready-made prerequisite but an emerging result" (Marx 1981: 45).

These two issues suggest why the whole weight of the analysis must be placed on exchange value, i.e. on the *manifestation* of value as *exchange value* (the "form of appearance" of value) and this is where Marx places it: he does not close his analysis of value with the concept of abstract labour but on the contrary devotes by far the greatest part of his analysis (107 of the 120 pages) to exchange value, or value as an exchange relation between commodities. Exchange value is the sole *objective materialisation* (form of appearance) of value.[22]

6. Digression: "Essence" and Forms of Appearance

On the basis of the theoretical positions outlined above, Marx introduced on the *methodological level* the theory of *forms of appearance* of economic and social relations. The forms of appearance are to be distinguished from the "essence", i.e. the internal, concealed, *causal regularities* (or *laws*) which govern social relations (without for all that being immediately visible on the level of empirically observable phenomena). It is stressed, that what the "common sense" spontaneously perceives is only an outer surface of what really "is", i.e. of what Marx alternatively describes as an "actual relation" or "hidden background" of bare appearance.[23]

As Marx had already explained in the first work of the period we are examining, the *Grundrisse*, the purpose of science is to start from empirically visible forms of appearance, proceed to a process of theoretical abstraction then return from the abstract to the concrete, thereby constituting the theoretical concept of the concrete, i.e. to expose the internal causality governing immediately observable phenomena (see Marx 1993: 100 ff.).

Dialectical method is the term used by Marx to denote the way of elaborating concepts on the basis of which one can intellectually appropriate reality, i.e. lay bare the internal causal relationships and the "regularity" of phenomena. The method involves taking concrete-empirical objects as a starting point and proceeding to intellectual abstraction.

Abstraction presupposes *starting from the concrete* and thus avoids the idealism of arbitrary – i.e. emerging from the predominant *theoretical* ideology – categorising. At the same time abstraction, as the first step in the dialectical method, transcends the reproduction of the ideological form of appearance of the concrete (which constitutes a *practical* dominant ideology of "everyday life") and the empiricism which is bound up with it – according to which reality is transparent, i.e. empirically observable and rationally interpretable without the necessity for conceptual elaboration (Heinrich 1999: chap. 5).

Marx perceives that abstractions alone do not constitute concepts of the empirically perceptible objects of reality. For the process of intellectual/scientific appropriation of reality to be consummated a second step is needed: The "return" from abstraction to the concrete object.

There thus emerges a theoretical procedure by means of which the *scientific concept of the concrete* is constructed. This is a concept which conveys the causal relationships that regulate empirical reality without ever themselves appearing as such in the realm of reality and of appearance, since they do not belong to the realm of empirically tangible entities and phenomena. The theoretical concept is real in the sense that it deciphers the phenomena, as for example the law of gravity deciphers the fall of a body. The transition from the abstract to the concrete object of scientific analysis is thus radically distinct from the method of rationalisation (but also from the way in which Hegel employs abstraction) because it does not constitute an autonomous process but the second phase of a process of conceptual decoding of the concrete (after the construction of the abstraction, the return to the concrete by means of it).

In this way, theoretical categories are generated which constitute conceptual determinants of concrete (contemporary or historical) reality. Thus, for example, the Marxist concept of capital "does indeed appear *only as an abstraction*; not an arbitrary abstraction, but an abstraction which grasps the specific characteristics which distinguish capital from all other forms of wealth – or modes in which (social) production develops" (Marx 1993: 449).

This methodological approach represents a break with the empiricism of Classical Political Economy, since it is grounded on the position that empirical observation does not suffice for comprehension of the causality which governs economic processes or the fact that the "essence" cannot be expected to manifest itself on the plane of immediate experience.[24]

The conclusion that may be inferred from the above theses is that the value of commodities never appears as such, as an immediately perceivable (empirically observable) and thus measurable entity. It finds expression only through the (distorted) forms of its appearance, i.e. commodity prices. These forms of appearance of value do not, as we have argued, relate to each commodity separately, that is to say, it is not a matter of isolated, of *initially mutually independent* expressions of the value of each commodity. The forms register the *relationship of exchange* between each commodity and *all other* commodities. They constitute material expression of the social homogenisation of labour in the capitalist mode of production (as delineated through the concept of *abstract labour*).

In order to be able to decipher the form of appearance of value as money, Marx starts from the scheme of simple barter relations, in which a quantity of a commodity is exchanged for a different quantity of another commodity. The Classical economists believed, as we have said, that all market transactions can be reduced to simple barter relations, which are merely facilitated by money.[25]

7. The Value Form and Money

7.1 "The Simple, Isolated or Accidental Form of Value"

This form corresponds to the simple case of barter:
x Commodity A = y Commodity B or 20 yards of linen = 1 coat,

of which Marx says that "the whole mystery of the form of value lies hidden in this simple form" (Marx 1990: 139). It is abstruse because it is simple, yet if deciphered it will reveal the secret of even its most developed configuration, that of money.

This relation does not amount to equality in the mathematical sense or a conventional equivalence but is characterised by a "polarisation", i.e. by the fact that each "pole" of the equality (the linen or –by the same token– the coat) occupies a qualitatively different position and has a correspondingly different function, such that, from a mathematical viewpoint, the converse (permutational) property does not apply [if a=b $\Rightarrow$ b=a]. The linen (commodity A) has the *relative value form*, the coat (commodity B) the *form of equivalent*, which means that "they play two different parts", i.e. while they "belong to and mutually condition each other (...), at the same time, they are mutually exclusive or opposed extremes, i.e. poles of the expression of value" (Marx 1990: 139-40).

This polarisation and this difference result from the fact that value (as content or "essence" deriving from capitalistically expended labour) is manifested (i.e., empirically, appears) *only* in the exchange *relation* between commodities, in exchange value. In the simple form of the exchange relation, the equivalent (the coat) constitutes the measure of value of the "relative". In other words the simple form of value tells us that twenty yards of linen *have the value of* one coat. "The value of the commodity linen is expressed by the physical body of the commodity coat, the value of one by the use-value of the other" (Marx 1990: 143). The reason for this is that the value of linen "must be related to another commodity as equivalent" (Marx 1990: 148). "The same commodity cannot accordingly appear in the same expression of value in its two forms simultaneously. These two forms are polar opposites and mutually exclusive" (MEGA II, 5: 628).

Thus commodity A (relative form) "makes the use-value B into the material through which its own value is expressed" (Marx 1990: 144). So B, or the coat (equivalent form) becomes the *measure of value* (the *"money"*) of A, of linen. The equivalent (commodity B or the coat), although itself a useful thing, through the process of exchange, functions as a "form of appearance of value", which means that concrete labour embodied in it (coat tailoring work) functions (for the moment only vis-á-vis the linen) as a manifestation of labour in general, of abstract labour. Value is manifested only through these forms of its appearance:

Within the value relation and the expression of value immanent in it, the abstractedly general [i.e. value] does not constitute a property of the concrete, sensorily actual (i.e. of exchange value) but on the contrary the sensorily actual is a simple form of appearance or specific form of realisation of the abstractedly general (...) *Only the sensorily concrete is valid as a form of appearance of the abstractedly general* (MEGA II, 5: 634, emphasis added).

The form of the equivalent, as tangible manifestation of value, is characterised by the following elements: a) Its use value constitutes the form of appearance of value, b) concrete labour (tailoring) constitutes the form of appearance of abstract labour, c) individual labour is manifested as directly social labour. The following schema reconstructs the simple value form (Altvater et al 1999).

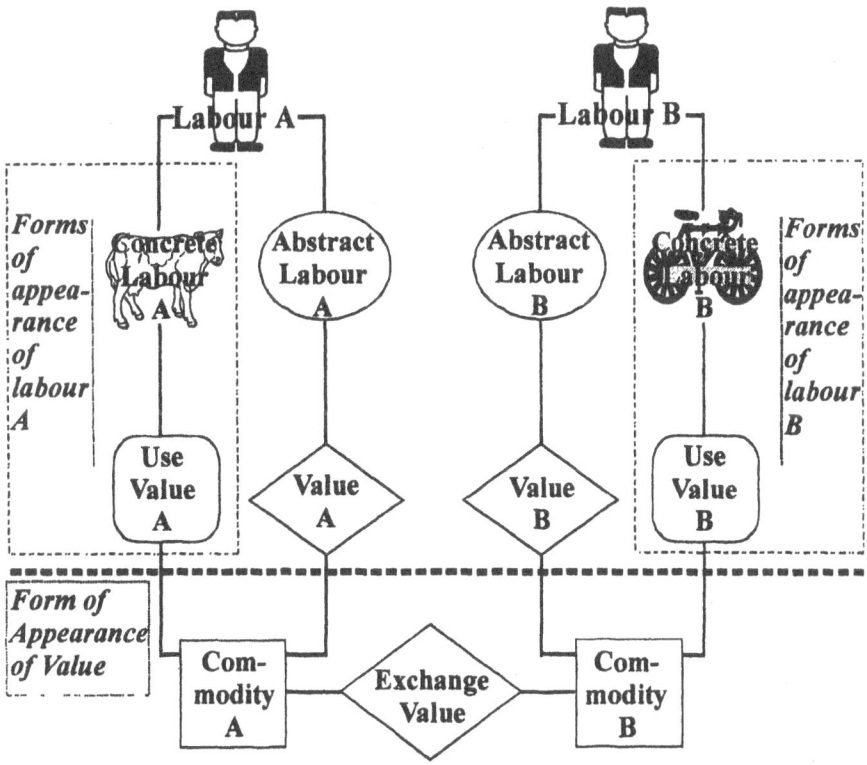

Figure 2.1 The Simple Form of Value: x commodity A = y commodity B or one unit of commodity A has the value of y/x units of B

Another important question concerns the value of the coat or of commodity B (equivalent form). To the extent that the coat remains in the position of the equivalent, its value remains latent, which is to say it "does not exist" in the world of tangible reality, of the forms of appearance:

> But as soon as the coat takes up the position of the equivalent in the value expression, the magnitude of its value ceases to be expressed quantitatively. On the contrary, the coat now figures in the value equation merely as a definite quantity of some article (Marx 1990: 147).

Just as the value of commodity A, i.e. of the linen (relative form) "cannot be related to itself as equivalent, and therefore cannot make its own physical shape into the expression of its own value" (Marx 1990: 148), so by analogy neither is the coat able to assume any tangible form of expression: "it cannot express its value in its own body or in its own use value (...) it cannot be referred to the (...) concrete labour contained in itself as a simple form of realisation of abstract human labour" (MEGA II, 5: 32). If that could happen with the coat, then the same would apply for the linen or for any other commodity and value would be a self-existent manifestation (form of appearance) of labour. The form and content of value would be identical.

Consequently the Marxian system of analysis could be considered synonymous with the Ricardian. But this is not the case.

7.2 Total or Expanded, General and Money Form of Value

From the analysis of the simple value form, Marx now has no difficulty in deciphering the money form. For this purpose he utilises two intermediate intellectual formulas, the *total or expanded* and the *general* form for expressing value.

The first formula connotes an endless series of acts of barter of the kind:

w Commodity A = v Commodity B = x Commodity C = y Commodity D = etc.

It is characterised by two deficiencies, a) that as an overall proposition it is endless, and so indeterminate since it conveys a random selection of successive commodities, in which a commodity may be seen either as a relative value form with a multitude of equivalents or as one of the multitude of equivalents of another commodity occupying the position corresponding to the relative expression of value and b) that it can be seen as a medley of endless sequences of simple value forms (Marx 1990: 156).

The second form in this developmental sequence is the general form of value, which is characterised by one and only one equivalent (e.g. of linen) in which all the other commodities express their value. These commodities are thus always in the position of *relative* value. The fabric has come to constitute the *universal relative form of value* (Marx 1990: 161). Every other commodity is now excluded from the status of equivalent, which is now occupied only by the general equivalent, the fabric. Given that for all commodities apart from linen fabric a "common form of appearance of value is now applicable, (...) the specific labour materialised in the fabric now applies (...) as a general form of actualisation of human labour, as *labour in general*" (MEGA II, 5: 37), and so as a form of appearance of abstract labour.[26]

Commodities are now exchangeable between themselves not *directly* but only through the general equivalent (of linen fabric). Their social "essence" (that all are products of capitalistically expended labour) is not expressed immediately but with the general equivalent playing the role of *intermediary*:

> Commodities do not then assume the form of *direct mutual exchangeability*. Their *socially validated form is a mediated one*. Conversely: through the relation of all other commodities to linen fabric as the form of appearance of their value, the physical form of linen material becomes *the form of direct exchangeability* between these commodities and all other commodities and as such their *direct* or *general social* form" (MEGA II, 5: 40). "All types of private labour acquire their *social* character only through *antithesis*, with all of them *equated* with an exclusive variety of private labour, in this case that of linen-weaving. Hence the latter becomes a direct and general form of abstract human labour (MEGA II, 5: 42).

When a commodity on the market definitively adopts the role of general equivalent, the form of the general equivalent leads directly to the money form. That commodity (gold) then becomes money, and the form of the general equivalent is the money form. Nevertheless, as we shall see later when we refer in more detail to the Marxist theory of money, it is no accident that Marx distinguishes the form of the general equivalent from the money form. We shall see, in other words, that he deliberately chose as his initial example a chance commodity (linen fabric) and not gold (money's historical "body") when he introduced the concept of the general equivalent. Money is much more than a commodity playing the role of the general equivalent.

Thus the relation of general exchangeability of commodities is expressed (or realised) only in an indirect, *mediated* sense, i.e. through money, which functions as *general equivalent* in the process of exchange, and through which all commodities express their value. The Marxian analysis does not therefore entail reproduction of the barter model (of exchanging one commodity for another), since it holds that exchange *is necessarily mediated by money*. This amounts to a monetary theory of the capitalist economy (a monetary theory of value) since money is interpreted as an intrinsic and necessary element in capitalist economic relations.

Having acquired the exclusive function of the expression and measurement of prices, money itself does not have a price (even if we are speaking of a commodity that has been withdrawn from circulation so as to be able to play the role of money: gold). As Marx puts it:

> Money has no price. In order to form a part of this uniform relative form of value of the other commodities, it would have to be brought into relation with itself as its own equivalent (Marx 1990: 189). It is the adequate form of appearance of value, that is a material embodiment of abstract and therefore equal human labour (Marx 1990: 184).

To summarise: Based on his monetary theory of value, Marx shows that the value of a commodity is expressed not through itself but through its distorted forms of appearance in prices. Moreover, it cannot be defined in isolation, but *exclusively in relation to all other commodities*, in a process of exchange. This relation of exchange value is materialised in money. In the Marxist system there cannot be any other "material condensation" of (abstract) labour, any other measure (or form of appearance) of value:

> It has become apparent in the course of our presentation that value, which appeared as an abstraction, is only possible as such an abstraction, as soon as money is posited (Marx 1993: 776).

The essential feature of the "market economy" (of capitalism) is thus not simply commodity exchange (as maintained by previous theories) but monetary circulation and money.[27] The Marxist theory of value points simultaneously to the concept of abstract labour (as causal determinant or "essence" of value) and of money (as its necessary form of appearance).

Value is described as "essence", magnitude and form: *it is the expression of a historically specific socio-economic relation and a distillation of the distinctive social homogenisation of labour under capitalism, which is manifested in the generalised exchangeability, mediated by money, of commodities on the market*: "The difficulty lies not in comprehending that money is a commodity, but in discovering how, why and by what means a commodity becomes money" (Marx 1990: 186. Also see Rubin 1972, particularly 107-23 and Rubin 1978).

From a quantitative viewpoint, the value of a commodity *would be* the quantity of *socially necessary labour* (i.e. of *abstract* labour with socially average characteristics of productivity and intensity) which is expended for its production. Nevertheless, the necessarily distorted form of appearance of all the internal-causal definitions of economic relations results in the formation of relative prices (ratios of exchange of quantities expressed through prices) between commodities which differ from what the relative values between them would be (ratios of exchange in values). Marx nonetheless supposed in the first and second Volumes of *Capital* that commodities are exchanged in accordance with their values. In this section of his analysis what chiefly concerned him was to study the causal determinants of the capitalist economy, and in particular capitalist exploitation as the motor of capitalist production and economic growth, as well as of the results created by increases in labour productivity (which "becomes manifest as an adequate embodiment of the *law of value* which develops fully only on the foundation of capitalist production" Marx 1990: 1037-38). In the third Volume of *Capital* he abandoned this assumption, focusing his analysis on the forms of appearance of capitalist production relations. Here he introduced the concept of *production prices* as the forms of appearance of value which secure the equalisation of the rate of profit for all individual capitals, which become interlinked, through competition, within the framework of a capitalist economy. According to Marx, the price of production constitutes what may be called the "gravitation centre" (or, in a Classical vocabulary, the "natural price") around which the actual market price oscillates, see Chapter 5). On the contrary, the Classics considered the "natural price" to be identical with the value of the commodity, i.e. they regarded prices and values as commensurable quantities. (See Smith 1981: I.vi.15).

What is more important, according to Marx, is that commodity exchange *presupposes* the (positive) prices of all commodities involved. In other words, prices are *not determined after* the establishment of a non-monetary equilibrium system of barter between "production sectors", like the Sraffian "linear production systems" (see Chapter 5). On the contrary, barter is for Marx non-existing, as all exchange transactions are made up of separate acts of exchange of commodities with money, which means that *commodities are by definition price-carrying products*. Prices are determined in the process of *commodity* production, i.e. in a historically unique process of (capitalist) production-for-the-exchange, a process which unites immediate production (in the narrow sense) with circulation. It is in this sense that, as Rubin (1978: 123) puts it, "exchange is the form of the whole production process, or the form of social labour".

Something that perhaps complicates the understanding of Marx's theory of value is that after completion of his analysis of the value form and the money form, and without any warning to the reader, he adopts a simplistic, resembling the Ricardian, approach to value, in order to make easier perceivable the quantitative aspect of his exegesis: he mentions the value of a commodity as if it was in itself an empirically measurable figure, e.g. "value created by n hours of labour of average intensiveness", "forgetting" that the labour deployed in this instance is *abstract labour* (a concept not to be counted among empirically tangible measures), and also ignoring the fact that value is measurable only by means of another "thing", as it can be manifested (appear) only in the form of, i.e. through, the general equivalent – in other words through money and so measured not in hours of labour time but in units of the general equivalent – precisely in units of money.

Notes

1. However there are also Marxists who expressly declare that Marx retained Ricardian economic theory and simply appended it to the dialectical philosophy of Hegel. The distinguished Italian Marxist Antonio Gramsci wrote characteristically: "It seems to me that in a certain sense we can say that the philosophy of praxis (meaning Marxism) equals Hegel + David Ricardo (...) Ricardo is to be conjoined with Hegel and Robespierre" (Gramsci 1977: 1247-8). A similar view shared also Lenin in his "Three Sources and Three Component Parts of Marxism" (1913): "Adam Smith and David Ricardo laid the foundations of the *labour theory of value*. Marx continued their work. He rigidly proved and consistently developed this theory" (Lenin-internet).
2. "By the money-price of goods, it is to be observed, I understand always the quantity of pure gold or silver for which they are sold, without any regard to the denomination of the coin" (Smith 1981: I.v.42). It is on this notion that Smith bases his view of the "neutrality of money" as a medium which simply facilitates the exchange of one commodity with another: "The gold and silver money which circulates in any country may very properly be compared to a highway, which, while it circulates and carries to market all the grass and corn of the country, produces itself not a single pile of either" (Smith 1981: II.ii.86). Consequently, it is the exchange of one commodity with another (on the model of non-monetary exchange - barter), not the circulation of money that is seen as the essential characteristic of the "market economy".

3. "Labour [is] the real measure of the exchangeable value of all commodities. (...) Labour alone, therefore, never varying in its own value, is alone the ultimate and real standard by which the value of all commodities can at all times and places be estimated and compared. It is their real price; money is their nominal price only" (Smith 1981: I.v.4 and I.v.7).
4. "The value of a commodity, or the quantity of any other commodity for which it will exchange, depends on the relative quantity of labour which is necessary for its production, and not on the greater or less compensation which is paid for that labour" (Ricardo 1992: 5).
5. "As soon as land becomes private property, the landlord demands a share of almost all the produce which the labourer can either raise, or collect from it. His rent makes *the first deduction from the produce of the labour* which is employed upon land. (...) Profit, makes a *second deduction from the produce of the labour* which is employed upon land" (Smith 1981: I.viii.6 and 7, emphasis added).
6. This in any case emerges from the *Classical Thesis* that the value of the wage ("of labour") is equal to the value of the worker's necessary means of subsistence. This magnitude is consequently something entirely different from the quantity of labour expended by the labourer and is not regulated either by the intensity or by the productivity of his labour.
7. This conviction is shared by almost all Neoclassical historians of economic theory. Thus Samuelson argued that we have to see Marx as "a minor post-Ricardian", while G.D.H. Cole, in a more nuanced treatment, wrote of the line of argument developed in the first volume of *Capital*: "Not one single idea in this theory of value was invented by Marx (...) Marx merely took over this conception from the classical economists. (...) There is nothing specifically Marxian about Marx's theory of value; what is novel is the use to which he puts the theory, not the theory itself" (Introduction to the Everyman edition of *Capital*, Vol. 1, London, xxi. Both citations in Meikle 1995: 185).
8. Bailey (1825), 4-5. This view is often regarded as a post-Marxist conception and so as something which Marx himself could not have taken into account. In fact Marx examines the view in *Theories of Surplus Value*, part 3. MEW Vol. 26.3: 122-167.
9. Schumpeter, for example, writes that Marx "was under the same delusion as Aristotle, viz., that value, though a factor in the determination of relative prices, is yet something that is different from, and exists independently of, relative prices or exchange relations. The proposition that the value of a commodity is the amount of labour embodied in it can hardly mean anything else" (Schumpeter 1952: 23, n. 2). The same view was also formulated by the Keynesian Joan Robinson: "One of the great metaphysical ideas in economics is expressed by the word 'value'. (...) Like all metaphysical ideas, when you try to pin it down, it turns out to be just a word" (Robinson 1964: 29). The distinguished Neoclassical theorist Vifredo Pareto (1848-1923) had already arrived at the same formulation, making even less of an effort to restrain his sarcasm: "In a recently published book, is said that 'price is the concrete manifestation of value'. We have had incarnation of Buddha, here we have incarnation of *value*. What indeed can this mysterious entity be? It is, it appears, 'the capacity which a good has to be exchanged with other goods'. This is to define one unknown thing by another still less known: for what indeed can this 'capacity' be? Of this 'capacity' or its homonym 'value' we know only the 'concrete manifestation' which is the price; truly then it is useless to entangle ourselves with these metaphysical entities, and we can stick to the prices" (Pareto 1971: 177). As aptly noted by Scott Meikle, according to such a view of value as (merely) an exchange relation "the argument would be that exchange value is a property like that of

'being married' which property depends on the relation 'being married to ...' in the sense that one cannot have the property unless one has the relation to someone. (...) The analogy with a property like 'being married', even if correct, is clearly not the whole story, because 'being married' is not a quantity and does not enter into relations of equality. (...) Aristotle explains in the *Categories* that 'All relatives, then, are spoken of in relation to correlatives that reciprocate, *provided* they are properly given. (...) For example, if a slave is given as of -not a master, but- a man or a biped or anything else like that, then there is not reciprocation; for it has not been given properly' (7ª22-30). If goods are to be related by equality, as they are in '5 beds = 1 house', they must be given as quantities; not quantities of goods, e.g. 5 beds, but quantities of whatever it is that 5 beds has in equal amount with 1 house, that is, exchange value" (Meikle 1995: 115-16).

10. It should be remembered that in this "labour purchased" variant, Smith rarely defined the value of a commodity simply as the "quantity of labour" which it could purchase. In most cases he supplemented this formulation with the phrase "or the quantity of products of labour". E.g. (Smith 1981: I.v.3): "Wealth, as Mr. Hobbes says, is power. (...) The power which that possession immediately and directly conveys to him, is the power of purchasing; a certain command over all the labour, or over all the produce of labour, which is then in the market. His fortune is greater or less, precisely in proportion to the extent of this power; or to *the quantity either of other men's labour, or, what is the same thing, of the produce of other men's labour, which it enables him to purchase or command*. The exchangeable value of everything must always be precisely equal to the extent of this power which it conveys to its owner" (emphasis added).

11. In terms of Pareto's ordinal utility, although the owner of a unit of a commodity A cannot exactly measure its utility (the benefit it offers him), nevertheless he is in a position to compare the (subjective) dimensions of this benefit with the corresponding benefit to be derived from the acquisition of another commodity B (or with the degree of pain resulting from non-acquisition of commodity B). Thus the owner of A will exchange it for B if and only if this exchange (the acquisition of B and loss of A) brings him at least as much utility as the possession of A brought him, and the same must apply conversely for the initial owner of B. Since it is a question of subjective utilities ("which in no way admit of comparison between themselves" – Pareto 1921: 34), the exchange could result in both partners to it acquiring a higher level of utility. At any rate, they will derive at least as much utility as they enjoyed before the transaction. As Pareto put it: "Exchange value is not derived directly but is the consequence of a relation established by any parties to a contract between the *use value* to the recipient and the *use value* to the giver. Truly, we do not buy commodities, we buy *use values*: The purchaser of coffee is not so much interested in whether that coffee is a seed of a certain chemical composition. What he buys is the pleasure he experiences as he drinks his coffee. And he compares that pleasure with the pleasure which he must deny himself giving in exchange for the coffee some economic good which he might similarly enjoy" (Pareto, 1921: 33). "Value is simply a relation" (Pareto, 1921: 45).

12. Referring to Bailey, Marx states: "S. Bailey (...), despite the narrowness of his own outlook he was able to put his finger on some serious defects in the Ricardian theory, as it is demonstrated by the animosity with which he was attacked by Ricardo's followers (...)" (Marx 1990: 155).

13. "The specific economic form in which unpaid surplus labour is pumped out of the direct producers determines the relationship of domination and servitude, as this grows directly out of production itself and reacts back on it in turn as a determinant" (Marx 1991: 927). Also, concerning wealth being under all social regimes a product of labour, Marx notes:

Marx Versus Ricardo 33

"The middle ages could not live on Catholicism, nor could the ancient world on politics. On the contrary, it is the manner in which they gained a livelihood that explains why in one case politics, in the other case Catholicism, played the chief part" (Marx 1990: 176).
14. In the first Edition of Volume One of *Capital* [1867] we read: "In the ancient Indian community labour is socially allocated without its products becoming commodities" (MEGA II, 5: 22). See also Marx 1990: 170.
15. "The concept of value is entirely peculiar to the most modern economy, since it is the most abstract expression of capital itself and of the production resting on it. In the concept of value, its secret is betrayed. (...) The economic concept of value does not occur in antiquity" (Marx 1993: 776 ff.).
16. "*The value form of the product of labour* is the most abstract, but also the *most general form* of the bourgeois mode of production as a particular kind of social production of a historical and transitory character" (Marx 1990: 174).
17. "The simple circulation is mainly an abstract sphere of the bourgeois overall production process, which manifests itself through its own determinations as a trend, a mere form of appearance of a deeper process which lies behind it, and equally results from it but also produces it –the industrial capital" (MEGA II, 2: 68-9). As Murray (2000) correctly notes, "*Marx's whole presentation of the commodity and generalised simple commodity circulation presupposes capital and its characteristic form of circulation.* It is perhaps the foremost accomplishment of Marx's theory of generalised commodity circulation to have demonstrated – with superb dialectical reasoning – that a sphere of such exchanges cannot stand alone; generalised commodity circulation is unintelligible when abstracted from the circulation of capital".
18. Moreover, under capitalism it is not only the products of labour that are commodities but also the labour power of working people, who during the course of historical development have forfeited all their property rights over the means of production (at the same time as being liberated from every unmediated form of personal dependency) and are obliged to sell their labour power to capitalists (owners of the means of production) as their sole recourse for obtaining the necessary means of subsistence. Marx however chooses not to speak of that issue until Part 2 (Chapter 4) of the first volume of *Capital*. When speaking about property, we always refer to the definition of Marx: "Property, then, originally means (...) the relation of the working (producing or self-reproducing) subject to the relations of production or reproduction as his own" (Marx 1993: 495).
19. Murray (2000 and 2001) defines as abstract labour the human labour in general in its physiological sense, as expenditure of human capacity, and uses the term "practically abstract labour" to define value producing labour (i.e. what we define here as *abstract labour*). He writes: "This concept of 'practically abstract' labour as a definite historical type of labour, namely, the labour that produces commodities and is socially validated once those commodities are exchanged for the universal equivalent (money), builds conceptually on the generally applicable notion of abstract labour". And he explains: "The 'free market' is not an independent phenomenon; it is a moment of capital's circulation. Consequently, any thought that the market *alone* makes labour 'practically abstract' misconceives the status of generalised commodity circulation in relation to the production process as a whole".
20. A characteristic instance is that of Rosdolsky. In his book *The Making of Marx's Capital*, which had a significant influence on post-World War II Marxist theoretical analysis, he maintains that decline from the "craftsmanship" of the pre-capitalist artisan led to concrete labour becoming "abstract labour". He writes: "Marx accepted the thesis of Ricardo, which is confirmed by the workings of the market, that what is involved is a

reduction of specialised labour to unspecialised" (Rosdolsky 1969: 609. Also see the English translation London 1977: 510 ff.).

21. "All labour is expressed as equal human labour and therefore as labour of equal quality" (Marx 1990: 152). By contrast Classical Political Economy never grasped the concept of abstract labour. It stuck to the empiricist inference that for there to be exchange there must be commensurability and that labour (although of a differing "quality" of usefulness in each case) creates this commensurability. As Meikle observes: "Ricardo, for instance, at the beginning of chapter 1, section 2 of his *Principles*, seems about to recognise the problem of the incommensurability of labours: 'In speaking, however, of labour, as being the foundation of all value (...) I am not be supposed to be inattentive to the different qualities of labour, and the difficulty of comparing an hour's or a day's labour, in one employment, with the same duration of labour in another'. (...) But in the next sentence he changes direction: 'The estimation in which different qualities of labour are held, comes soon to be adjusted in the market with sufficient precision for practical purposes (...)'. If he had at first got the matters of quality, end, and commensurability in his sights, which is at best doubtful, he vees away from it in his second sentence (...)" (Meikle 1995: 188). On the same question Smith wrote: "But it is not easy to find any accurate measure either of hardship or ingenuity. In exchanging, indeed, the different productions of different sorts of labour for one another, some allowance is commonly made for both. It is adjusted, however, not by any accurate measure, but by the higgling and bargaining of the market, according to that sort of rough equality which, though not exact, is sufficient for carrying on the business of common life" (Smith 1981: I.v.4).

22. In *Capital* Marx introduces his readers to these questions through the following phrase: "The reality of the value of commodities differs in this respect from Dame Quickly, that we don't know 'where to have it'. The value of commodities is the very opposite of the coarse materiality of their substance, not an atom of matter enters into its composition. Turn and examine a single commodity, by itself, as we will, yet in so far as it remains an object of value, it seems impossible to grasp it. (...) *Value can only manifest itself in the social relation of commodity to commodity*. In fact we started from exchange-value, or the exchange relation of commodities, in order to get at the value that lies hidden behind it. We must now return to this form under which value first appeared to us" (Marx 1990: 138-39, emphasis added).

23. Marx writes: "That in their appearance things are often presented in an inverted way is something fairly familiar in every science, apart from political economy" (Marx 1990: 677), and he explains that "the forms of appearance are reproduced directly and spontaneously, as current and usual modes of thought" (Marx 1990: 682), thus concealing the "hidden background" (Marx 1990: 682) and the "actual relation" (Marx 1990: 580). He thus connects the traditional philosophical dichotomy between *being* ("einai") and *appearing* ("fainesthai") with the process of creating scientific concepts that confronts common persuasion.

24. To quote Marx: "the form of appearance (...) makes the actual relation invisible, and indeed presents to the eye the precise opposite of that relation. (...) A scientific analysis of competition is not possible, before we have a conception of the inner nature of capital, just as the apparent motions of the heavenly bodies are not intelligible to any but him, who is acquainted with their real motions, motions which are not directly perceptible by the senses" (Marx 1990: 680, 433).

25. "But when the division of labour first began to take place, this power of exchanging must frequently have been very much clogged and embarrassed in its operations. One

man, we shall suppose, has more of a certain commodity than he himself has occasion for, while another has less. The former consequently would be glad to dispose of, and the latter to purchase, a part of this superfluity. But if this latter should chance to have nothing that the former stands in need of, no exchange can be made between them. (...) In order to avoid the inconveniency of such situations, every prudent man in every period of society, after the first establishment of the division of labour, must naturally have endeavoured to manage his affairs in such a manner as to have at all times by him, besides the peculiar produce of his own industry, a certain quantity of some one commodity or other, such as he imagined few people would be likely to refuse in exchange for the produce of their industry. (...) In all countries, however, men seem at last to have been determined by irresistible reasons to give the preference, for this employment, to metals above every other commodity" (Smith 1981: I.iv.2 and I.iv.4).

26. Through the expression of the value of each commodity in quantities of fabric, "the value of every commodity is now not only differentiated from its own use-value, but from all use-values, and is, by this very fact, expressed as that which is common to all commodities. By this form, commodities are, for the first time, really brought into relation with each other as values, or permitted to appear to each other as exchange-values" (Marx 1990: 158).

27. In distinction to the Marxian theory, a non-monetary theory of labour value (à la Ricardo) could be reconciled with the Neoclassical variant of ordinal utility, as Pareto demonstrated in a critique of what he regarded as the Marxian theory of value, since he too thought that "K. Marx simply follows the theories of Ricardo" (Pareto 1921: 28). He wrote: "If we suppose that the water consumer is a shoemaker paying the water carriers in shoes, what reveals to us the fact of the exchange is the shoemaker's assumption of equality between the effort expended in making a pair of shoes and the deprivation he would experience if left without water, which would be the recompense. And the same applies for the other similar assumption of equality made by the water carriers when they equate the trouble involved in their transporting a new quantity of water and the inconvenience they would suffer if deprived of shoes. (...) In order to come to grips with the theory of Karl Marx, let us acknowledge that this trouble is proportionate to the straightforward task of making the shoes as it is to that of transporting the water. That, however, is not enough. We must also suppose that there is no circumstance (...) that would prevent the shoemakers from changing profession such that it would be indifferent to them whether they should be provided with the commodity directly or through exchange. (...) So, since both instances of inconvenience are calculated on the basis of simple labour, which in any one place is relative, it follows that equal quantities of simple labour are contained in the shoes and the water. We thus have before us the hypothesis of Karl Marx" (Pareto 1921: 34, 35).

3 Money and Capital (Marx's Theory of Money and the Circuit of Capital)

1. Money-Mediated Exchange

From the above it has become apparent that for Marx value can be expressed (or manifested) only through money, as a "money-mediated" form of appearance registering the general exchangeability of commodities. According to the Marxist approach and in contrast to the Classical and Neoclassical schools, even the most straightforward act, that of exchanging two commodities[1] must be understood as a procedure consisting of two successive monetary transactions, a sale followed by a purchase, in accordance with the formula C-M-C (where C symbolises the commodity and M the money).

Thus, whereas in "simple commodity production" each sale is carried out with a view to making a purchase, already in this introductory scheme Marx is allowing it to be inferred that on the one hand one may buy without previously selling (an inference which introduces credit as a constitutive element in the "market economy") but also sell without buying ("hoarding" or, in present-day economic terms "saving"). But since there are no grounds for believing that an act of purchase by an economic agent should presuppose the same person selling anything (and conversely that a sale must be followed by the same person purchasing anything), Say's law ceases to apply and it becomes apparent that economic crisis is an inherent potentiality of the "market economy".[2]

In other words, the splitting of the whole business of the exchange process into two separate processes is a primary prerequisite for economic crises, which Classical economists (following Say's law) were not in a

Money and Capital 37

position to comprehend because they expunged money from their analysis and approached exchange on the basis of a barter model (exchange in kind).

2. Money as a Measure (of Value) as a Medium (of Circulation of Commodities) and as an End in Itself ("Money")

Marx initially describes money in the context of its functions as a measure of value (in its form of appearance)[3] as a standard of prices[4] and as a medium of circulation – during the process of exchange, in accordance with the formula C-M-C.[5] In these functions, money serves the purpose of facilitating commodity transactions; it is the *medium* of commodity circulation in the broadest sense of the term. In this sense, these functions of money correspond to the *classic conception of money*, since, as we have said, the Classical School (and for that matter the Neoclassical School also) perceives commodity transactions as actions analogous to barter, which are merely facilitated in a technical sense by money.

But Marx's analysis transcends the classic notional framework, as it refers to three additional functions of money: money as a means of hoarding, as means of payment and as "world money". All three of these functions of money according to Marx belong in the same category, denoting the same type of function, which is the function of *money "as money"*. By this Marx means that in all three cases money functions as an *end in itself, not as a medium* of commodity circulation:

In the case of *hoarding*, "commodities are thus sold not in order to buy commodities, but in order to replace their commodity-form by their money-form. From being the mere means of effecting the circulation of commodities, this change of form becomes the end and aim" (Marx 1990: 227-8).

As a *means of payment* money can be used in all cases where there is a commodity market based not on immediate deposit of money but on an agreement (a contract) of payment at a specific time in the future.[6] And in this case "money has now become the self-sufficient purpose of the sale" (Marx 1990: 234). Of course this function of money as a means of payment develops under that form of economy where *money is already an end in itself*: "The movement of the means of payment expresses a social connection which was already present independently" (Marx 1990: 235). We know from fragmentary comments by Marx in the first three chapters of the first volume of *Capital*, which we are examining here, and also from what follows in the fourth chapter, that the "social connection" in question is capitalism.

But also in its function as *world money* what predominates is its "function as means of payment in the settling of international balances" and for the "transferring wealth from one country to another" (Marx 1990: 243).

3. Money as Capital

3.1 A Question of Methodology

Marx's entire analysis of money as an end in itself (as "money") essentially refers to the function it performs as *capital*. Nevertheless, Marx chose to present *"what is value?"* and *"what is money?"* in the first three chapters of *Capital* before formulating the concept of capital and the capitalist mode of production. So, for instance, his treatment of the concept of "money as a means of payment" is necessarily carried out in reference to money's function as loan *capital*, and characteristically Marx in fact states that "the seller becomes a creditor, the buyer becomes a debtor" (Marx 1990: 233), but without having introduced the concept of interest (precisely because he has not defined what capital, and thus interest-bearing capital, is) although it is indispensable that he should do so for the functions of the creditor and the debtor to be comprehensible.

In the first volume of *Capital*, perhaps the most important section of the theory of money in the capitalist mode of production (money as capital) is contained in Part 2, Chapters 4-6 ("Transformation of money into capital"), where the analysis of money as a means of payment is "deciphered". There we read:

> Capital is money, capital is commodities. In truth, however, value is here the subject of a process, in which, while constantly assuming the form in turn of money and commodities, it at the same time changes in magnitude, throws off surplus-value from itself considered as original value, and thus valorises itself independently. (...) *The circulation of money as capital is an end in itself,* for the expansion of value takes place only within this constantly renewed movement. *The circulation of capital is therefore limitless.* (...) As the conscious bearer of this movement, the possessor of money becomes a capitalist (...) it is only in so far as the appropriation of ever more and more wealth in the abstract is the sole driving force of his operations, that he

functions as a capitalist, i.e. as capital personified and endowed with consciousness and a will (Marx 1990: 255, 253-4, emphasis added).[7]

To come to grips, then, with Marx's analysis of money, it is necessary to define the concept of capital and describe the function of money as capital. Before doing so, however, let us take the liberty of dwelling for a little on the consequences that have arisen vis-á-vis interpretation of Marx's work from the fact that in *Capital* value and money are initially defined in Chapters 1-3 without any reference to the concept of capital.

In the first three chapters of Volume 1, having chosen not to introduce the concept of capital, Marx to some extent restricts himself to the context of Aristotle's analysis of money, in which the distinction between money as a medium of circulation of commodities (in accordance with the formula C-M-C' which he himself coined) and its function as an end in itself (in accordance with the Aristotelian formula: M-C-M') was first introduced.

For Aristotle, the essence of commodities is to be found in their use-values, and accordingly that essence is not lost in the course of circulation C-M-C', since a useful thing (C) which is surplus to our needs is employed for the purposes of acquiring another similarly useful thing (C'). By contrast, in the formula M-C-M', the useful essence of the thing (C) is transformed into a means for acquiring more money (since M<M'), that is to say, money becomes an end in itself, so that the essence of the goods, and/or the natural purpose of the human activity which produced them, is lost.[8]

Characteristic of Marx's analysis of money as end in itself (as "money") being a first approximation to the concept of money-capital (money in its function as capital) is the fact that he chooses not to include in his analysis the Aristotelian formula of M-C-M', describing the movement of capital as end in itself, until he gets to the fourth chapter of Vol. 1, (where he introduces the notion of capital).

The manner in which Marx presents money (and value) prior to introducing the concept of capital has given rise to two significant instances of theoretical confusion among Marxists.

The *first confusion* is that whereby a distinction is drawn between the theory of value and the theory of the capitalist mode of production, with a more comprehensive content being assigned to the former. According to this concept, value is not a constitutive category of the concept of a capitalist mode of production but rather points in principle to a (supposed) historical epoch of generalised *simple* commodity production preceding capitalism. This means at the same time that value is a concept which (may) pertain to various modes and forms of production, including the "socialist mode of production".[9] This overlooks all those formulations by Marx himself according to which "*the value form of the product of labour is the most abstract but also the most universal form of the bourgeois* mode of production" (Marx 1990: 174).[10]

Apart from the "delinkage" of the concept of value from the capitalist mode of production and its consideration in relation to a whole host of "commodified" modes and forms of production,[11] the introductory reference to value "as such" has *a further consequence* for Marxist theory. It creates the illusion that the first three chapters of Vol. 1 of *Capital* contain (*can* contain) a consummated and definitive theoretical investigation of the concepts referred to.

This is particularly true of money, which in the context of Marx's original analysis (Chapters 1-3) is defined as the "adequate form of appearance of value, that is a material embodiment of abstract and therefore equal human labour" (Marx 1990: 184). This approach leaves outside of Marxist theory all of Marx's analysis, above all in the 3rd volume of *Capital*, of the function of money as capital, of the interpretation of interest, etc.[12] We shall return to this question. Let us now proceed to the concept of money as capital.

3.2 The Concept of Capital and its Origins in Surplus Value

Marx formulated and then developed the theory of capital on the basis of the concept of value. Capital is value which, though created by the working class, has been appropriated by capitalists. Precisely because it constitutes value, capital makes its appearance as money and commodities. But the commodities that function as capital are certain specific commodities: the means of production (fixed capital) on one hand and labour power (variable capital) on the other.

For labour power to constitute a commodity, it must have undergone a long historical process of social transformation and revolution from which there emerges the free worker.[13] The formation of the capital - wage labour relationship is thus a historically specific form of class power which is inseparable from the institutional, legal and ideological structure of the "free individual" and of equality. As already stated, Marx describes the internal interdependencies which condition this historic social order of things as the capitalist mode of production. The *capitalist mode of production* (and not the "economy" in general) is thus constituted as the pre-eminent object of

Marxian theory. (For the concept of mode of production and specifically the capitalist mode of production see Chapter 1 but also Chapter 6 below).

The use-value of the labour-power purchased by the capitalist consists in that it produces commodities which contain value in excess of its own value. If we denote as (v) the value of a unit of labour power (the variable capital advanced by the capitalist), then the new (net) value produced by it will be (v + s), where s is *surplus value*, the part of the value produced which is appropriated by the capitalist. The labour process is thus simultaneously a process of *valorisation* (production of value) and *surplus-value production*.

The working day is divided into the *necessary labour time* (during which the labourer produces a value equal to that of his labour-power) and the *surplus labour time* (in which surplus-value is produced). If (c) is the (pre-existing) value of the means of production which are worn out in the production process (or the amortisation), then the (gross) value of the produced output will be c+v+s.

Money, functioning as capital, unifies the capitalist production process and the process of circulation, in accordance with the Aristotelian formula M-C-M' (or M-C-[M + ΔM]). However, unlike in the age of Aristotle, where commerce was a marginal economic activity in the framework of a non-monetary and non-commercial economy (most useful goods were not commodities), within which ΔM could emerge as *direct appropriation of wealth* through exploitation of local peculiarities, or, as Aristotle wrote "through mutual deception" (quoted by Marx 1990: 177), in the capitalist mode of production the Aristotelian formula is nothing more than the "outer husk" of the overall process of capitalist production, i.e. the *circuit of (social) capital* (O'Hara 1999):

$$M—C \ (= Mp+Lp) \ [\rightarrow P \rightarrow C'] —M'$$

The capitalist appears on the market as the owner of money (M) buying commodities (C) which consist of means of production (Mp) and labour power (Lp). In the process of production (P), the C are productively used up in order to create an outflow of commodities, a product (C') whose value exceeds that of C. Finally he sells that outflow in order to recover a sum of money (M') higher than (M). Thus the "circulation of money leads (...) to capital" (Marx 1993: 776). Money appears to possess "the occult ability to add value to itself" (Marx 1990: 255). This is particularly so in the case of loan (or interest-bearing) capital, which the banker or finance capitalist lends to the industrial capitalist. The surplus value created in the process of production is then divided into profit and interest, and the latter appears to emerge automatically from the loan capital itself.

Surplus value (s = M'-M) acquired by the capitalists, and, according to the above representing the product of exploitation of the working class by capital (the class of capitalists), is transformed partially into means of private consumption for the capitalists themselves and partially into additional fixed and variable capital (i.e. additional means of production and labour power) for the expansion of production. The latter process (i.e. the conversion of surplus value into capital) is defined as *accumulation*. Through accumulation, the capitalist economy reproduces itself on an expanded scale.[14]

With the production process consuming (using up) one part of the pre-existing material capital, which is not only replaced by the (gross) product but also increased through invested (capitalised) surplus value, after a certain point the entire material capital becomes a product of (capitalised) surplus value. Surplus value (as the process of capitalist production and capitalist exploitation of labour) is produced by − and also produces − capital.

Surplus-value production is a process of exploitation of the labourers by the capitalist. Marx defines as *exploitation rate* (or surplus-value rate) the quotient s/v. Capitalist production aims at increasing surplus-value and the rate of exploitation. This is a moment inherent in the capital relation, which shapes the will of its "bearer", the individual capitalist, who functions "as capital personified and endowed with consciousness and a will" (Marx 1990: 254). Surplus-value increases accruing from a prolongation of the work-day or the intensification of labour are regarded by Marx as production of *absolute surplus-labour*. However, increases in s/v also result from increases in productivity of labour, which suppress the value of unit commodities and consequently reduce nominal wages if real wages remain unchanged (or even increase at rates lower than the increase rates in labour productivity). This process is defined as production of *relative surplus-labour*. From the point of view of prices (the "adequate form of appearance of value"), absolute surplus-value production designates an increase in the profit share due to reductions of the unit labour costs − in a given technological environment, whereas relative surplus value production designates profit share increases due to technological change (which lowers both the nominal wage and the constant capital costs).

So according to Marx's theory, the capitalist productive process is simultaneously a process of exploitation and domination of the working class by the class of capitalists. The class struggle is an immanent motive force of that process and the object over which the struggle is waged is first of all the magnitude of the capitalist exploitation (increase, stabilisation or curtailment of capitalist exploitation).

There thus emerges the radically amended Marxian version of *Thesis 4* of Classical Political Economy (see Chapter 2 Section 1 of this text). Surplus value is not conceived as a simple "subtraction" or "deduction" from the product of the worker's labour but as *a social relation, a result of and prerequisite for capitalist exploitation, which necessarily takes the form of (more) money, as the increment in value brought about by uniting the process of production with the process of circulation. The concept of surplus value is inseparable from that of value*, since under the capitalist mode of production value is mobilised for the sake of surplus value (money as an end in itself) and is made possible through surplus value.[15] Capital is a "self-valorising value" and

> as the dominant subject of this process (...) value requires above all an independent form by means of which its identity with itself may be asserted. *Only in the shape of money does it possess this form.* Money therefore forms the starting-point and the conclusion of every valorisation process (Marx 1990: 255).

From the above it emerges that money, to paraphrase a previously quoted extract from Marx, constitutes the most general form of appearance of capital. It is *the adequate form of appearance of value, that is a material embodiment of abstract and therefore equal human labour, which the capitalist has appropriated, and which in the framework of capitalist relations of exploitation is accumulated and functions as a "self-valorising value".* "Capital essentially produces capital" (Marx 1991: 1020). Capital is therefore not merely "the means of production" in general as held by the Classical and Neoclassical Schools. It is the social relation of capitalistic economic exploitation and domination, which is put in motion by money. *Money* is not a mere "medium" for facilitating economic transactions. It *is the necessary form of appearance of "self-valorising value", of capital.* A highly specific role in the activation of money as capital is played by interest-bearing capital, the operations of which Marx attempts to come to grips with above all in that part of his *Manuscripts 1863-67* which appeared as Part Five of the third volume of *Capital*, particularly in chapters 21-24.

In the Marxist system both value and money are concepts which cannot be defined independently of (or before) the notion of capital. They contain (and are also contained in) the concept of capital.

> This circulation of money in turn leads to capital, hence can be fully developed only on the foundation of capital, just as, generally, only on this foundation can circulation seize hold of all moments of production (Marx 1993: 776).

We will now test the theoretical consequences of the abovementioned theses, starting from what is known as the quantity theory of money.

4. Marx's Critique to the Quantity Theory of Money

4.1 Description of the Quantity Theory

Even before the formulation of Adam Smith's labour theory of value, the view had been put forward that price levels are determined by the quantity of money in circulation in a country. This idea was first propounded as an interpretation of the price rises that occurred in Europe during the 16th and 17th centuries, since it coincided with a mass influx of precious metals from the new South American mines. At the same time it was the basis for critique of the mercantilist views that "wealth" could be equated with money. If only price levels are regulated by the quantity of money, then this is a question merely of a nominalistic consequence. "Real" wealth consists in commodities' total value, irrespective of the quantity of precious metals which serve to put those commodities in circulation.

A further consequence of this quantity theory of money is that, *given that the analysis concerns metallic money*, it will be necessary at the same time to adopt the nominalistic view of money, i.e. the view according to which money is a public "symbol of value" (or "imaginary value") and not a commodity: Conversely, according to the Classical labour theory of value, whether in its Smithian version of expended labour or its Ricardian variant, money is a commodity and as such has "intrinsic value", whose dimensions are determined by the quantity of labour expended on producing and bringing it to market (see above).

Money and Capital 45

In fact it is in the work of David Hume, who first systematised the quantity theory of money, that we find its theoretical grounding in the nominalistic stance towards money:

> Money having chiefly a fictitious value, the greater or less plenty of it is of no consequence, if we consider a nation within itself; and the quantity of specie, when once fixed, though ever so large, has no other effect, than to oblige every one to tell out a greater number of those shining bits of metal, for clothes, furniture or equipage (D. Hume, *Of Interest*, quoted in Rubin 1989: 82).[16]

In more up-to-date mode, the quantity theory of money can be formulated as follows:

$$M \cdot V = P \cdot Y \quad (1),$$

Where M is the quantity of money in circulation, in other words the nominal money supply, V the speed of circulation (the multitude of transactions in which on average each monetary unit participates in the course of a given period of time), P is the level of prices and Y the real income (in material terms) of the economy. Thus $P \cdot Y$ is the nominal income (in monetary terms).

We can accordingly record relation (1) as follows:

$$M/P = Y/V \quad (2).$$

Relation (2) has as its left-hand component the "real money supply" (money as "purchasing power") and so the right-hand component must refer to the real demand for money. Given that money demand is regarded as a function of real income and interest rate, we may postulate that the speed of circulation registers the consequences of the level of interest rate on real money demand (Heinrich 1999: 244 ff.).

Assuming that at any given moment not only real income (Y) but also the speed of circulation (as determined by "standard business practice" but also by the levels of interest rates) is correspondingly stable, it follows that real money supply must also be stable, i.e. that:

$$M/P = \text{const.} \quad (3).$$

46 Karl Marx and the Classics

This means that any variation in the nominal money supply (M) *will lead to a corresponding variation in price levels (P).*

4.2 Non-Marxist Criticisms of Quantity Theory

From all the preceding it is not hard to understand that the quantity theory of money is open to criticism from three perspectives:

a) From the perspective of the Classical theory of value, according to which money is a commodity with "intrinsic value" which is determined by duration of production time (quantity of expended labour).

b) From a questioning of the thesis that speed of circulation (V) remains stable despite the alteration in the nominal money supply, i.e. questioning that real money demand is constant or that relation (2) can be reduced or converted to relation (3).

c) From an reversal of the flow of cause and effect introduced by quantity theory, i.e. from questioning the thesis that nominal money supply (M) may be considered an exogenous quantity (or as the independent variable in relation 3). Thus, even if relations (1)-(3) apply and real money demand is stable, price increases are not regarded as a consequence of the increase in nominal money supply, but on the contrary the increase in nominal money supply is regarded as a consequence of price increases (the cause of which must be located outside the realm of monetary circulation, in the sphere of production).

The key representatives of the Classical School were exponents of the first type of criticism (point a). Criticism of the quantity theory was voiced unequivocally by Adam Smith, who argued that the quantity of money in circulation (M) is determined by the inherent features of economic activity, i.e. endogenously, and cannot be modified (increased) even when metallic money is replaced by paper money.[17]

Somewhat more obliquely, Ricardo criticised the quantity theory of money on the basis of the argument that money "has an intrinsic value".[18] Nevertheless, in contrast to Smith, Ricardo adopted the view that the value of coins is something separate from the value of the *precious metal* they contain, and so finally arrived at the quantity theory of money. In Chapter VII, entitled "On foreign trade", of his *Principles of Political Economy and Taxation*, he grounds the famous theory of "comparative costs" in the quantity theory of money, thus assuming that in the context of international competition between different countries, price increases will emerge (in country A) on account of the attraction of precious metals in consequence of a positive trade balance,[19] with corresponding price reductions (in country B) due to an outflow of precious metals in consequence of a negative trade balance. Thus, in contrast to Smith, Ricardo equates the value of money with its nominal and not with its "real" price.[20] In short we might say that while Smith was an inconsistent critic of the quantity theory of money (on the basis of his thesis on the intrinsic value of gold), Ricardo was an inconsistent exponent of the quantity theory of money.

The second criticism of the quantity theory, i.e. that increase (fall) in the nominal supply of money may be accompanied by a parallel fall (increase) in the speed of circulation (point b), which may be equivalent to the outflow (or correspondingly the inflow) of money to (or from) circulation, was elaborated in the framework of non-Marxist economic theories, however not from the Classics but from Keynes and Keynesian-inspired macroeconomic analysis (see Mollo 1999: 6 ff.).

The third criticism of the quantity theory of money, according to which the quantity of money in circulation is an endogenously established magnitude, determined by the total income and the characteristics of the transactions (point c) is indirectly implied in Smith's argument concerning the intrinsic value of money. In Smith's account not only is the value of money always to be equated with the value of the precious metal it contains, but not even the issue of paper money or even promissory notes (money in the form of credit) can increase the quantity of money beyond what it is *necessary at any given time*, which is why paper money and promissory notes of necessity correspond to the value of the precious metal which they have replaced and which they "represent". Nevertheless, the view concerning the intrinsic character of the quantity of money in circulation was specifically formulated by Thomas Tooke (1774-1858)[21] (and later by John Stuart Mill), in the framework of the so-called Banking School. Tooke maintained, on the basis of extensive empirical documentation, that the value of bank-notes can never exceed what is necessary to cover the real needs of the economy.

4.3 Marx's Approach in the Context of the Theory of "Simple Commodity Production"

Marx knew and subscribed to critiques of the quantity theory of money quite a few years prior to commencing the researching and writing of his theoretical system for the Critique of Political Economy. On 3 February 1851, in a long letter to Engels:

What I want to take issue with is the fundamental essence of the matter. Specifically, I argue: *Even in the situation of a purely metallic currency, its expansion or contraction has nothing whatever to do with the inflow and outflow of precious metals, with a favourable or unfavourable trade balance, with favourable or unfavourable rates of exchange*, except in unusual circumstances, which in practice never arise, but can be designated theoretically. Tooke makes the same assertion. In any case I found no evidence in the *History of Prices*. (...) So the *currency* functions here not as a *cause*. Its increase is in the final analysis a *consequence* of a larger capital being activated, not the opposite (MEW Vol. 27: 174-5).

For this reason, Marx maintained, contraction in a country's reserves of metals would have to be confronted with an expansionary monetary policy and not a restrictive one, as had been the case until then.[22]

As early as 1851, Marx's remarks were suggesting that accumulation and the process of expanded reproduction of social capital determines (and is not determined by) expansion of the amount of money in circulation, in other words "the money supply". Of course this analysis cannot be formulated in the framework of the preliminary approach to the capitalist mode of production that is pursued by Marx in the first three chapters of *Capital* (or in *A Contribution to the Critique of Political Economy*), when he introduces the concept of money before that of capital. Marx limits himself initially to repeating the criticism that derives from the theses of the "Banking School" (see point (c) above). In his *Contribution to the Critique of Political Economy* he writes:

If the velocity of circulation is given, then the quantity of the means of circulation is simply determined by the prices of commodities. Prices are thus high or low not because more or less money is in circulation, but there is more or less money in circulation because prices are high or low (Marx 1981: 105).[23]

Marx's "self-limitation" to the conceptual framework of simple commodity production, in the first section of his analysis of money, thus leads him to restrict his critique to a reversal of the flow of cause and effect in the relation between prices and the available money supply. This reversal nevertheless continues to allow of a quantitative relation between the two variables (amount of money and prices). In the context of simple commodity production Marx in fact accepts the validity of Smith's analysis of the circulation of paper money, in fact postulating a "law peculiar to the circulation of paper money".[24]

It thus becomes clear that in the context of a theory of simple commodity circulation, in which money is a measure of value and a medium for circulation, the critique of the quantity theory of money cannot progress beyond the logic of the Classical arguments (Smith, Tooke). Marx is only able to elaborate his theoretical system from the moment that he introduces the concept of money as capital, even in the preliminary form of money as an "end in itself", i.e. the formula of "money as money".

4.4 "Money as Money" and the Quantity Theory

As soon as Marx makes reference to "hoarding" (as the preliminary concept of saving and credit money), the quantitative relation between alterations in the nominal money supply on one hand and price level on the other ceases to apply, given that *the money supply is no longer to be equated with the quantity of coins or paper money in circulation* and that the quantity of money in circulation is regulated endogenously by the movement (expanded reproduction) of capital, from which is derived the expansion or contraction of credit.

Even if one does not mention the ability of the credit system to create money whenever that becomes necessary for the process of expanded reproduction of overall capital (see below), a certain portion of the money (fluctuating in accordance with the economic conjuncture) remains out of circulation "stagnating" as a "hoard", thereby abolishing whatever quantitative relation exists between total money funds and price level. This position complements and provides an interpretative context for the preceding one, whereby the flow of cause and effect starts from prices and is directed towards the quantity in circulation. The new theoretical framework thus allows for the introduction, retrospectively, of the concept of credit money, which is produced by the credit system within the framework of the debtor-creditor relation. Marx writes in relation to the formation of "hoards":

> The total quantity of money in circulation must therefore perpetually increase or decrease in accordance with the changing aggregate price of the commodities in circulation, that is in accordance, on the one hand, with *the volume of their metamorphoses which take place simultaneously and, on the other hand, with the prevailing velocity of their transformation.* This is only

possible provided that *the proportion of money in circulation to the total amount of money in a given country varies continuously*. Thanks to the *formation of hoards* this condition is fulfilled. (...) The solidification of circulating money into hoards and the flowing of the hoards into circulation is a continuously changing and oscillating movement, and the prevalence of the one or the other trend is solely *determined by variations in the circulation of commodities* (MEGA II, 2: 197-8, poorly translated in Marx 1981: 136, emphasis added).

It follows therefore, that Marx's critique of the quantity theory of money cannot be brought to a conclusion, as is true also of the concept of money as such, prior to analysis of the function of money as capital. Nevertheless, from what has been said previously in the course of the present analysis, we are enabled to apprehend the Marxist argumentation implicit in the extract just quoted:

a) The "circulation of commodities" is merely a manifestation of the movement of capital, of expanded reproduction of the social capital (the circuit of social capital).

b) The fluctuations in this movement are to be sought for in the Marxist theory of crises, of the economic cycle and of fluctuations in the rate of profit.

c) The *result* of this movement and of these fluctuations is the expansion or contraction of the sphere of money and credit.

In this framework, relation (1), reflecting the quantity theory of money, is transformed by Marx into an identity, which equates the price of the total output of a time period with the total sum of *all money forms* circulating during this period plus the payments that balance one another:

$$P \cdot Y \equiv M \cdot V + \text{Mutually Balanced Payments (MBP)} \Leftrightarrow M \cdot V \equiv P \cdot Y - MBP$$

Marx also makes reference to the payments which still fall dew at the end of the period; he writes:

"The law regarding the quantity of money in circulation as it emerged from the examination of simple circulation of money is significantly modified by the circulation of means of payment. If the velocity of money, both as means of circulation and as means of payment, is given, then the aggregate amount of money in circulation during a particular period is determined by the total amount of commodity-prices to be realised [plus] the total amount of

Money and Capital   51

payments falling due during this period minus the payments that balance one another" (Marx 1981: 147).

5. A Note on the Relation Between Interest and Profit

The question that is raised on the basis of the above argument is the following: If the total amount of all forms of money in circulation is determined by the price of the total output, and with given the fact that an expansion of the monetary circulation is implemented mainly through the expansion of credit, then what is the type of relationship between, on the one hand, interest and the credit sphere and on the other average profit and the circuit of social capital?

Like the Classical economists, Marx's point of departure is the thesis that interest is a "derivative revenue",[25] more precisely that part of profit which the active capitalist is obliged to pay back to his lenders (the money-capitalists) for lending him (part of) his initial money capital.

In contrast to the Keynesian theory, Marx explicitly argues that the accumulation of capital in the industrial or service sectors is not determined by the movements of the interest rate (due to developments in the sphere of money and credit) but on the contrary, that the circuit of social capital determines more or less, depending on the economic conjuncture, the expansion or contraction of the financial sphere and influences the long-run trend of the interest rate. To put it somewhat differently, the rate of profit and its fluctuations, as the indicator which reflects the movement of total-social capital and the economic conjuncture, and not the interest rate (the indicator which correlates with fluctuations in the sphere of money and credit) is the determinant variable for the accumulation of capital ("economic development", as one might say in non-Marxist terminology). In the third volume of *Capital*, Marx makes clear the power of the above-mentioned theses.[26]

Furthermore, Marx argues that the "antithesis" between industrial capital and interest bearing capital appears only on the surface of capitalist economic and social relations, disguising their essential characteristics, i.e. the surplus-value production through exploitation of the labour-force. This "antithesis" cannot thus provide any scientific explanation in regard to the source or even the magnitude of profit, or the rate of capital accumulation:

The characteristic movement of capital in general, the return of money to the capitalist, the return of capital to its point of departure, receives in the case of interest-bearing capital a completely superficial form, separated from the real movement whose form it is. (...) All that we see is the giving-out and the repayment. Everything that happens in between is obliterated. (...) From the *quantitative* point of view, the part of profit that forms interest seems to be related not to industrial and commercial capital as such but rather to money capital, and the rate of this part of the surplus-value, the interest rate, confirms this relationship. This is firstly because the rate of interest – despite its dependence on the general rate of profit – is separately determined, and secondly because it appears, just like the market price of commodities, as something hard and fast, for all its changes: a palpable and always given relationship as opposed to the intangible rate of profit. (...) Taking the average profit as given, the rate of profit of enterprise is determined not by wages but rather by the rate of interest. It is either high or low in inverse proportion to the latter. (...) The purely quantitative division of profit between two persons with different legal titles to it has been transformed into a qualitative distinction that seems to arise from the very nature of capital and profit. (...) These two forms, interest and profit of enterprise, exist only in their antithesis. Thus they are neither of them related to surplus-value, of which they are simply parts, under different categories, titles or names, but rather related to each other. It is because one part of profit has been turned into interest that the other part accordingly appears as profit of enterprise (Marx 1991: 468-9, 471, 500, 503, 502).

According to Marx, credit, as the form of money anticipating and facilitating future production (i.e. the expanded reproduction of the social capital), constitutes the par excellence manifestation of capital's innate "essence", its ability to function as self-valorising value, which constitutes its sole aim: an "end in itself".

6. Credit and the Question of Commodity-Money

6.1 The Developed Marxian Argument

A final question to complete the theory of money from the viewpoint of Marxian analysis is the question of the "money commodity", i.e. the question of how far money must be reduced to the material substance of a manufactured medium, which was subsequently a commodity prior to becoming entirely (or partially) separated from the world of commodities and confined to the monetary function (or the function of both money and of the commodity: precious metal).

We know that not only in the time of Marx but even as early as the time of Adam Smith (see for example Kindleberger 1993: 79ff.) the money available for utilisation in the economy does not include only the so-called "monetary base", i.e. the disposable liquid assets in circulation and the disposable liquid assets of lending institutions, but that monetary base augmented through loans from the above-mentioned institutions to individuals and companies (the credit system as a producer of money), which loans always involve sums many times greater than the disposable liquid assets of the banks (irrespective of whether they consist of disposable assets in the form of bullion, metallic coin or of paper money). Credit money circulates in the form of promissory notes, overdraft loan accounts,[27] government securities, etc. while at the same time the actions of clearance carried out through the credit system make it possible for there to be transactions without any actual cash changing hands, etc., so that the overall amount (supply) of disposable money and money in circulation will differ to a greater or lesser extent from the total sum of liquid assets, and even more so of coin.

It is quite possible to come to an understanding of these different forms of money in the framework of Marxist theory, since this theory perceives money as *the necessary form of appearance of value* (and so of *capital*) and value not as a quality of each individual commodity but as a *comprehensive social-economic* relation (mediated through money).[28] It is a relation derived from (and linked to) the structural characteristics of the capitalist mode of production, which is why comprehension of it presupposes the concept of capital. Value, as Engelskirchen (2001) correctly argues, being the social relation uniting all "independent commodity producers", can be conceptualised as a claim on the labour product of others.

Money is not the representative of a material or of a commodity, but the embodiment of the capital relation: It can thus be produced within the framework of the expanded reproduction of this relation (i.e. independently of any commodity or material), and this is exactly what happens when the bank opens an advance credit account for a businessman client. The loans and the credit of every bank always amount to a sum many times greater than its liquid assets. In the first place, the bank does not simply transfer some already existing sum of paper money or gold (belonging to itself or to its depositors). It creates additional credit money (since credit money is created at precisely the moment the loan is concluded, e.g. through loan-consolidation services), without making demands on some treasury or other. That is to say it expands, depending on the conjuncture (the expected rate of profit, etc.) the boundaries of the formula M—C(= Mp+Lp) [→P→C′]— M′, in which the client(s) is (are) implicated. Credit is a demand on *future* production, but it functions as money (exchange value) in the present. Through this procedure the bank will cream off, in the form of interest, a part of the profit (ΔM=M′-M) which will enable it to expand further, at a multiplying rate, its credit and loans. In this way it creates the prerequisites for production of profit to an extent *regulated by the particularities of the specific conjuncture*. It becomes thus clear that:

> this social character of capital is mediated and completely realised only by the full development of the credit and banking system (Marx 1991: 742).

The implication of the above is that the creation of credit money (the expansion of credit) takes place under preconditions which make possible the expanded reproduction of capital at a given rate.[29] In other words, they allow the expansion of the process of surplus-value extraction from labour, as well as the process of surplus value accumulation. These preconditions are judged by the economic parties concerned (banks, entrepreneurs) to secure a) the existence of an additional supply of means of production and labour power, in quantities and at prices which make possible the expansion of the individual capitals resorting to borrowing, b) the capacity of these individual capitals, through expanding their production, to manufacture a product in quantities and at prices that will secure its absorption by demand capable to pay, c) the ability of capitals in question to secure by this means a sufficient rate of profit to make it worthwhile for them to have concluded the loan (and thus expanded the credit).[30]

At the level of the economy as a whole, Marx studied the issues connected with points (a) and (b) in the 2nd volume of *Capital*, part three, where he examined the conditions of "reproduction and circulation of the total social capital" (see Chapter 5). The issues bearing on point (c) were examined by Marx in the 3rd volume of Capital, both in relation to fluctuation of the average rate of profit and economic crises (sections 1-3) and in relation to money capital and the credit system (sections 4 and 5. See Chapters 7-9). Under the preconditions mentioned, money capital appears to have:

the power of producing surplus-value in geometric progression by way of an inherent secret quality, as a pure automaton, so that this accumulated product of labour (...) has long since discounted the whole world's wealth for all time, as belonging to it by right and rightfully coming its way (Marx 1991: 523-4).

Money, according to the Marxian analysis of credit and expanded reproduction of the total social capital cannot be reduced to a "commodity" with "intrinsic value". Money (and credit money) is a form of appearance of the capital-relation:

> It is the foundation of capitalist production that money confronts commodities as an autonomous form of value, or that exchange-value must obtain an autonomous form in money. (...) This must show itself in two ways, particularly in developed capitalist countries, which replace money to a large extent either by credit operations or by credit money. (...) In former modes of production, this does not happen, because given the narrow basis on which these move, neither credit nor credit money is able to develop (Marx 1991: 648-9).[31]

6.2 Digression: On the Contradictions of the Classical Approach

Before closing this chapter we would like to refer again in more detail to the Classical approach of money as a "commodity with intrinsic value" and its contradictions when approaching credit money.

Conversely to the Marxian analysis, understanding of credit money within the context of the Classical system becomes a vexed issue, since it is considered that the value of every commodity is formed separately and exists in isolation, with money perceived as one among many commodities (with "intrinsic" value), which in every transaction simply activates other commodities of equal value. The point is of significant importance for Marxist economic theory, because Marx's choice to take for his point of departure the Classical definition of value and the (Classical) schema of simple commodity circulation (albeit as the "surface" of the capitalist economy) meant transferring a part of the contradictions and misunderstandings of the Classical system into Marxist analysis and discourse.

It is in the work of Adam Smith that we can, again, best pinpoint these contradictions of Classical Political Economy.

a) Since money is a commodity of a value corresponding to the labour time required for bringing it onto the market, each non-metallic form of money (paper money, securities) must be seen as comprising a substitute for a specific quantity of the money commodity, by means of which substitution the economy succeeds merely in reducing circulation costs.[32] b) But if it is simply a question of replacing expensive gold with cheap paper securities of negligible "intrinsic value", the gold should be withdrawn from circulation. But nothing of this kind is acceptable since, in the Classical mode of though, money is perceived exclusively as a medium for circulation (and not, at the same time, as a "hoard"). The metallic money that has been replaced by paper money and promissory notes cannot be withdrawn from circulation and hoarded. Since however the quantity of money in circulation cannot be increased either, because the quantity of money that must circulate is in each instance regulated (at its fixed level, as it was prior to the introduction of non-metallic money) by the circulation itself, we are faced with an inherent contradiction. What happens finally to the additional money generated by the credit functions of the banks, from the issue of promissory notes?

Smith tries to resolve the contradiction, asserting that the bullion that is replaced will be exported abroad as foreign exchange for the purchase of commodities manufactured in other countries.[33] But if the circulation of commodities abroad *can* be increased through utilisation of the (domestic) surplus gold, why *cannot* domestic circulation also be increased? If the additional money can increase circulation anywhere (abroad), then something similar is theoretically also possible in the country in question (domestically). It is obvious that Smith displaced, but did not resolve, the contradiction into which his theory led him (the Classical theory of value and money as a commodity).

The Classical system of thought cannot cope with this contradiction, and it is therefore not by chance that it often abandons the thesis about the "intrinsic value" of money to adhere to the quantity theory. This contradiction does not exist in the Marxist system, unless one insists on reading Marx through the prism of the Classical system of concepts, perhaps misled by the manner of presentation of his theory in the 1st part of the 1st volume of *Capital*. Because even if one combines the Classical thesis of money as a commodity possessing an intrinsic value with the position that any excess supply of money goes into hoarding, still the fact cannot be explained how in certain conjunctures a volume of credit is created which constitutes a multiple of all forms of liquid assets or reserves.

The analysis of Marx shows that the capital *relation* necessarily manifests itself in the form of a *"thing"*, of an "object", this "thing" being money. For the analysis of money Marx takes as his point of departure the model of simple barter exchange ("the simple, isolated or accidental form of value"), and so he initially presents the "thing" which measures value and embodies the capital relation as a produced commodity. However, it is not a pre-existing material body which allows the expression of value, but, on the contrary, it is the expanded reproduction of the capital relation, the circuit of social capital functioning as "self-valorising value" which creates the (quantity of the) "thing" "materialising" value and capital.

A *social relation* creates the *thing* to which it is expressed: The scheme relates to what Marx described as *fetishism*, which will be our main object of analysis in the next Part of this book.

Notes

1. An act during which "all commodities are non-use-values for their owners, and use-values for their non-owners" (Marx 1990: 179).
2. "Nothing could be more foolish than the dogma that because every sale is a purchase, and every purchase a sale, the circulation of commodities necessarily implies an equilibrium between sales and purchases. If this means that the number of actual sales is equal to the number of purchases, it is mere tautology. (...) No one can sell unless some one else purchases. But no one directly needs to purchase because he has just sold. Circulation bursts through all the temporal, spatial and personal barriers imposed by the direct exchange of products, and it does this by splitting up the direct identity present in this case between the exchange of one's own product and the acquisition of someone else's into the antithetical segments of sale and purchase" (Marx 1990: 208-9).
3. "The first main function of gold is (...) to represent their values as magnitudes of the same denomination, qualitatively equal, and quantitatively comparable. It thus serves as a universal measure of value (...)" (Marx 1990: 188).
4. "[Money] is the standard of price inasmuch as it is a fixed weight of metal. As the measure of value it serves to convert the values of all the manifold commodities into prices, into imaginary quantities of gold; as the standard of price it measures those quantities of gold. The measure of values measures commodities considered as values; the standard of price measures, on the contrary, quantities of gold by a unit quantity of gold, not the value of one quantity of gold by the weight of another. In order to make gold a standard of price, a certain weight must be fixed as the unit of measurement" (Marx 1990: 192).
5. "The circulation of money is the constant and monotonous repetition of the same process. The commodity is always in the hands of the seller; the money, as a means of purchase, always in the hands of the buyer. (...) This realisation transfers the commodity from the seller to the buyer and removes the money from the hands of the

58 *Karl Marx and the Classics*

buyer into those of the seller, where it again goes through the same process with another commodity" (Marx 1990: 210-11).

6. Of course, at the prearranged deadline "the means of payment enters circulation (...) after the commodity has already left it. (...) The price fixed by contract measures the obligation of the buyer, i.e. the sum of money he owes at a particular time" (Marx 1990: 234).

7. We see, then, that money is reduced to *an end in itself* in the economic process when it functions as capital and that Marx's analysis of money as "money" (an end in itself) has begun to introduce us to this function it has as capital, as is evident in formulations like the following: "as the hart pants after fresh water, so pants his [the bourgeois's] soul after money" (Marx 1990: 236). Unlike for Marx, for Classical Political Economy, perceiving money as it does as a simple *means* of facilitating transactions (which are interpreted as acts of mutual exchange of commodities on the barter model) the purpose of (capitalist) economy cannot be other than the acquisition of useful things (use values), in the final analysis goods for individual consumption: "To maintain and augment the stock which may be reserved for immediate consumption is the sole end and purpose both of the fixed and circulating capitals" (Smith 1981: II.i.26). Keynes was aware of money's function as an "end in itself" but he did not develop a conception of capital comparable to that of Marx. In contrast even to Aristotle, who saw the root of money's function as an end in itself in the inherent qualities of money as such (i.e., ultimately, in the social relations through which it is articulated or which it tends to establish, see Meikle 1995), Keynes sought for the source of money's function as an end in itself in quasi-psychological conceptions of "human nature", in which were grounded both the "marginal propensity to consume" and the "propensity to save" or the "propensity to hoard".

8. As Scott Meikle remarks, "this is the main contrast Aristotle draws between the circuit M-C-M' and C-M-C'. He says that the aim or point of C-M-C' lies in the fact that C and C' are different use-values. The aim is to acquire the specific usefulness of C' which is needed, and the sale of C is simply a means to that end. Once C' is acquired in this way, exchange reaches a natural terminus. (...) But the M-C-M' circuit has no natural terminus. It has no end outside of circulation. 'Money is the starting point and the goal' of this form of activity, as Aristotle observes (1257^b22 f.), and since there is no difference of quality between one sum of money and another, the only possible difference being one of quantity, this quantitative growth of exchange value in the form of money is the only aim that M-C-M' can have. But if M can be advanced to become M', so can M' be advanced to become M'', and so on, without limit. Aristotle says of this kind of exchange that 'there is no limit to the end it seeks; and the end it seeks is wealth of the sort we have mentioned (...) the mere acquisition of currency' (1257^b28 f.)" (Meikle 1995: 58-9). It is recommended that the reader compare the extracts from Aristotle quoted by Meikle to the following formulations by Marx: "The hoarding drive is boundless in its very nature. (...) But at the same time every actual sum of money is limited in amount. (...) This contradiction between the quantitative limitation and the qualitative lack of limitation of money keeps driving the hoarder back to his Sisyphean task: accumulation" (Marx 1990: 230-31).

9. Socialism does not constitute a social regime corresponding to some particular mode of production but a social regime of transition from capitalism to communism: the regime of labour power. Given that social relations and structures corresponding to the

Money and Capital 59

capitalist mode of production will be overturned constantly, workers' class power leads to the classless society of Communism, that is to say to the abolition of all forms of domination. See Milios 1995. Also see Bettelheim 1974, 75: "If the value form is preserved in present-day transitory social formations, this is due to the fact that *defined social relations are also preserved which objectively take on 'the fantastic form of a relation between things'*".

10. We should bear in mind that Engels himself in his Preface to the third volume of *Capital* hastened to assert that in Volume 1 Marx "takes simple commodity production as [the] historical presupposition" of capitalism, i.e. that he is "proceeding from this basis, to come on to capital - (...) he proceeds precisely there from the simple commodity and not from a conceptually and historically secondary form, the commodity as already modified by capitalism" (Engels in Marx 1991: 91, emphasis added). Also see Hecker 1998: 73ff.

11. The delinkage is reinforced by the empirical fact of the existence of commodities, money, interest-bearing loans, etc. within the structures of pre-capitalist societies. Nevertheless, no pre-capitalist society has been a society of generalised commodity production, or generalised monetary circulation and extensive credit relations. In other words only capitalism has, or is, a "market economy". Nevertheless, having opted for not yet introducing the concept of capital, in the first three chapters of Volume 1, Marx derives many of the examples he cites from these pre-capitalist forms of money, interest, saving, etc. thus facilitating a misconstrual of the content of his analysis.

12. A characteristic example of entrapment in the view that there can be a Marxist theory of money without prior formulation of the concept of capital (money as capital) is a 1994 text by Lapavitsas, where we read: "Marx's own theory had a highly structured view of the functions of money. (...) His theory started with the essence of money (the 'universal equivalent' or 'independent form of value'. (...) From this starting point, three functions were derived in strict logical sequence: measure of value, means of circulation and money as money (which includes the dimensions of money as hoard, as means of payment and as international money)" (Lapavitsas 1994: 449). Following the general rule, the author considers that the first three chapters of Vol. 1 contain the basic components of the Marxist theory of money. Nevertheless, most treatises on Marxist economic theory are completely indifferent to the Marxist theory of money. In other words, they seem not to perceive the monetary character of the Marxist concepts of value and capital, but to accept the Classical dichotomy between the "real" magnitudes and money as a simple means for facilitating the workings of the "real" economy, or even – in a more "Marxist" variant, its "concealment". Note – by way of illustration - the eloquent absence of the Marxist theory of money and capital as money in Sweezy, (1970) Meek (1973), Dobb (1973), Howard and King (1985), Catefores (1989). Some other Marxists, such as Elson (1979) and Levine (1985) in fact seem to believe that Marx introduced two measures for value, labour time and money.

13. "One thing, however, is clear: Nature does not produce on the one side owners of money or commodities, and on the other men possessing nothing but their own labour-power. (...) Had we gone further, and inquired under what circumstances all, or even the majority of products take the form of commodities, we should have found that this only happens on the basis of one particular mode of production, the capitalist one" (Marx 1990: 273).

14. In the special case of non-accumulation, i.e. when all the surplus value goes into the private consumption of the capitalist, we have *simple reproduction*. In Volume two of *Capital*, Marx formulates the conditions of uninterrupted – simple and expanded – reproduction of a pure capitalist economy comprising two sectors, one of which produces means of production for the whole economy, and the other means of consumption for all labourers and capitalists. (See Chapter 5).
15. As Arthur correctly notes: "*To be self-grounded, value must be produced by value.* This means that only those goods produced by capital itself count as values, as true commodities in both form and content. Only capitalistically produced commodities have adequacy in both form and content of value in and for itself. The activity of production is an activity of labour. Hence, capital must make that activity its own activity" (Arthur 1993: 85). However, the author combines his approach with a Hegelian interpretation of Marx's theory, which we regard as unpersuasive. We rather approve Murray's (2000) argument: "Marx does not leave the circle of Hegelian systematic dialectics unbroken; he objects to the 'presuppositionlessness' of Hegelian systematic dialectics and insists that science has premises. (...) These premises (...) reappear in *Capital* and testify to Marx's explicit and frequently reaffirmed divergence from strictly Hegelian systematic dialectics".
16. In the same author we find the idea that the quantity theory applies not for the total sum of money that exists in a country as a whole but for that part of it which functions as a means of circulation for commodities: "Prices do not so much depend on the absolute quantity of commodities and that of money, which are in a nation, as on that of the commodities which come or may come to market, and of the money which circulates. If the coin be locked up in chests, it is the same thing with regard to prices, as if it were annihilated; if the commodities be hoarded in magazines and granaries, a like effect follows. As the money and commodities, in these cases, never meet, they cannot affect each other" (D. Hume, *Of Money*, cited in Rubin 1989: 83).
17. "The increase of paper money, it has been said, by augmenting the quantity, and consequently diminishing the value of the whole currency, necessarily augments the money price of commodities. But as the quantity of gold and silver, which is taken from the currency, is always equal to the quantity of paper which is added to it, paper money does not necessarily increase the quantity of the whole currency. (...) The proportion between the price of provisions in Scotland and that in England is the same now as before the great multiplication of banking companies in Scotland. (...) In 1751 and in 1752, when Mr. Hume published his Political Discourses, and soon after the great multiplication of paper money in Scotland, there was a very sensible rise in the price of provisions, owing, probably, to the badness of the seasons, and not to the multiplication of paper money. (...) A paper currency which falls below the value of gold and silver coin does not thereby sink the value of those metals, or occasion equal quantities of them to exchange for a smaller quantity of goods of any other kind. The proportion between the value of gold and silver and that of goods of any other kind depends in all cases not upon the nature or quantity of any particular paper money, which may be current in any particular country, but upon the richness or poverty of the mines, which happen at any particular time to supply the great market of the commercial world with those metals. It depends upon the proportion between the quantity of labour which is necessary in order to bring a certain quantity of gold and silver to market, and that which is necessary in order to bring thither a certain quantity

Money and Capital 61

of any other sort of goods" (Smith 1981: II.ii). Nevertheless, with the inconsistency for which his work is notorious, Smith at other points in the *Wealth of Nations* accepts the quantity theory of money: "Any increase in the quantity of silver, while that of the commodities circulated by means of it remained the same, could have no other effect than to diminish the value of that metal. The nominal value of all sorts of goods would be greater, but their real value would be precisely the same as before" (Smith 1981: II.iv.11).

18. "Gold and silver, like other commodities, have an intrinsic value, which is not arbitrary, but is dependent on their scarcity, the quantity of labour bestowed in procuring them and the value of the capital employed in the mines which produce them" (Ricardo 1810: 2).

19. "Whenever the current of money is forcibly stopped, and when money is prevented from settling at its just level, there are no limits to the possible variations of the exchange. The effects are similar to those which follow, when a paper money, not exchangeable for specie at the will of the holder, is forced into circulation. Such a currency is necessarily confined to the country where it is issued: it cannot, when too abundant, diffuse itself generally amongst other countries. The level of circulation is destroyed, and the exchange will inevitably be unfavourable to the country where it is excessive in quantity: just so would be the effects of a metallic circulation, if by forcible means, by laws which could not be evaded, money should be detained in a country, when the stream of trade gave it an impetus towards other countries" (Ricardo 1992: 91).

20. "While gold is exclusively the standard in this country money will be depreciated when a pound sterling is not of equal value with 5 dwts. and 3 grs. of standard gold, and that whether gold rises or falls in general value" (Ricardo 1992: 93).

21. His three-volume work, *A History of Prices and of the State of the Circulation from 1792 to 1847 inclusive*, was published in 1848.

22. "I now maintain that the Bank [of England] should increase its discounting when there is a reduction in the amount of available metals (...) for example through the purchase of government securities, exchequer bills, etc" (Marx, in MEW Vol. 27: 174).

23. Nevertheless, even at this stage of his analysis, Marx warns the reader that the analysis cannot be brought to completion within the theoretical framework of "simple commodity production": "If the aggregate prices of the commodities in circulation rise, but to a smaller extent than the velocity of currency increases, then the volume of money in circulation will decrease. (...) But the causes occasioning a rise in the level of prices and at the same time an even larger rise in the velocity of currency, as also the converse development, lie outside the scope of an investigation into simple circulation. We may mention by way of illustration that in periods of expanding credit the velocity of currency increase faster than the prices of commodities, whereas in periods of contracting credit the velocity of currency declines faster than the prices of commodities" (Marx 1981: 105). In *Capital*, where the corresponding analysis is much briefer, Marx notes: "credit-money take[s] root spontaneously in the function of money as means of payment" (Marx 1990: 224).

24. "The issue of paper money must be restricted to the quantity of gold (or silver) which would actually be in circulation and which is represented symbolically by the paper money" (Marx 1990: 224).

25. "Whoever derives his revenue from a fund which is his own, must draw it either from his labour, from his stock, or from his land (...) The interest of money is always a derivative revenue, which, if it is not paid from the profit which is made by the use of the money, must be paid from some other source of revenue" (Smith 1981: I.vi.18).
26. "Since interest is simply a part of profit (...) which the industrial capitalist has to pay to the money capitalist, the maximum limit of interest would seem to be the profit itself, in which case the share that accrues to the functioning capitalist would be zero. Leaving aside those special cases (...), we might perhaps consider the maximum limit of interest as the whole profit minus the part of it reducible to the 'wages of superintendence'. (...) The minimum limit of interest is completely indeterminate. It could fall to any level, however low. (...) If we consider the turnover cycles in which modern industry moves (...) we find that a low level of interest generally corresponds to periods of prosperity or especially high profit, a rise in interest comes between prosperity and its collapse, while maximum interest up to extreme usury corresponds to a period of crisis. (...) Yet low interest can also be accompanied by stagnation, and a moderate rise in interest by growing animation. (...) But there is also a tendency for the rate of interest to fall, quite independently of fluctuations in the rate of profit. (...) The prevailing average rate of interest in a country (...) cannot be determined by any law. (...) The coincidence of demand and supply means nothing at all here. (...) There is no reason at all why the average conditions of competition, of equilibrium between lender and borrower, should give the lender an interest of 3, 4, 5 per cent, etc. on his capital, or alternatively a certain percentage, 20 per cent or 50 per cent, of the gross profit. Where, as here, it is competition as such that decides, the determination is inherently accidental, purely empirical, and only pedantry or fantasy can seek to present this accident as something necessary" (Marx 1991: 480, 482-5).
27. "Instead of a paper note, the bank can open a credit account for A, so that A, as its debtor, becomes an imaginary depositor" (Marx 1991: 589).
28. This explains why "exchange value" (price), as the form of appearance of value, adheres to nearly "everything" in the capitalist system, and not only to "produced goods". In this connection, we remind the reader that money has no price, and its "value" can only be assessed through the Marxian formula of "total or expanded form of value": it is the series of commodities (given the role of the "equivalent") that can be purchased with one monetary unit. For this reason, not even metallic money is a commodity like others, but an "object" in the body of which value finds representation and which, in the words of Marx "it is universal wealth in an individual form" (Marx 1981: 125). In the *Grundrisse* this position of Marx is formulated with even greater clarity: "In order to realise the commodity as exchange value in one stroke, and in order to give it the general influence of an exchange value, it is not enough to exchange it for one particular commodity. It must be exchanged against a third thing which is not in turn itself a particular commodity, but is the symbol of the commodity as commodity, of the commodity's exchange value itself, *which thus represents, say, labour time as such*, say a piece of paper or of leather, which represents a fractional part of labour time. (Such a symbol presupposes general recognition; it can only be a social symbol; it expresses, indeed, nothing more than a social relation)" (Marx 1993: 144). In the 1st Volume of *Capital*, Marx explains that often there is no point in distinguishing between the different forms of money: "In a crisis, the antithesis between commodities and their value-form, money, is raised to the level of an absolute contradiction. Hence,

money's form of appearance is here also a matter of indifference. The monetary famine remains whether payments have to be made in gold or in credit-money, such as banknotes" (Marx 1990: 236-7). (For the question of the "money commodity" but also the extensive Marxist discussion around this question, see Heinrich 1999: 233-44. For a convincing vindication of the thesis that the reduction of money to a commodity constitutes a confusion of categories within Marx's system, see Williams 1998. For the opposite position, according to which money has to be a commodity with intrinsic value, see Giussani 1999, Matsumoto 2001. For a similar argument, according to which the "value of money" can be determined by itself, as a definite quantity of abstract labour, see Moseley 2000, Ramos-Martínez and Rodrigues 1996.)

29. For an intruding analysis of the endogeneity of money in Marx's system see Mollo 1999.

30. "The limits of this commercial credit, considered by itself, are (1) the wealth of the industrialists and merchants, i.e. the reserve capital at their disposal in case of a delay in returns; (2) these returns themselves. They may be delayed in time, or commodity prices may fall in the meantime, or again the commodities may temporarily become unsaleable as a result of a glut on the market. (...) The development of the production process expands credit, while credit in turn leads to an expansion of industrial and commercial operations. (...) The maximum of credit is the same thing here as the fullest employment of industrial capital, i.e. the utmost taxing of its reproductive power" (Marx 1991: 611-12, 612, 613).

31. The above cardinal thesis enables Marx to come to grips to the relative autonomy of *money crises* from "actual" economic crises of capital overaccumulation (see Part III): "As long as the *social* character of labour appears as the *money existence* of the commodity and hence as a *thing* outside actual production, monetary crises, independent of real crises or as an intensification of them, are unavoidable. It is evident on the other hand that, as long as a bank's credit is not undermined, it can alleviate the panic in such cases by increasing its credit money, whereas it increases this panic by contracting credit. The entire history of modern industry shows that metal would be required only to settle international trade and its temporary imbalances, if production at home were organised. The suspension of cash payments by the so-called national banks, which is resorted to as the sole expedient in all extreme cases, shows that even now no metal money is needed at home" (Marx 1991: 649). As Williams (1998: 32, 18) puts it: "Marx's categorical development of the value form soon transcends commodity aspects of money. (...) If confidence in all currency were to collapse, value may take refuge in particular commodities characterised by intrinsic scarcity (...) including bullion. But this process becomes not the flight into a particular manifestation of money, but the flight *from* money in all its functionality, as part of the flight from capital".

32. "The substitution of paper in the room of gold and silver money, replaces a very expensive instrument of commerce with one much less costly, and sometimes equally convenient" (Smith 1981: II.ii.26). "A particular banker lends among his customers his own promissory notes, to the extent, we shall suppose, of a hundred thousand pounds. As those notes serve all the purposes of money, his debtors pay him the same interest as if he had lent them so much money. This interest is the source of his gain. Though some of those notes are continually coming back upon him for payment, part of them continue to circulate for months and years together. Though he has generally in

circulation, therefore, notes to the extent of a hundred thousand pounds, twenty thousand pounds in gold and silver may frequently be a sufficient provision for answering occasional demands. By this operation, therefore, twenty thousand pounds in gold and silver perform all the functions which a hundred thousand could otherwise have performed (...) the whole circulation may thus be conducted with a fifth part only of the gold and silver which would otherwise have been requisite" (Smith 1981: II.ii.29).

33. "Let us suppose, for example, that the whole circulating money of some particular country amounted, at a particular time, to one million sterling, that sum being then sufficient for circulating the whole annual produce of their land and labour. Let us suppose, too, that some time thereafter, different banks and bankers issued promissory notes, payable to the bearer, to the extent of one million, reserving in their different coffers two hundred thousand pounds for answering occasional demands. There would remain, therefore, in circulation, eight hundred thousand pounds in gold and silver, and a million of bank notes, or eighteen hundred thousand pounds of paper and money together. But the annual produce of the land and labour of the country had before required only one million to circulate and distribute it to its proper consumers, and that annual produce cannot be immediately augmented by those operations of banking. (...) The channel of circulation, if I may be allowed such an expression, will remain precisely the same as before. (...) One million eight hundred thousand pounds are poured into it. Eight hundred thousand pounds, therefore, must overflow, that sum being over and above what can be employed in the circulation of the country. But though this sum cannot be employed at home, it is too valuable to be allowed to lie idle. It will, therefore, be sent abroad, in order to seek that profitable employment which it cannot find at home. But the paper cannot go abroad; (...) Gold and silver, therefore, to the amount of eight hundred thousand pounds will be sent abroad, and the channel of home circulation will remain filled with a million of paper, instead of the million of those metals which filled it before" (Smith 1981: II.ii.30).

PART II:
THEORY OF VALUE
AND IDEOLOGY

4 The Question of "Commodity Fetishism"

1. Introduction

As stated in Chapter 1, Marx's economic theory is firmly embedded in his analysis of class power within class struggle, i.e. it is connected with a theory of the political and ideological "superstructures" of capitalist societies. In Marx's analysis of the Capitalist Mode of Production and more precisely in his theory of value, the key to decipher the political and ideological practices and structures is to be found. In this context, many Marxists believed that the analysis of "commodity fetishism" in Volume 1 of *Capital* renders the basis for understanding ideological domination and political coercion under the capitalist rule.

Marx introduced the notion of *commodity fetishism* in Section 4 of Chapter 1, Volume 1 of *Capital*, to describe the "mysterious character of the commodity-form", which consists in the fact that "the definite social relation between men themselves (...) assumes here, for them, the fantastic form of a relation between things" (Marx 1990: 164, 165).

Commodity fetishism has become, ever since, one of the classic themes in the Marxist bibliography.[1] Not only is it of direct importance in the framework of the Marxist theory of value and deployed widely in analyses of the bourgeois state and bourgeois law. It also constitutes a "major theoretical construction of present-day philosophy" (Balibar 1993, 56).[2] But what is interesting about these studies is primarily attributable to the fact that the analyses of fetishism are linked to issues which are controversial among Marxists, i.e. that they function as a point of departure for certain political strategies and as a symbol for them. All of which helps to explain the variety of viewpoints propounded, and the ardour of those who propound them, in the discussion on what Marx said in the section of fetishism in the first chapter of Vol. 1 of *Capital*, which is usually considered to exhaust his theoretical deliberations on the subject.

2. From the Fetishes of "Indigenes" to Alienation and Anti-Humanist Marxism. The Evolution of Fetishism

2.1 Ethnographers and their Fetishes

Even though the question of fetishism is inseparably linked to the works of Marx and Freud, the term "fetish" is much older.[3] The first colonists characterised as "fetishes"[4] the religious objects and ceremonies of the peoples they conquered. The term "fetishism" was to make its appearance in 1760 in the work of Charles de Brosses *Du culte des dieux fétiches* (*On the Worship of Fetish Gods*), which analyses the religions of "primitive peoples". He defines as fetishism the worship of objects, plants and animals, constituting a form of primitive religion: "Primitive people's" ignorance about and fear of nature leads them to deify various natural phenomena and entities. Fetishism is an early stage in the development of mankind. "Primitive thought" remains frozen at this stage, attributing the inexplicable to objects in its cultural environment and attempting to assimilate it through (ill-conceived) symbolic interpretations.

The most celebrated political philosophers of the modernity, and also many researchers and ethnographers, were to concern themselves with the analysis of "fetishes" and the description of the "primitive mentality". There were to be sharp disputes between them over whether fetishism was a stage in the development of all peoples, whether it had emerged autonomously at different points on the planet or had spread from a single initial source, whether it constituted a "degenerate" form of some primary divine revelation or could be attributed to the inability of primitive people to understand God's truth, etc. One common element in these approaches was the definition of fetishism as a nonsensical form of worship and the idea that there exists a hierarchical scale of peoples, at the summit of which are those who have been freed from fetishism by civilisation, passing from the concrete to the abstract, from the tangible image of God to the worship of the idea of Him.

We shall not concern ourselves here with the exact content of these theories or their character as the ideology of colonists confronted by people they do not wish to understand but to exploit, so that they project the "immaturity" of the conquered in validation of the conquest as historical and cultural "progress". What interests us is that from the methodological viewpoint they adopt the perspective of the outside observer, who with his knowledge and his position of superiority in relation to phenomena which do

The Question of "Commodity Fetishism" 69

not concern himself or his own social milieu, develops a theory of description and exegesis of a foreign culture through exclusive deployment of his own knowledge and (ideological) representations. This observer is able to diagnose the illusions of the "underdeveloped" and offer an interpretation of them because he is in possession of the truth concerning physical – and also metaphysical – phenomena. Thus "fetishists" are to be placed at the opposite pole from scientific knowledge and cultural maturity and are shackled to a superstition which proper knowledge has the ability to dispel (Iacono 1992: 63).

This traditional theory of fetishism is characterised by the following points: Existence of two different cultures, outward observation of an inward phenomenon, belief in the ability of knowledge to banish fetishism, emancipating the inferior culture. The viewpoint of the observer can be achieved only through the existence of a radical distance/difference, that is to say through the exclusion of the culturally "other" from a certain kind of humanity (the "civilised").

2.2 The Transformation of Fetishism in Marx (Methodological Reference)

The problem of fetishism in Marx will be examined in the next section of this chapter, but it is nonetheless necessary to make some reference to its methodological position in the Marxist *oeuvre*. From the days of his youth Marx was familiar with the statements of ethnographers on the subject of fetishism and, it is worth mentioning, used the term in his own writings (MEW Vol. 1: 89 f.; MEW Vol. 40: 532 f., 552). Marx's *Capital* – like the later work of Freud – is of particular interest for the way it *inverts* the outlook of the ethnographers. Both were to aspire to an analysis of fetishism in their "own" community and culture, that is, fetishism in which of necessity they themselves participate as inward-looking observers.

If the philosophers and ethnographers of colonialism found themselves confronted with the methodological question of how it is possible to achieve an outward description of fetishism corresponding to the inward reality of the primitive community, Marx and Freud are obliged to portray inward observation ("experience") as externally valid, i.e. as an objective description of the phenomenon of misapprehension, in which they themselves are implicated (Iacono 1992: 75, 78).

The endeavours of the former are by definition doomed to failure. The latter proved particularly fruitful, but perpetually obliged to answer the classic question: Should we believe someone who says he is a liar? Who is on "the neutral ground of the inward observer"? (Iacono 1992: 82). To this question Marxism gives a variety of answers: through the dialectic of Being and Consciousness, through epistemological studies of bias and analyses of the functioning of ideology and its transcendence.

In relation to fetishism a dual answer may be given. On the one hand because of its origins the concept of fetishism has the advantage of retaining its outward connotations, notwithstanding its being employed with inward reference. Being transferred by analogy from observation of an indigenous community to the community of the observer, it retains an external reference which enables the internal observer to carry out a distanced analysis of the elements of "illusion" which the members of a community of necessity – albeit unconsciously– experience in their social relations.

The second element in the answer is that Marx avoids the unqualifiedly inward dimension by employing the comparative method. He contraposes capitalism to communities real and imaginary where in the place of fetishism there is the "transparency" of social relations, finding points of support in the comparative material so derived that enable him to come to an understanding of fetishism by using external points of reference.

This nevertheless does not solve the problem of what stance the observer should take, i.e. how he can maintain an equally distanced position from his own society and from another society. It does however show why observation from within is objective. Marx does not see things unqualifiedly either from without or from within. Through the parallels he draws with various other societies he situates himself simultaneously inside society and outside it. He shows the reader what fetishism is without "transcending" it himself, but comprehending it as a necessary manifestation of concrete social relationships.

It is from analogy and metaphor that the descriptive power of fetishism and its critical function are derived. They constitute a genuine symbolic system in certain communities (Iacono 1992: 89-91, 99-100, 111). It thus emerges that Marx's immanent analysis, being external in a twofold way, is immanent in two senses. Firstly, he employs a concept imbued with the remoteness of the external observer of primitives, and secondly the concept of fetishism is not used only metaphorically but also comparatively, being so subjected to a simultaneous comparative-metaphorical treatment.[5]

2.3 Fetishism of Marxists

The theory of commodity fetishism is not hard to understand and there are no disagreements between Marxists as to its content. If the concept functions as a kind of touchstone of Marxism, this is attributable, as previously indicated, to disagreements about its soundness and its implications, i.e. to its association with other philosophical constructions and political strategies.

In what follows, we will reconstruct and critically evaluate the basic arguments of the Marxist controversies over the concept of fetishism, starting from the works of George Lukács. We will then turn to the writings of Marx himself, taking into consideration the conclusions of Part I of this book. Finally, we are going to formulate some concluding remarks with respect to the relation of the fetishism-problematic to ideology and politics.

2.3.1 The Fetishistically "Alienated" Society (Lukács)

2.3.1.1 The Subject-Object Dialectic and Consciousness

In this section, we will take as our point of departure Lukács' work *History and Class Consciousness* (1923), where commodity fetishism serves as the central theoretical concept. In highly repetitive fashion, the following theses are propounded:[6]

a) *The theoretical position of fetishism*. The key to the understanding of all aspects of capitalist society must be "sought for in the solution to the enigma of the commodity *structure*" (170). This structure constitutes an "archetype" for every form of existence of objects and every form of subjectivity (170). The essence of the commodity structure is defined as "a relation between persons acquiring a reified character (...), which through its strict –and to all appearance completely closed and rational– autonomy, conceals every trace of its fundamental essence, i.e. as a relation between human beings" (170/171).

Comprehension of the ideology of capitalism and of the prerequisites for its elimination presupposes comprehension of the fetishistic character of the commodity as a "form of objectivity" but also as a basis "for subjective behaviour" (171). In this way commodity fetishism is treated as the quintessence of Marxism and basis for the theory and politics of the transition to socialism.[7]

b) *Structure of fetishism*. Wherever the "rule of the commodity" (172), i.e. wherever the commodity form is imposed as the "universal form" (173), social development and the forms of consciousness are subjected to the basic element in the rule of the commodity, "reification" (174). Lukács describes the "primary phenomenon of reification" (174), quoting the best-known extracts of Marx's analysis of fetishism in the first chapter of the first volume of *Capital*. Human labour is "counterposed" to the human being as "something objective, independent of him, which rules over the human being with an autonomy that is alien to him" (175).

From an objective viewpoint commodities are counterposed to the human being as "a world of ready-made things and relations between things" (...), as "powers which act autonomously" (175). From a subjective viewpoint, human activity takes the form of the commodity and is "reified", i.e. moves on the basis of the laws of "an objectivity alien to the human being" (175/6). When the commodity form is universalised (capitalism), human labour is rendered an "abstraction" (175) which is objectified in commodities, becoming a "thing" which is sold (193). This leads to a "perpetually increasing rationalisation, to an ever intensifying exclusion of the qualitative, individual-human characteristics of the worker" (176/7). In economics, in science, in politics and philosophy, what prevails is measurability and rational calculability, in the sense that the human element is excluded (176/177, 187 ff., 195 ff.).[8]

c) *Consequences of fetishism*. The human being is rendered "a mechanised component of a mechanical system" to which he is helplessly subordinated (179, 292). Everything subjective has the appearance of an "element of error" (178). A new "structure of consciousness" is imposed on all groups in society (191).[9] The activity of the worker loses its "character of activity" (sic) and becomes a *"contemplative stance"* in relation to the closed system of machines which is levelling all before it (179). The person incorporated into this system becomes a "helpless spectator" (180), "a cog in the wheel of economic development" (296, 313). The further the extension of capitalism, the deeper the penetration of the "structure of reification" into human consciousness (185). It is engraved on all interpersonal relations without exception, which become commodified and determine the way in which the individual regards his own qualities and abilities: the elements of personality become objects which the individual "possesses" and can "alienate" (194). "The human being is objectified as a commodity" and his consciousness becomes *"the self-consciousness of the commodity"* (294-95).

At the same time fetishism "misshapes" the reified character of the object (184), quantifies objects into "fetishised exchange prices" (299). The totality of social phenomena undergoes a "process of transformation" in the direction of reification (187, 299). Under conditions of fetishism people become things and things lose their material character, being transformed into anonymous quantities.

d) *Political prospects*. The point of departure is the position that reification is synonymous with dehumanisation and debasement (268, 301).[10] Even though the "reification of every life-manifestation" strikes at all social classes in capitalism, the proletariat experiences it in its most extreme form, being subjected to the "most profound dehumanisation" (268, 291, 300). The proletarians find themselves "directly and *wholly* on the side of the object" and are "an object and not an active factor in the work process" (294-95).

The proletariat begins to come to an understanding of history as it acquires "self-knowledge of its social position", i.e. that absolute reification ("inhuman objectivity" - 307) is necessary to capitalism (282). This is of particular political importance: while the slave who becomes aware that he is a slave changes nothing in his situation, i.e. in the object of knowledge, the proletarian who comprehends that his fate is to be dehumanised acquires knowledge with direct practical consequences: the knowledge changes the object of knowledge (295-6, 309). The proletarian discovers the "vital core" behind the reified integument, i.e. he understands that in reality what exists is not things or relations between things but relations between people (296). This is how the fetishistic character of "commodities" is exposed and their real character as a relation between humans is brought to light (295-296, 309).

Thus the proletariat is able to make an empirical break with the bourgeois (quantitative) way of thinking and to regard society "as a dialectical unity" (297, 301, 338). When the consciousness of the proletariat becomes "the self-consciousness of the whole community" (313) checks will be imposed on the "full capitalistic rationalisation of the entire social Being" (299). The quantified objects ("*the reified structure of Being*") are dissolved into shifting processes and relationships, demonstrating the possibility and necessity of "*overthrow of the reified forms*" (321, 339). The proletariat thus becomes the "simultaneous subject-object of history" and the practice which changes reality (339).

2.3.1.2 Questions of Idealism

The centrality which Lukács ascribes to the problem of fetishism presents a number of questionable aspects. For a start it is ahistorically idealistic, presupposing that human beings are born in possession of a kind of "essence", i.e. that they have a preformed consciousness, type of behaviour, thought, etc. which, confronted by objective factors, is "alienated" under capitalism and becomes a thing, imitating the structure of commodity exchange.

In parallel with the *essentialism*, the formula of fetishism as the matrix of alienation is patently reductionist. Social life is reduced to a "principle", which is not the "material base" as supposed by mechanistic Marxism, but the way in which the bearers of productive relations conceive of this "base". It is the policy of ignoring the multiplicity of social practices (history, class struggle, the activity of state ideological apparatuses) that is responsible for the over-simplifications of Lukács, e.g. for the position that labour is characterised by the "contemplative stance" of the observer of machines and that every form of thought is associated with the quantification of commercial calculation.

Equally reductionist is the view of ideology as a false consciousness (concealment of the true character of the relations of production) as something which emerges "automatically" from the form of exchange. In "creating" fetishism, capitalism safeguards the absence of transparency of exploitative relations. This simplification elevates fetishism to a primary and indeed unique ideological dynamic. It is counterbalanced by the hope that the Messiah-proletariat will recognise the "truth" and, constituting itself as a subject, overturn all existing reality. For those who do not believe in the wondrous dialectical leaps anticipated by Lukács, following the young Marx,[11] it remains inexplicable how the absolute thing is to be divested of the huge weight of ideology and succeed in overthrowing capitalism on the strength of its "consciousness".

There is no room in this ideological framework either for questions such as how the erroneous conception of the relations of production has the power to shape every aspect of the existent, or for refutations of the schema by existing reality which indicate that the course of science and politics is not interpretable through schematic models of "decline". Also unexplained is the passage from commodity fetishism to transformation of everything under the sun into alienated and reified objects.[12]

Lukács attributes to Marxism a specific core, which for him is the analysis of fetishism. When the products of man's labour come to dominate man irrespective of his class position and when every person becomes a thing, Marxism is reduced to a theory of interpretation and exposure of this "automated" false consciousness. The theory of ideology is then restricted to the discovery of a simple secret: the subject becomes a thing, but it can return to itself, linking up again with the true human "core" of history, thanks to a revolutionision in apprehension.[13]

2.3.2 The Continuity of Fetishism

Another orientation in the reading of the situation is to be found in historians of the Marxist *oeuvre* who draw attention to the continuity of the fetishism problematic. A typical instance is that of Rosdolsky, who claims that the *1844 Manuscripts*, the *German Ideology* and other texts of the young Marx contain the theory of fetishism "in philosophical garb". Though not theoretically grounded until *Capital*, fetishism is dealt with in the "earliest economic writings of Marx" (Rosdolsky 1969: 157 and 159). Rosdolsky endeavours to demonstrate the intellectual continuity through references to money as an expression of "alienation", the domination of man over man manifesting itself as a generalised domination of things over people, etc. From them the inference is drawn that in appearance – and also unavoidably – things rule over people.

There are two problems with this outlook. On the one hand it presupposes the continuity of the Marxist oeuvre, which simply "evolves", grounding to ever greater standards of perfection the "philosophical" ideas of the young Marx, into which fetishism is incorporated as symptomatic of the decadence of bourgeois society. On the other hand fetishism is considered synonymous with the rule of things over people, leading to "alienation" and/or enslavement.

2.3.3 The Pashukanis Approach

2.3.3.1 Fetishism, the Bourgeois State and Law

The Soviet jurist Evgeny Pashukanis developed his conception of the forms of the bourgeois legal system on the basis of a particular finding.[14] If we define law as a system of social relationships corresponding to the interests of the ruling class and safeguarded by institutionalised violence, we certainly capture the class content of legal forms (correspondence with the interests of the ruling class, and not with the general interest, peace, justice, etc.) but we provide no answer to the decisive question "why does this content take this form?" (59).

Perceiving the blind alley entailed in the view of law as coercion, Pashukanis develops a theory of law as *consent* (Müller-Tuckfeld 1994), which utilises an analysis of commodity fetishism incorporating the following positions:

a) *The matrix of the legal system*. A specific element of the legal system is that it concerns "isolated, separate subjects", the people who have rights and demands (77).

b) *The law as "private" and capitalist law*. "The legal form of the subject vested with rights arises in a society comprised of selfish, isolated bearers of individual interests", i.e. a society based "on an agreement between free individual wills" (80). Public law is imitating the structure of civil law, though it organises the interests of the society's dominant class, and its role is not to guarantee the rights of the individual. The legal form cannot exist in a guise other than that of individual interest and will, and so public law becomes a "reflection" of civil law (80, 83-4). The bourgeois state (an "impersonal abstraction" which is "merged entirely into the abstract objective rule") is a "reflection" of the subjective structure of law (118, 123 f.).[15]

The result of this is that Pashukanis perceives as law only the law of capitalist society, which is based on the individual as commodity owner. It thus excludes from the realm of law systems of social regulation from other modes of production which were ignorant of the concept of the subject as a status common to all people (123 ff.).[16]

c) *Legal fetishism*. The question arises as to how certain sentient beings are transformed into abstract and equal subjects of law (93). Following the "private approach", Pashukanis notes that the analysis of the form of the subject must take as its point of departure an analysis of the commodity form, which demonstrates that social relations take on the characteristics of relations between things (89 f.). The legal subject arises from the act of exchange, in which the human being realises his/her absolute and abstract freedom of will. As a subject he/she is the owner of the commodity-object and he/she exchanges it. It is in this way that there arises that legal fetishism which complements commodity fetishism. In economic fetishism things are the bearers of value in a natural way. In legal fetishism the subjects which move the things are "natural" vehicles for domination, reflecting an ascendancy which is being guaranteed by the legal system.

In this way social relations take on a form which is doubly mysterious. They appear as relations between things and at the same time relations between subjects (95 f.). Abstract labour, the abstract subject, abstract legal rules, impersonal state power. This is the specifically bourgeois mechanism of assimilation, creator of capitalist law by "inducing" social entities[17] whose material foundations are to be found in the act of exchange.[18]

d) The withering away of the law. Pashukanis's celebrated, and radical, stance may be deduced from this. For as long as market or value determined relations are preserved, the attendant legal system will also be preserved. In countries where proletarian power has prevailed, the withering away of the law will become possible only with the abolition of economic relations based on contract and the resolution of differences in courts of law (110 ff.). And here there is an obvious parallel between law and economics. Just as commodity fetishism will be abolished only when capitalism too is abolished, so the fate of bourgeois law and its subjects are likewise indissolubly linked to capitalism.

2.3.3.2 Economism or Structural Interpretation?

The analogy between the commodity as a "natural" bearer of value and the subject as a "natural" vehicle for the human will (and with the state as abstract macro-subject) is based on the hypothesis that there exists a structural similarity of a causal type, and through this an attempt will be made to interpret the legal system. Pashukanis thus adopts the classically Marxist schema of base-superstructure, searching in the former for the "secret" of the latter.

Pashukanis is commonly charged with economism, i.e. with ignoring the relative autonomy of law.[19] But the charge is not well-founded. Pashukanis does not assert that the legal system lacks autonomy, nor that the "base" determines what is to become law (legal statutes, court decisions, legal theory, etc.). His analysis aims at demonstrating in what way the structure of a society (the operating principles which comprise the semantic core of a mode of production) make it necessary for there to be a system of rules for social regulation adopting certain assumptions and forcibly imposing them as generally applicable (free and equal subjects, contract, structuring of public law on the basis of private, free will).

This system of rules functions on the basis of "free negotiations" between "sovereign individuals" (see also Engelskirchen 2001). Pashukanis gives the name of "law" to this system of rules. To explain the necessity for it under capitalism he demonstrates the similarity of its principles to the structure of generalised commodity circulation. Establishing this causal linkage (the principles of law reflect the structure of production), Pashukanis is in a position to transcend the theory of coercion (law is the product of a dominant will). He gives an interpretation of the structural reasons for consent to it (correspondence with the structure of production, i.e. with the "fetishistic" representations which are imposed on individuals by the laws of the economy) and succeeds in explaining why the law has a specific content and specific codes in bourgeois societies.[20]

It is certainly possible for law to be defined more broadly so that it includes the legal systems of other modes of production. Pashukanis' absolute stance (capitalism = bourgeois law = civil law = law) aims at showing that a legal system with the structural characteristics of bourgeois civil law did not exist prior to capitalism and will not exist subsequent to capitalism because it is derived from a historically *specific* regulation of "sociability" (establishment of the social character of a particular productive process, type of political structure and ideological identity) through the circulation of commodities. This kind of law is of a historically unique character because of its form and – we might add – because of the universalisic character of its implementation, in contrast with previous "laws".[21]

Through this "absolute" stance, Pashukanis avoids the idealistic trap of giving a general, i.e. purely formalistic, definition of law as a concept. The formalistic definition has two consequences. On the one hand capitalist civil law appears as the concrete historical expression of the legal regulation necessary in every human community (ubi societas ibi ius).[22] On the other, law is linked to the "idea of Justice" (or of Ethics) so that in order for one to be able to speak of justice in general despite the huge differences between the various systems of social regulation and coercion, there must be a common element between them. This leads to the appearance of bourgeois civil law as the best, "most human", etc. form of law (freedom, equality, separation of powers, contractuality, moderation in punishment, etc.). Neither the other viewpoints positing the uniform purpose or origin of law (the "spirit" of a certain people, expression of the collective will of a community, observance of the prescriptions of the legislator, will of the authorities charged with implementation of the law, etc.) nor the critical assumption that violence (and not justice) is the essence of law escape from this idealistic trap.[23] The latter view has the advantage of realism. It establishes the "law = power" paradigm and provides a satisfactory explanation of the origins of a rule which is represented as just, necessary, etc. Nevertheless, above and beyond its genealogical accuracy, it is incapable of explaining the specialised character and the specific mode of operation of the bourgeois legal system, as Pashukanis correctly perceived.

The position opted for by Pashukanis cannot therefore be described as economistic, unless we regard as economistic any analysis which considers that legal and ideological phenomena are linked to the structure of production. His approach reflects the well-known observation of Marx, in the *Grundrisse* (1856/57):

> Equality and freedom are thus not only respected in exchange based on exchange values but, also, the exchange of exchange values is the productive, real basis of all *equality* and *freedom*. As pure ideas they are merely the idealised expressions of this basis; as developed in juridical, political, social relations they are merely this basis to a higher power (Marx 1993: 245).

This view is repeatedly expressed by Marx in *Capital* and the *Critique of the Gotha Programme*, regarding the legal concepts of equality and freedom "as the internal reflection of commodity production and circulation" (Balibar 1997, 194).[24] He therefore treats fundamental legal statutes as ideological conceptions necessary to capitalism, as the religious system was "necessary" to feudalism.

These positions are susceptible to an economistic reading, if we suppose that Divine Grace produces a superstructure perfectly suited to a certain base, i.e. if the process of production of the superstructure is treated ahistorically (automatic adjustment to the base), which would entail the process of formation of the base taking place in an ideological and political void, or in connection with an adverse superstructure.[25] If on the other hand we perceive the formation of bourgeois societies as a derivative of ideology and law *in parallel with* the violent imposition of capitalist relations, the position of Marx, and of Pashukanis, is entirely sound. It shows why the creation of a legal system of universal application, based on free contractual relations between legal subjects of equal status is, from a theoretical (and also historical) viewpoint, inseparable from capitalism as an economic system. Other interpretations of the character of bourgeois civil law (progress of humanity, civilisation, rationalisation of the state apparatus as an expression of the general interest, etc.) are not able to demonstrate this.

A prerequisite for the avoidance of "economist" reductionism is thus that one does not start from an assumption of the commodity as something "straightforward" (i.e. independent of the capitalist mode of production), which enables one to posit a "fetishistic" law. The Marx/Pashukanis analysis is based on a semantic abstraction, because it does not invoke a historically existent point of departure for everything. The deduction is not chronological or developmental but attributes to the base (the "material foundation") a logical and/or functional priority which has never been confirmed historically.[26]

Inspired by economic fetishism, Pashukanis designates as *legal fetishism* the view that there exist sovereign (free and equal) subjects which rule over objects and enjoy freedom in their relations between themselves. This particular element of correspondence is overlooked by those who regard as legal fetishism the belief that law has a power in itself to impose its prescriptions, not due to any particular balance in class forces. The belief that the rule of law "applies because it applies" is nevertheless an ideological consequence of its everyday application ("this is what the law says") and to characterise it as fetishism is a choice which is linked methodologically to the schema of idolatry, i.e. the pre-Marxian usage of the term fetishism (law has supernatural power to move the world, like an inanimate idol). In contrast, Pashukanis' interpretation of fetishism aims at demonstrating the concrete transformational effects of legal fetishism (imposition of a model of interpersonal relations corresponding to the structure of exchange but which cannot prevail socially in the absence of legal regulation). With this "enriched" concept of fetishism, Pashukanis is able to offer an interpretation of the *distinctive structural specificity* of bourgeois civil law.[27]

2.3.4 The Rejection of Fetishism ("Althusser School")

The common element in the above approaches is that they accept the Marxist analysis of fetishism in the first chapter of Volume 1 of *Capital*, elaborating it in different directions.[28] The Lukácsian outlook is *extensive-universalising*. Commodity fetishism is seen as a process of alienation, which is not confined to production of a "false" image of acts of exchange but extends to all social activities (reification of subjectivity, quantification of thought on the model of economic calculation). Fetishism is thus treated as the matrix of a structure of alienation which destroys the authentic structure of social relations. The hope is that this descent into total ignominy will implant in the proletariat the consciousness and the spirit of revolt that will put an end to the alienation.

Pashukanis' approach is *extensive-comparative*. It links the codes of exchange (value, equivalence) with those of the legal system (subject, will), exposing the structure of the legal system and its inextricable connection with commodity exchange. Legal fetishism may be compared with economic fetishism, being a consequence of it. Here too the view is clear that capitalism has a "flattening" function (homogenising things into exchangeable commodities and people into equalised vehicles of free will). Nevertheless it is not Pashukanis' purpose to deplore "alienation". He analyses the effects of the functioning of a symbolic (but also profoundly political) order which shapes the relations of production in accordance with certain codes. He solves the riddle of the legal framework, stressing that without the "fetishistic" structuring of capitalistic exchange concrete law would not be conceivable. This, fundamentally, is where he differs from Lukács. Pashukanis notes the *need for simultaneity* in the abolition of the state, its law and the market by means of class struggle and he perceives that the "flattening" operation of fetishism does not in itself have political implications for the process of transition.

At the opposite extreme to this approach is the philosophical-theoretical questioning of the fetishism analysis by the "Althusser School". Apart from a text by Althusser, published postmortem, this includes a study by E. Balibar that must be considered part of the sequel to the collective volume *Reading Capital*.

2.3.4.1 Commodity Fetishism as Idealism I (Balibar)[29]

Embarking on "a critical analysis of the definition" of fetishism and its place in the work of Marx (213), Balibar maintains that:

a) Fetishism is a bourgeois-idealist theory. Marx carries out his analysis of fetishism before introducing the concept of capital, of the capitalist mode of production or its overall process of reproduction. Without these notions it does not clearly emerge in what context fetishism can be seen operating (bourgeois ideology, a legal system based on contracts and other elements with a bearing on the circulation of commodities: 218-9, 221). The analysis of fetishism in the first chapter of *Capital* is based on the bourgeois ideological concepts of law and political economy (person/thing, freedom/coercion, natural/social, plan/market). The consequence of this is that ideological misinterpretation is seen as an automatic consequence of the circulation of commodities, with the commodity represented as subject or the "reason" for the ideological misinterpretation (227).

b) *Theoretical significance of fetishism.* Marxists who have based their analyses on fetishism have elaborated idealistic anthropologies (Lukács), while materialists (Lenin) have ignored it (220). There are two reasons for this. From a philosophical viewpoint, the theory of fetishism is an impediment to materialist investigation of ideology, being based on a problematic concerning the origins of the Subject. It does not treat the Subject as an ideological category but as a scientific concept which provides an interpretation of ideological findings. Fetishism is therefore "enthusiastically elaborated" by the "alienation" school of thought (what is decisive is the consciousness of the Subject) but also by the formalistic-structuralist tendency which is likewise founded on the problematic of the Subject (its position in the process of production leads to the formation of certain representations and illusions: 225-229, 231).

From a methodological viewpoint, those who insist on the "theory" of fetishism assume that *Capital* is imbued with an attitude of continuity: from the simple initial abstraction of the commodity everything is deduced from elaboration of its concrete determinants. But in fact Marx shifts the object of his inquiry in the course of the exposition of *Capital.* The references are not to the commodity and to the value form in general but to the dual character of labour and the process of exchange (222-3).

The fetishism discussion therefore has to do with a "pre-Marxist *philosophical* problematic" (224). At most it represents a "preparatory dialectic" (220), i.e. a critical deflection of the economic categories against themselves, against their utilisation for apologetical purposes (223), given that Marx attempts to criticise economists without having previously developed a theory of ideology (227).

c) *Fetishism against ideology.* The materialistic theory of ideology is obliged to take into account the existence and the operation of "actual *ideological social relations*" which are established in the class struggle, expressed through ideological apparatuses and differentiated from the relations of production, which determine ideological relations only in the final analysis (225).

d) *Political consequences.* The theory of fetishism, despite the fact that it avoids economism, is an impediment to proper understanding of the revolutionary transition because it presents social "transparency" and the end of illusion as an automatic consequence of the proletarian revolution leading to the abolition of the market. Communism is thus presented as the overcoming of alienation and its opposite (the end of history) emerges immediately from the transformation of the economic base (229).

2.3.4.2 Commodity Fetishism as Idealism II (Althusser's Reading of Fetishism)[30]

In the context of a multi-levelled 1978 analysis of the state, of Marxist readings of it, and the "impasses" in which they find themselves, (an analysis included in his studies on the "crisis of Marxism"), Althusser referred to the question of fetishism.

Although ostensibly in dialogue with Marx, in fact Althusser undertakes no systematic reading or critique of his positions. He intervenes in fully-formed ideological fronts which make use of commodity fetishism as raw material for elaborating their positions. This emerges from a comparison of Althusser's views with other currents in the Marxist debate but also from the fact that he does not take into account the analyses of his own close collaborators concerning Marx's conception of fetishism.[31]

Succinctly rephrased, his theses were as follows:

a) *Fetishism as a legal ideology*. Marx's fetishism is founded on the idea that human labour relations in commodified societies appear as relations between things. This presupposes that the relations of people between themselves and/or the things they produce *are transparent* (when the ideology of fetishism does not act) because they *are immediate*. But this presupposition is groundable only in legal ideology, which projects into legal relations the "transparency" of relations of ownership (the object belongs absolutely, directly, indisputably, etc. to the owner-subject). In legal ideology the relations between people are equated with the relations between things (e.g. two quantities of commodities are brought into correlation in the exchange of equivalents, because two people decided to exchange them and vice versa). Whether we claim that there is an exchange of things or that there is an exchange between subjects, we are in effect saying the same thing (487 ff.).

b) *Fetishism against ideology*. Marxian fetishism is a logical (and ideological) game whose terms are in constant flux: we cannot distinguish the real from the apparent, the immediate from the mediated. To escape from the closed ideological circuit we must abandon the legal categories of antithesis between person and thing on which Marx bases his conception of fetishism in Chapter 1. His analysis does not identify the productive mechanisms of fetishism, which is interpreted in terms of the state apparatuses generating mystifications much more complex and effective than the reduction of human relations to relations between things. To put it somewhat differently, the ideological operation – which also effects the naturalisation of what is essentially historical – has to do chiefly with the state and not with commodity exchange (487 ff.).

c) *The reasons for Marxian idealism.* The question arises of why Marx plays this game, defining the concepts of subject and thing in accordance with whatever he has to demonstrate. Althusser suggests three possible interpretations (490-92):

- One political explanation is that according to Marx every type of community to its own members appears to be something self-evident, immediate, necessary, just, etc. but in fact is neither natural nor eternal. Everything changes, so that one day capitalism too will cease to be. This corresponds to the definition Althusser gives to the concept of fetishism (the tendency for that which exists to be considered "natural": 495). But this provides no satisfactory explanation of Marx's digression into fetishism. Marx has expressed this view repeatedly and much more persuasively, so that there is no need for this game of the obvious/non-obvious, truth/appearance in order to show the historical mutability of representations of a society.

- A more plausible explanation is that Marx wanted to criticise economists who regard social relationships as relationships between things, but also to justify them, attributing their misconception to the fetishism generated by the commodity exchange mechanism. The price for this is that Marx elevates labour into an Essence which takes "predicates" (actual and imaginary, material and social) and that he considers the material elements in production the merely apparent aspect of the Labour-Essence (coal becomes a "material appearance") (495). Thus Marx bases the theory of fetishism on the postulate that social relations possess a "material appearance", a profoundly idealist view.

- The most comprehensive explanation is that Marx wanted to find "easy" arguments at the beginning of the first chapter, speaking only about the concept of value. This is attributable to his "fundamental inability" to commence *Capital* with the "simplest abstraction" (491). The analysis of fetishism is thoroughly makeshift and fanciful because it is in the wrong place. In the chapter on value Marx is unable to speak about capitalism, about the state and the existence of social classes, i.e. about the notions which help to account for the illusions and the fetishisms of the economists and of the dominant ideology. At the beginning of *Capital*, the philosopher "by the name of Marx" became a prisoner of the legal categories on which the concept of the commodity depends. He became entangled in the bourgeois way of treating value, linking fetishism to the commodity form as such.

d) *Political consequences*. The analyses of fetishism are of political significance within Marxism, because they make possible a dissociation from economism. They are, however, the basis both for humanistic interpretations and for workerist positions supporting proletarian subjectivity and insurrection. In either case the theory of fetishism boils down to a particular form of the theory of "alienation" (487), i.e. they belong to a philosophical approach which Althusser fibrously criticises.

2.3.5 The "Other" Fetishism: Gramsci

Before we move on to an examination of the question in the work of Marx it may be of interest to quote two references to fetishism by Gramsci.

The first quotation concerns the relationship between the individual and the collectivities into which he is integrated (Gramsci 1977: 1769; 1771).[32] When the individuals who constitute a "collective organisation" perceive it as something external to themselves, functioning without their participation, then that organisation essentially ceases to exist. "It becomes a mental apparition, a fetish". What is paradoxical is that this fetishistic (critical or simply passive) relationship of individuals to organisations is not to be found only in coercive organisations of a traditional kind (the Church), but also in "non-public", "voluntary"[33] organisations such as parties and trade unions. A deterministic-mechanistic viewpoint thus arises which portrays these organisations as a "phantasmagorical amalgam". By contrast, for revolutionary organisations the need for "immediate and direct" participation by individuals, i.e. the overcoming of fetishism even if this creates a situation of apparent chaos, is absolutely vital.

In the second quotation Gramsci (1977: 1980-81) describes as "fetishistic history"[34] the dominant interpretation of Italian history. Those represented as protagonists are various mythological figures such as the Revolution, the Union, the Nation and Italy. The historical horizon ends at the national borders and the past is interpreted in the light of the present on the basis of a deterministic linearity. The historical problem of the reason for the establishment of the Italian state, and the manner in which it was established, is transformed into the problem of discovering the eternal essence of that state, as a Union or as People or more generally as Italy, which in all preceding history existed in exactly the way that the bird must exist inside the fertilised egg.

The former reference has to do with the pre-Marxist meaning of the term "fetishism". An inanimate entity acquires substance as a vehicle for will and action, concealing the real agents. Gramsci's aim is clearly to criticise the authoritarian and elitist policies of the Communist parties, by implementing an individualistic, "anti-organic" outlook on social institutions.

In the latter Gramsci exerts a timely critique of the fundamental mode of thought of nationalism (the nation is perceived as the perennially existent subject, unchanged over time, which is the motive power of history), but also of the nationalistically constituted science of states which extends theoretical support to this construction.

What is interesting about the quotations from the viewpoint of the present problematic is that Gramsci completely ignores the economic dimension of fetishism, although obviously he would have been familiar with Marx's analysis, diagnosing fetishistic phenomena in the ideological apparatuses of the state (church, parties, trade unions, "nationally"-oriented scholarship). The functioning of certain institutions generates illusions of historical evolution, depicting it as product of the actions of non-existent entities, so that not only is there a misapprehension of reality (classes, individuals, etc.) but also the creation of a distorted image of it conveying an impression of omnipotence of bourgeois institutions.

Even though it does not take into account the complex meaning that Marx attributes to the term "fetishism", the quotation from Gramsci is a positive foreshadowing of Althusser's critical remarks to the effect that fetishism is associated with the different stages of ideological production.

3. The Question of Fetishism in Marx's *Capital*

3.1 The Manner of Presentation of the Theory of Value in "Capital" and Some of its Consequences

Althusser's and Balibar's (critical) outlook refocuses attention on a significant methodological problem in *Capital*: the fact that Marx examines the question *what is value* and subsequently *what is money* in the first three chapters of the first volume of Capital before offering a definition of the capitalist mode of production (CMP). As argued in Part 1, Chapter 2 of this book, the method of exposition chosen by Marx has led certain Marxists to the view that value is not a constituent category of the concept of the CMP but that it gives a preliminary description of the (supposed) historical epoch of generalised *simple* commodity production, which preceded capitalism (see also Maniatis and O'Hara 1999).

As argued above (see Chapter 2), Marx introduces that concept of generalised commodity production only as an intellectual construct that will help him to approach and then to establish the concept of capitalist production.

Apart from the detachment of the concept of value from the CMP and its examination in correlation with a plethora of "commodity"- forms and - modes of production, the introductory reference to value "in itself" creates again the illusion that in the first three chapters of the first volume of *Capital* there is (or may be) a comprehensive theoretical investigation of the Marxian concept of fetishism.

According to this illusion the concept of "fetishism" is adequately formulated in the first chapter of Volume 1, (the fourth section of which is entitled "The Fetishism of the Commodity and its Secret"). Here too Marx's initial conclusions, which flow from a presentation of "generalised commodity circulation", are treated as if they represent developed Marxist theory, with the result that the concept of the CMP and the ideological forms produced within that framework are not taken into account. The same is true of the analyses in Volume 3 of the *fetishism of capital* (e.g. of interest and interest-bearing capital), which can be decoded in the light of what is written in the first three chapters of Volume 1 about "commodity fetishism".

It is not only Lukács and those who saw in "commodity fetishism" the whole essence of a theory of alienation "of mankind" that have fallen victim to these illusions, but also Althusser and more generally those who have believed that one can speak seriously of the theory of Marx taking into account only the analyses of the first part of Volume 1 of *Capital*.

The paradox is that a) Althusser had already noted that to introduce the concept of value independently of the concept of capital in the first section of *Capital* was to put the cart before the horse and b) that colleagues of his (e.g. Rancière 1972) had concerned themselves with Marx's development (in the subsequent sections) of concepts insufficiently defined in that first section. On the basis of this consideration we asserted that Althusser's text refers more to (or is more constrained by) Marxist writings on fetishism than by the (overall) analysis of Marx.

In that (and only that) sense there is some justification for Althusser's position on the "makeshift and fanciful" theory of fetishism (of certain Marxists), deduced from the passages in the first section of Volume 1 on commodity fetishism and subsequently projected onto the entirety of capitalist society, with the analysis grounded in the ideological categories of law and bourgeois economics and not on Marxist concepts or research findings. This criticism was directed at those who "are more interested in the form and less in the content of Marx's theoretical work" (Godelier 1977: 201). Nevertheless it did not provide a comprehensive solution to the problem, as was the intention of Althusser, who was similarly misled by appearances and overstated the case for the significance of Marx's method of exposition, turning it into something absolute and overlooking the subsequent analyses in *Capital*. We shall return to this point.

In any case, the whole discussion we referred to and the analysis undertaken in Section 1 enables us to comprehend the analytical significance (or "weakness") of the reference to Chapter 1 of Volume 1. The commodity is truly the simplest economic form, albeit that in the first section of the Volume 1 it is presented without even the slightest reference to the most characteristic commodity of the CMP, labour-power. Consequently, from the "simplest form" of the CMP a "model" is constructed of an economy of independent self-employed commodity producers, something which does not encapsulate the differentia specifica of the CMP (see also Reuten 1993).

Even if we accept that the "model" of independent self-employed commodity producers is legitimate as a first approximation to a *capitalist* economy (one feature of which is the institutional independence of the producer-capitalists[35]), because – for example – to establish the concept of money as general equivalent it is not necessary to refer to capitalist exploitation relations, we nevertheless believe that Marx's analysis would be more successful if he had made it clear from the outset what is involved. The distinguishing feature of the capitalist economy is that all active agents of production are commodity *owners*, because even if they are not commodity *producers* (capitalists), they possess the commodity of labour power. The preliminary formulation of this position was not to constitute the slightest obstacle to the evolution of Marx's theoretical views in the first section of Volume 1 (e.g. the development of the concept of the general equivalent) while at the same time it would make it clear beyond the slightest shadow of doubt that the *only* economy of generalised commodity *exchange* is capitalism. On this basis, the ensuing analysis of the movement of capital

The Question of "Commodity Fetishism" 89

(M-C-M´, see Chapter 3, Section 3.2), the production of surplus value, etc. would emerge as a logical consequence.

3.2 Capitalist Mode of Production, Ideological Forms, "Fetishism". From Commodity Fetishism to Fetishism of Capital

When he introduces the concept of the CMP in Chapters 4-6 of Volume 1 Marx makes it clear that that the basic structural relation of the CPM is the capital - wage labour relation, whose foundation is the separation of the workers from the means of production and the transformation of labour power into a commodity.[36] This relation is not just economic. It constitutes at the same time a historically specific political and ideological structure.

Domination by the CMP has as one of its necessary concomitants the establishment of the worker (on the legal-political level and on the level of ideology) as a free citizen (subject of law), with all that entails for the structural features of the state and the dominant ideology: hierarchical-bureaucratic configuration of the machinery of state, "classless" functioning of the state on the basis of the rule of law and the so-called formal legitimity etc. Correspondingly, the dominant bourgeois ideology prescribes the materiality of the civilisation of the "free human being", "natural rights and equality before the law", the common/national interest which arises from the harmonisation of individual vested interests etc.

The dominant ideology therefore represents a procedure for consolidating capitalist class interests, through its materiality as an element in the institutional state-juridical functioning but also as a life practice, a "way of life" not only of the ruling classes but also, in modified form, of the subordinate classes.[37] In this sense, the dominant ideology is a component element of the CMP, i.e. of the *structural core of capitalist relations of domination and exploitation.* The dominant ideology conceals the class relations of domination and exploitation, not so much by denying them as by presenting them and/or imposing them through many different practices as relations of equality, freedom and common interest. Their hard core – as pointed out by Althusser/Balibar – is the juridical ideology that is inextricably linked to the functioning of the legal system. As Marx puts it:

> The sphere of circulation or commodity exchange, within whose boundaries the sale and purchase of labour-power goes on, is in fact a very Eden of the innate rights of man. There alone rule Freedom, Equality, Property and Bentham. Freedom, because both buyer and seller of a commodity, let us say

of labour-power, are determined only by their own free will. They contract as free persons, who are equal before the law. Their contract is the final result in which their joint will finds a common legal expression. Equality, because each enters into relation with the other, as with a simple owner of commodities, and they exchange equivalent for equivalent. Property, because each disposes only of what is his own. And Bentham, because each looks only to his own advantage. The only force bringing them together and putting them into relation with each other, is the selfishness, the gain and the private interests of each. Each pays heed to himself only, and no one worries about the others. And precisely for that reason, either in accordance with the pre-established harmony of things, or under the auspices of an omniscient providence, they all work together to their mutual advantage, for the common weal, and in the common interest (Marx 1990: 280).

This function, inherent in capitalist domination, of *concealment of the exploitative and coercive character of social relations* is called "fetishism" by Marx, in all cases where the relations of class domination and exploitation *appear*, in the framework of the dominant ideology, *in a "material" form*: When social relations (money, capital[38]) or the functions which derive from social relations (profits, interest) appear as objects (gold, means of production) or as qualities of objects (the means of production produce profit, money generates interest, etc.), and so "the forms which stamp products as commodities" appear as "natural forms" of "fixed quality" (Marx 1990: 168. See also Rubin 1972, chap. 1).

The concept of fetishism was simply introduced by Marx in the first section of Volume 1 in regard to the commodity, in order to show that "the value of the commodity no longer appears as that which it is, i.e. a social relation between producers, but as a quality of the thing, no less natural than its colour or its weight" (Labica 1985: 465).[39] In the course of his further investigations Marx made it clear that the concept of fetishism does not refer only to the commodity but to *all forms of capital* (money, means of production in the framework of the productive process). In reality Marx does not expound a theory of *commodity fetishism* but a theory of *the fetishism of capital, of capitalist relations*. He introduces the commodity as a form of capital and as a result of capitalist production. In this context, he introduces commodity-fetishism as a form or a result of capital-fetishism. This explains the anticipatory hints concerning *the fetishism of capital* that are put forward in the first section of Volume 1.

The Question of "Commodity Fetishism" 91

3.3 The Concept of Fetishism and its Place in "Capital"

3.3.1 The Fetishism of Capitalist Relations

We perceive, then, that contrary to what many Marxists seem to believe,[40] Marx makes comprehensive reference to fetishism in the subsequent sections of his work and above all in sections of the third volume of *Capital*.[41] The reason for this is that the forms of appearance of capitalist relations are analysed chiefly in the third volume:

- The subordination of labour to capital imposes the capitalist as the producer of commodities and regulates exchange ratios between commodities in accordance with production costs (and not values). Profit is presented as proportion of the advanced capital, so that "surplus-value itself appears as having arisen from the total capital, and uniformly from all parts of it" (Marx 1991: 267). This:

> completely conceals the true nature and origin of profit, not only for the capitalist, who has here a particular interest in deceiving himself, but also for the worker. With the transformation of values into prices of production, the very basis for determining value is now removed from view (Marx 1991: 268).

- The development of credit and the split of profit into business profit (which accrues to the capitalist entrepreneur) and interest (which accrues to the lender, the money capitalist) has the following consequence:

> One portion of profit, in contrast to the other, separates itself completely from the capital-relation as such and presents itself as deriving not from the function of exploiting wage-labour but rather from the wage-labour of the capitalist himself. As against this, interest then seems independent both of the wage labour of the worker and of the capitalist's own labour; it seems to derive from capital as its own independent source. If capital originally appeared on the surface of circulation as the *capital fetish, value-creating value*, so it now presents itself once again in the figure of interest-bearing capital as its most estranged and peculiar form (Marx 1991: 968, emphasis added). Interest-bearing capital displays the conception of the *capital fetish* in its consummate form, the idea that ascribes to the accumulated product of labour, in the fixed form of money at that, the power of producing surplus-value in geometric progression by way of an inherent secret quality, as a pure automaton, so that this accumulated product of labour (...) has long since

discounted the whole world's wealth for all time, as belonging to it by right and rightfully coming its way (Marx 1991: 523-4, emphasis added).

The same applies with incomes, which in fact reflect nothing other than the relations of distribution of the value produced and appear in the framework of capitalist property relations and the ideological forms associated with them as *sources* of value. Labour "produces" the wage, the means of production the profit and "natural resources" the rent:

> *Firstly*, because the commodity's value components confront one another as independent revenues, which are related as such to three completely separate agents of production, labour, capital and the earth, and appear therefore to arise from these. Property in labour-power, capital and the earth is the reason why these different value components of the commodity fall to their respective proprietors, transforming them therefore into their revenues. But value does not arise from a transformation into revenue, it must rather be already in existence before it can be transformed into revenue and assume this form (Marx 1991: 1007).

It becomes apparent that Marx's ideas on the "fetishistic" form of appearance of the *capitalist relations* at the surface level of circulation (or in the context of the dominant and self-reproducing bourgeois ideology) cannot be conveyed adequately if the capital-relation itself is not analysed, i.e. if we do not extract ourselves from the ideological framework of the legal-economic concepts of the first section of Volume 1 where, as Balibar points out, the critical view of fetishism serves a preliminary educational purpose, as ironic-critical comment on the intellectual limitations of bourgeois thought. Through this comment Marx dissipates the unquestioned false assumptions in the spontaneous views of economists, which correspond to "collective self-deception" (Godelier 1977: 212/3, 221).

3.3.2 Concluding Remarks on Commodity Fetishism

Bearing in mind that Marx wrote the introductory first section of Volume 1 of *Capital* only to arrive at the concept of the "fetish of capital" which we have just outlined,[42] we should appreciate that the reference to commodity fetishism does not constitute a theory of alienation or estrangement presupposing an essence in the subject and assessing the existing reality as in contradiction with that essence (see also Heinrich 1999: 228 ff.). Moreover fetishism does not possess, as is often believed, an ideological strength: it does not conceal social relations of exploitation, nor does it "alienate" anything.[43] It consists in the examination of a "symptom", not an ideological causality or force.

In reference to fetishism of capital, Marx does not play out a simple game of subject and object. He demonstrates the various ways in which capitalist relations are imprinted on things, leaving the traces of its movement during the process of accumulation. These traces subsequently appear – in a "spontaneous" co-optation – as qualities of the things. It is wrong, therefore, to conclude that fetishism transforms the subject into an object (that relations between humans become relations between things), matter into ideas and things into masters of human beings. However, it is an excessively hasty reaction to reject for that reason the problematic of fetishism as idealistic, a view put forward with particular intransigence by Balibar, who regards as authentic the extensive-universalising interpretation of fetishism by Lukács.

In fact, even if we adopt philosophical terminology, saying that fetishism constitutes an inversion of the qualities of subject and object, it cannot be a question of a simple inversion. The social features of labour do not appear, as in a mirror image, as natural qualities of things. The image of fetishism is not the exact opposite of reality (such that an "enlightening" critique would enough to put things right). The fetishistic image is modified in relation to the reality it "reflects".

Representing the social as natural, its effect is to cause misrecognition of the social character of "human" relations, which are naturalised (whereas in reality they constitute the "hypostatised consequence of effaced beginnings" –Goux 1975: 116). The "relation of things" does not constitute mere symbolism of active individuals (as with a board game when a piece of wood symbolises a certain player, such that one can always at any moment bring about a conversion to what is symbolised), but a permanent alteration in perceiving reality (what is social becomes natural) which does not permit individuals to become aware of the transition from labour relations to relations between things.[44]

Here we have to do not with equivalence, whose terms can be inverted at will. What is involved is "fetishistic" configuring as *part of the structure of capitalist reality* which conceals "the relationship between the social character of the commodity and the social relations mobilised in its production" (Iacono 1992: 87) and it does not entail a mere inversion but is the product of a process of repression of certain elements of reality (Goux 1975: 189) and their replacement with others.

But what is decisive is that, as indicated by J. Rancière, the question of fetishism cannot be posed in terms of inversion:

> The relevant terms are not subject, predicate and thing but relation and form. The process of estrangement (...) does not signify the externalisation of the predicates of a subject into something foreign but shows what happens to capitalist relations when they assume the most highly mediated form of the process (...) The social determinants of the relations of production are thus reduced to the material determinants of the thing. Which explains the confusion between what Marx calls material foundations (things which exercise the function of a bearer) and social determinants. The latter become natural *qualities* of the material elements of production. In this way the capital relation is constituted as a *thing*. (...) The reification of social determinants of production and subjectivisation of the material foundations of things. (...) Marx explains that this dual movement was already perceptible in the simplest determinant of the CMP in the commodity form of the product of labour. (...) Fetishism does not involve the relation between a subject and an object but the relation of each of these entities with the relations of production that determine them. The relations which determine the capitalist system can only exist under conditions of concealment. The form of their reality is the form in which their real movement disappears. (...) [In *Capital* Marx formulates] the theory of the process and the theory of the reasons for its misrecognition (Rancière 1972, 108, 110, 111, 133, 121-2, 123-4).

We can now return to the "weaknesses" in Marx's analysis in the first chapter of Volume 1, where mention is made of fetishism without the capital relation itself yet having been defined. Because of this restriction Marx is obliged to refer to "social relations" in general or to relations between humans. (What social relations? What kind of "human" relations? Simply relations between "autonomous commodity producers"?) He does indeed record the reified forms in which these relations appear, assuming "the fantastic form of a relation between things" (Marx 1990: 165). However, neither the "social relations" (capitalism) nor the "things" have been defined.[45]

The further we progress in this preliminary analysis by Marx of *commodity* fetishism, the more we come up against this absence of the concept of capitalist relations. Let us reflect further on the "material" element in commodity exchange. The producer fabricates something which he himself does not need (which does not possess use-value for him personally). He subsequently takes what he needs, exchanging with others the *thing* which for him is useless. For the individual producer to be socialised, what is needed is a *thing* which at the individual level is useless, and the mediation of the thing as such is demonstrated to be its (indirect) use-value for production, (its social use value). By means of the "thing" the individual producer is, or appears to be, made part of the social mechanism of production. This analysis in a way illustrates the relations of capitalists among themselves but it could be generalised as a description of the forms of appearance of social relations in capitalism only if one regarded labour-power too as a "thing". Moreover, and more importantly, the market is not a prime mover of, or the reason for, this socialisation. It is itself a manifestation of the CMP.[46]

In a pertinent extract Marx make the point that:

> the capitalist mode of production, like every other, constantly reproduces not only the material product but also the socio-economic relations, the formal economic determinants of its formation. Its result thus constantly appears as its premise, and its premises as its results (Marx 1991: 1011).

It thus emerges that, seen as a whole, Marxist analysis is very far from being an ideological game of deriving everything from the "simple" commodity. The fetishism (of capitalist relations) does not consist in the mistaken view that the fate of human beings is regulated by the products of their labour, but in a necessary form of engaging with reality in a capitalist society, which will only disappear with the disappearance of capitalism itself.[47]

If, however, fetishism consists in an "objective" or "internal" illusion, analysing it would require us to transfer ourselves mentally to other forms of production. This is facilitated by the comparative framework of Marx's authentic and imaginary paradigms.[48] But owing to its objective nature the fetishism of capital cannot be dissipated as may happen with other illusions that are structurally inessential for capitalism (e.g. the existence of God). As we saw in section 2.2, the external/internal viewpoint of Marx makes it possible for the mechanisms of its creation to be demonstrated, but not for the phenomenon to be eliminated.

3.3.3 A Comment in Relation to Constructivism

Fetishism, like other social constructs (e.g. the gender socially assigned to every individual, the national identity, racial classification, the stigmatisation of certain individuals as criminals, etc.) is a phenomenon which can be deconstructed given a "constructivist" theoretical viewpoint. Deconstruction means comprehending on the one hand their own historicity (the way in which they were constructed) and on the other the reasons for their construction, i.e. the interests to which they correspond. Nevertheless capital will go on making profit and earning interest, just as individuals cannot cease having a certain sex, national identity, tribal membership, social profile and criminal record etc. even if through the right readings and political experiences it is established that what are represented as natural elements are the distorted forms of appearance of a social structure and so are susceptible of transformation.[49]

Constructivism poses the question of how our representations of reality are created, i.e. what are the foundations of our relevant knowledge. This prospect transcends the traditional dilemma of "objectivity or subjectivity of knowledge". It does not consider either that the subject creates the "real" object or that the object-reality is imposed on the subject of knowledge. Constructivism thus refuses to speak of reality as a datum which pre-exists knowledge but also of the subject which creates it. It examines only the procedures for shaping different kinds of knowledge, through which reality is created in the form of valid assertions as to what it "is".[50]

We do not propose to examine here either the different variations of constructivism or the elements deriving from it which can be summarised as a falling into the dual trap of the idealism or realism from which they are seeking to escape (Müller-Tuckfeld 1997: 467 ff.). What is interesting is that even though Marx's method can be differentiated in general terms from constructivism, Marx adopts the constructivist viewpoint on the question of fetishism. He refuses to distinguish between truth and falsehood, ideology and truth, on the question of fetishism and asserts that on the bases of certain facts concerning the structure of social production, individuals construct a conception of reality which – without being true – corresponds to that certain structure, i.e. is the only possible way of conceiving reality.

In the constructivist view, individuals' representation of reality is a construct but not something false or artificial. It is also asserted that it can be replaced – in a different socio-historical context – by a representation which will be subject to different criteria of truth and may be politically desirable but in any case will be equally artificial as that of the present day (e.g. the "transparency" prevailing in human labour relations in a Communist society will not constitute the "truth" of those relations deriving from the division of labour or a conception of "actual reality" freed from ideology, but a different way of human subjects' conceiving social data). The weak element in constructivism from a practical viewpoint (the theoretical awareness of being a construct changes nothing in this) is met with in the self-same form in Marx's analysis of fetishism.[51] It shows its – from the cognitive viewpoint – particularly "modern" character but also its limited ideological-political significance. No ideological struggle is possible here and no transcendence conceivable within the framework of capitalism. The advantages of the analysis are to be found in its reliable knowledge of the mechanisms of conception of reality in a particular society and thus of the *constitution of subjects* in that society.

It thus becomes possible to deduce conclusions concerning the character of ideology and politics in societies where identities and differences are constant and the volatile data of history are naturalised for purposes of legitimisation. What has been said of constructivism in general may be asserted also of Marx's approach: it is nothing less, but also nothing more, than a precondition for ontologised discourse to be able to be exposed to fundamental criticism (Müller-Tuckfeld 1997: 487).

3.4 Fetishism Without Ideological State Apparatuses (ISA)?

It is a central premise of Althusser/Balibar's critique that Marx constructs his analysis of fetishism without reference to the legal system and the ideological activity of the state. The criticism is justified given that, as previously indicated, (commodity) fetishism can emerge only in an already functioning capitalist society and not quasi-spontaneously from the simple act of exchange of two commodities in non-capitalist conditions. Without a continual "education" of subjects to the capitalist regulations and "values", the necessary illusion is not created.

Here emerges a major problem, given that Marx speaks of fetishism without having defined the concept of ideology and the ISA, so that there is no explanation of the status of fetishism (illusion? symbol? truth?) and, as we shall see in the last section of this chapter, the consequence could be a tacit insertion of "feticism" in the place of ideology, thus constituting a kind of ideology without "material action" of state-type apparatuses.

Nevertheless, Althusser/Balibar overlook a distinctive feature of fetishism. Fetishism is the *self-generating consequence of the concealment of social relations through the operations of the economy* as such and so is not directly linked to the ISA. It is therefore proper that speaking of fetishism Marx should "forget the state" – and so provide no interpretation for the framework of creation of fetishism – but this does not amount to an argument against the analysis as such.

In two quotations from *Capital*, Marx comments that:

> When the political economists treat surplus-value and the value of labour-power as fractions of the value-product (...) they conceal the specific character of the capital relation, namely the fact that variable capital is exchanged for living labour-power, and the worker is accordingly excluded from the product. Instead of revealing the capital-relation, they show us the false semblance of a relation of association, in which worker and capitalist divide the product in proportion to the different elements which they respectively contribute towards its formation (Marx 1990: 670). In slave labour, even that part of the working day in which the slave is only replacing the value of his own means of existence, in which he therefore works for himself alone, appears as labour for his master. All the slave's labour appears as unpaid labour. In wage labour, on the contrary, even surplus-labour, or unpaid labour, appears as paid. In the one case, the property-relation conceals the slave's labour for himself; in the other case the money-relation conceals the unrequited labour of the wage labourer. (...) All the notions justice held by both the worker and the capitalist, all the mystifications of the capitalistic mode of production, all capitalism's illusions about freedom, all the apologetic tricks of vulgar economists, have as their basis the form of appearance discussed above, which makes the actual relation invisible, and indeed presents to the eye the precise opposite of that relation (Marx 1990: 680).

In both cases (capitalism, slave ownership) there exist in the mode of production self-generating consequences of concealment, but their tendencies are in opposite directions. This is of particular importance for the political relations of domination and the formation of ideological constructs in each mode of production. However, it is not the specific result of ideological activity but a necessity in the mode of production (which, as previously mentioned, is effectively unattainable in the absence of a functioning "superstructure", although it is not created by it).

This is the time to mention an unexpected consequence of Althusser/Balibar's critique. Although they explicitly seek to take issue with the universalising outlook of Lukács, their criticism strikes just as forcefully at the comparative viewpoint of Pashukanis. If the economic analysis of fetishism presupposes the state-legal framework, the derivation of legal fetishism from the economic (Pashukanis) is shown to be an implementation of what is required. It is represented as implying a further consequence of Marx's critique, despite the fact that the self-same implication is already contained in economic fetishism and in a way provides it with its grounding!

In our opinion this is not altogether damning for Pashukanis' viewpoint. If we take into account our methodological reference to simultaneous exteriority/interiority, to which any analysis of fetishism is de facto condemned, it becomes clear that there cannot be any absolute principle, i.e. an external point of reference which can exist prior to the appearance (on the historical and semantic plane) of all then determinants of capitalism. As a result, neither can the analysis of commodity fetishism and the fetishism of capital be deduced from a pre-existent legal ideology, nor on the other hand can a "pure structure" of commodity exchange depict the structure of the legal system as contingent to itself.

If it seems impossible to disentangle the threads of interior vs. exterior there is a way out: simultaneous analysis of the various phenomena through the concepts which emerge enriched from the dialectical method of Marx. On this point the analysis of Pashukanis retains its full force as a negative conclusion, notwithstanding its hesitancy to designate the economic as something primary, from which there emerges a legal structure. The "negative" conclusion is that in the absence of the CMP it is impossible for there to be a civil law based on specific legal codes. The inverse formulation (without bourgeois civil law there can be no capitalism) is logically possible but meaningless from the materialist viewpoint. It presupposes a power or will which lays down a certain law thus making feasible a mode of production! This is what proves the correctness of the priority of the economic postulated by Pashukanis, though it must become comprehensible only as a process of simultaneous formation of the interacting elements of the CMP, comprising among other things the formation of the (bourgeois civil) law and the ideology/philosophy which accompanies it.

3.5 Transparency of Other Modes of Production?

The comparative reference to capitalism and the slave mode of production enables us to touch on another issue. On the basis of Marx's reference to the transparency of other modes of production, the impression has been created that capitalism, in contrast to other modes of production, is characterised by a unique ideological loading which prevents individuals from realising what they are doing. But it is facile, to say the least, to surmise that the "transparency" that Marx attributes to other modes of production concerns only the social relations of the division of labour and not the absence of illusions in general (Balibar 1976: 217). In the Asiatic community, for example, the division of labour is conscious and immediate because it precedes production and decides what each individual will produce and how the product will be distributed. In the CMP, by contrast, this occurs through the market-price mechanism, i.e. "behind the back" of the active agents of production, even the most "powerful" of them.

Every mode of production ends up developing *self-generating* forms of concealment. The difference is that in capitalism class domination is linked ideologically to individual freedom and not to other legitimations (the will of God, the superiority of certain social groups). This does not occur out of the choice of certain "ideological centres" but is the consequence of necessary forms of appearance of its structural characteristics.[52] If we consider that a class rule legitimated by the will of the "subject" himself is less transparent ideologically than a rule legitimated by external commands, the superior ideological effectiveness and stability of capitalism, when it functions through a powerful market (and so in "freedom") is implied.

4. Ideology, Fetishism and Politics. Certain Conclusions

The point is often made that in *Capital* Marx does not employ the concept of ideology, which was very much present in the youth works of Marx/Engels and returns as a powerful theoretical element in the later works of Engels.[53] The analysis of fetishism in *Capital* is not only precocious (i.e. it precedes the reference to the state and to the mechanisms of ideological production) but in a way it replaces the focus on ideology that is absent from *Capital*. As we have repeatedly pointed out, this leads to the view that ideology is produced by the structure of exchange independently of ideological or state instances.

The antagonism between problematics of ideology and of fetishism resulted in the formation of two different orientations in Marxism.[54] Certain theoreticians concentrate their attention on the state, analysing the processes by means of which ideologies are developed and imposed (the "political" viewpoint). Other theoreticians attach decisive importance to the structure of commodity exchange, linking the misapprehensions and illusions of bourgeois societies to fetishism (the "economic" viewpoint). The former emphasise the general or universal element (the state), the latter the concrete-subjective (individual, action, exchange), developing a theory of the symbolic in everyday life.

The exponents of the "political" orientation either ignore the analysis of commodity fetishism (Gramsci) or directly express opposition to it (Althusser and School). The theoreticians of the second orientation starting from Lukács depoliticise the question of ideology, detaching it from specific bourgeois strategies and ending up in phenomenologies of alienation in everyday life (consumerism, cultural decline, politics as spectacle, etc.) which are essentially outside the boundaries of Marxism, regarding ideological formations as a kind of cultural datum which imposes on "man" an inhuman life model.

This established, there is no doubt that the fetishism of capitalist relations is not either a synonym for ideology or a more comprehensive definition for it, which leads to the conclusion that the line which should be followed is the "political" one. But this raises the question of the influence of analyses of fetishism on the definition of ideology. Logically there are three possible ways of defining ideology.

Firstly, it may be seen as a false, deluded conception or illusion which is cultivated by those in possession of power or knowledge so as to conceal actual processes of exploitation and domination. The model is that of religious ideology (respect must be shown for the dominant order of things because this is commanded by God, who is not only omniscient but also omnipotent and so will punish you if you disobey his commands). It can assume more "modern" forms, for example, with replacement of the category of "God" by that of "democratic legitimation through elections", the institution of "hell" by that of "prison and/or social stigma" etc. The propagation/imposition of conceptions of this kind is of much greater benefit to society's masters than the appearance of social class as a product of violence exercised by the powerful.

Secondly, ideology can be defined more comprehensively and dialectically as a delusion (also) of the producers of ideology themselves. It is much more reasonable for us to consider that the representatives of God or of Democracy themselves believe what they proclaim and do not pursue their activities in a spirit of cynical deceit. This postulate provides an explanation for the organic character of ideology, in contrast to the former which postulates a kind of conspiracy of the powerful, who resolve to elaborate and then disseminate a lie to a huge crowd of dilettantes, who are eager to maintain the faith at the expense of their own personal well-being.

Thirdly, ideology can be defined organically, unrelated to false consciousness, i.e. the contrast between truth and falsehood (freedom and unfreedom, being correct and being in error). If ideology expressed only violence concealed behind falsehood (or ideas corresponding to particular vested interests) it would be neither persuasive nor stable. The only way its persistence can become comprehensible is for it to be regarded as truth, as *the truth which is both necessary and self-evident in a given society*. The starting point must be a view of ideology as a totality of practices (behaviours) which are produced, taught and implemented is ideological institutions openly or tacitly linked to the state and operating as a category for reproducing the general conditions underlying social relations. The main element is not that ideology is materially grounded nor that it is associated with various forms of indirect coercion but that the "ideas" in which it is codified are organic, i.e. they contribute to the reproduction of the relations of production. As such not only do they become acceptable to all members of society but they are experienced by them as expressions of the "truth" of social life. In this sense they are the foundations of a *necessary relation between subjects and the conditions of their* lives.[55]

To avoid reference to the "idea" as the opposite of reality (and of the truth) it is expedient for the ideological level to be regarded as symbolic, that is to say as a level of reality which exists in parallel with the others and establishes behaviours and beliefs of social subjects, producing an "actual illusion" (Haug 1993: 51), i.e. constituting the symptom and the "displaced" mode of expression of reality (Althusser 1974: 20-21).

This does not mean that it is impossible for the ideological determination (or distortion) of certain view to be demonstrated, i.e. to be shown, through suitable methods of criticism and comparison, to correspond to a "truth" useful for the reproduction of a system with immediate consequences for individuals' behaviour.[56] What it does mean is that ideology is not something that can be overridden through enlightenment or dialogue and that it is intimately linked to the socially produced "truth" and the necessity of certain behaviours.

In this outlook of "true and necessary" ideology, the fetishism of capitalist relations is a detail of the ideological production process. Nevertheless it is of significance as an indicator of the production mechanisms involved. It makes clear the functionality of ideology, the mechanism of interiority/exteriority (which enables us to overcome the antithesis between truth and falsehood by relegating it to the plane of symbolism) and the resultant consent through the naturalisation of the social order. Still, the most important point is that fetishism links ideological representation to ideas such as the subject and his/her subordination, which Marx conceptualises in a way entirely different to that of philosophical tradition.

As has been shown (Balibar 1993: 64 ff), it emerges from Marx's analysis that it is not only the thing, the entity, the real, that is objective but also the "illusions", the "hypersensory object" ("übersinnliches Ding"). These constitute necessary components of reality, even though they amount to a misapprehension of it and a naturalised projection of historical constructs. Just as real are the non-transparent and ideologically coerced behaviours which emerge from this "reality". In this way Marx transcends the classical distinction between the world and the subject, showing that *there are no subjects outside of society but practices which constitute subjects on the basis of historical elements (subjective identity is the product of particular society)*. The subject does not constitute the world, as asserted by idealism, but the world gives birth to the "subjectivity" of the individual in bourgeois society as possessor of himself and his commodities in continuous simultaneous-parallel coexistence with the world of things. This entails an inversion of the philosophy of consciousness and the subject.

Fetishism consists in an analysis of the process of *subordination* of subjects by means of the market, which in capitalism is a site for the constitution of objects and subjects (also see Balibar 1993: 75-76). Fetishism does not therefore make available interpretative schemes for politics and the exercise of power, i.e. for the production of ideology as such, but is one element in a theory of *ideology*, showing up the mechanisms for conceiving reality, which are linked not with subjective wills but with the overall conditions of a mode of production that are "transmitted" to subjects.

Let us make a closing observation. In the context of ideological production, fetishism provides significant raw material: it explains the viewpoint of the primacy of the individual. Depending on the balance of forces at any given time, this viewpoint is either activated (parliamentary regimes is periods of neo-liberal hegemony) or recedes into the background (fascist and dictatorial regimes of the between-war period which projected the "historical commune", the "duty of sacrifice in the name of the fatherland or race", etc.). It thus emerges that ideological apparatuses can make political use of the mechanism of fetishism. However, in no case does fetishism ever appear "in the raw", nor can it be present if a fully integrated ideological-political social formation does not exist. There is neither a fetishist "destiny" in capitalism, nor an unavoidable economic necessity which forces all individuals to act in a specific way. This is the basis of the relative autonomy of the political level, which provides the point of departure for revolutionary transformations.

Notes

1. See for example the bibliography referred to in Iacono 1992: 82-83.
2. This formulation tacitly revises the author's earlier position that the text in Vol. 1 leads to an ideological-realistic "theory" of fetishism (Balibar 1976, 211 and 222/5).
3. For more details on what follows see Iacono 1992: 5-76 and 116-126.
4. The word made its way into the different European languages from the Portuguese, where feitiço means the fabricated or a artificial, and by extension the object of "magic".
5. Freud's concept of fetishism is utilised in a similar way and has a similar function. Within a theoretical framework comparable to that of Marxism yet fundamentally different from it (see Althusser 1977 and 1984-a for detailed treatment of this) fetishism is expressive of the "perversion" whereby the object of love is not a person but a part of a person or an object associated with the person. In Freud fetishism betrays not an inversion, as in Marx, but a *displacement* of the engagement with the desire (see Iacono 1992: 107 ff.). For linkage of the two problematics in the framework of a comprehensive critique of idealism and essentialism through the fetishism of money and of language, see Goux 1975, 130 ff. and 179 ff.
6. The extracts quoted simply by page reference in the present chapter section come from Lukács 1988.
7. "The chapter on the fetishistic character of the commodity contains all of historical materialism, all of the self-knowledge of the proletariat as the consciousness of capitalist society" (297/8).
8. The reference is to the "principle of rationality based on calculation, on *calculability*" (177), on "quantification of objects" and on their determination by "abstract thought categories" (291), which conceal the real character of the world, functioning as a "reifying and reified integument" (293).
9. "Reification is *general*, a fundamental structural phenomenon of the *entirety* of bourgeois society". (192, note 22). The human being becomes a "number" or a "mechanised and rationalised implement", he is "broken down (...) into an element in the movement of commodities" (291/2).
10. The terms "exploitation" and "class domination" are used rarely in the text and in a manner unrelated to the analysis of fetishism.
11. "Where then is the *"positive"* potential of German emancipation? *Answer*: In the formation of a class which is *radically shackled:* (...) which constitutes in a word the *total loss* of the human and can thus find itself again only through the *full reacquisition of the human:* this dissolution of society as a particular caste is the *proletariat*:" (Marx, in MEW Vol. 1: 390).
12. There is an obvious affinity between Lukács' outlook and that of the theorists who attribute to capitalism "now" an exclusively symbolic and spectacular function: labour

The Question of "Commodity Fetishism" 105

and politics are no more. War is waged on television. The economy is determined by the VDU monitors in the stock exchange, etc.
13. For Lukács' views also see the critical presentation in Projekt-Ideologie-Theorie 1986, 39 ff. with reference to the similar views of Korsch and GDR Marxists. The universalising outlook is also conspicuous in the 1975 analysis of Goux, who maintains that: "Speech-centredness is the linguistic term for the universal and dominant principle of marketability, based on abstract labour", 140. At another point he considers that "the enslavement of the worker by capital, which is perpetuated by the institution of money, is also implemented through the repression of the operative form of writing, which is debased along with the element of meaning, and repressed through subordination to speech-centredness" (147. Also see 182-184, 190-191). A highly elaborated version of the alienation-problematic was formulated by Sohn-Rethel (1990, particularly 53 f., 68 f., 91 f., 96). The author stresses the fact of the dissociation of intellectual from manual labour, and considers the concepts formulated by the bourgeois philosophy as "the alienation of an alienation".
14. The extracts quoted in the present chapter section, citing only page numbers, are from Paschukanis, 1929.
15. For the state as macro-subject linked with legal subjects and the contradictions of "dual sovereignty" of individual and state, see Dimoulis 1996: 582 ff.
16. "The contract (...) expresses the idea of law is a constitutive part of the concept of law" (100). "Every legal relation is a relation between legal subjects" (87).
17. "Every human being has become the human being in general; all work has become socially useful work in general; every subject has become the abstract legal subject. At the same time the rule also acquires the perfectly logical full legal form of abstract and general law" (99 f.).
18. "The legal form (...) also finds its material foundation in the act of exchange (...), the act of exchange brings together (...) the essential elements both of political economy and of law" (100).
19. See the recent work of Müller-Tuckfeld 1994: 189.
20. It sounds at least paradoxical to neglect this contribution of Pashukanis. More paradoxical is the recently posited allegation that he simply equates law with exchange, thus not investigating the specificity of the law! (La Torre, 1999: 398-400).
21. Legal historians speak of an "extensive-mass" implementation of law under capitalism, in contrast to a "restricted-selective" application of mediaeval and "absolutist" law as a means of social control (Sabadell 1999: 169-72).
22. Thus, for example, the important German constitutionalist –of social-democratic persuasions– of the inter-war period H. Heller (1934: 196) reproached Pashukanis for "ignoring" that even the most homogeneous society requires its positive law and thus governing will capable of framing it and safeguarding it.
23. For the implication of a general definition of law see Dimoulis 1996: 30 f., 47 f.
24. "All the notions of justice held by both the worker and the capitalist, all the mystifications of the capitalist mode of production, all capitalism's illusions about freedom, all the apologetic tricks of vulgar economics, have as their basis the form of appearance discussed above, which makes the actual relation invisible, and indeed present to the eye the precise opposite of that relation" (Marx 1990: 680). Marx puts forward the same idea more clearly in a letter to Engels, dated April 2, 1858: "This simple circulation taken in and of itself, and we are talking about the surface of

bourgeois society on which are made manifest the deeper functions from which it emerges, does not reveal (zeigt) any difference between the subjects of exchange, with the sole exception of some obvious formal differences. This is *the realm of freedom, equality and property that is erected on the basis of 'labour'"* (MEW Vol. 29: 317). As a site for (and process of) exchange of equivalents, the market, even when it is the labour market, embodies the realm of equality and freedom which is a prerequisite for the implementation of "equal exchange".

25. This is criticised by Althusser when he writes: "Marx did of course attempt in his 'A Contribution to the Critique of Political Economy' to 'deduce' a commodity law from (...) commodity relations, but – unless we believe in a providential self-regulation of the commodity relations in question – we do not see how they could function without there being a state-issued currency, without transactions registered by state apparatuses and without courts of law for resolving disagreements" (Althusser 1994: 493).

26. Norrie argues correctly that a historical synchrony exists between law and exchange; then he extends this argument to the thesis of logical synchrony: "The logical relationship between exchange and the juridical form is not one of onesided priority: it is one of true symbiosis. (...) Marx does not imagine for a moment that exchange is logically prior to the juridical" (Norrie 1982: 423). However, if we abandon the thesis of logical/functional priority of the economic over the juridical social level, then we shall also abandon the Marxian scheme of basis/superstructure and accept that specific (juridical) norms (as well as the state apparatuses which implement them) may shape the mode of production. This is undoubtedly an approach contrary to the Marxist theory in general, and in any case to the analysis of Pashukanis, who constantly refers to law as a product, an effect, a reflection, etc. of commodity exchange, fully accepting the derivation of law from the economy (see the references to the original Russian text in Naves 2000: 53-54, 69-78). To our opinion, the question of logical priority cannot be resolved be a simple choice of either approach. In order to determine the relationship between the economic and the legal level of society a definition of each one of these levels is needed, which should confront their "common sense" comprehension.

27. Pashukanis' analysis has to do exclusively with the structure, i.e. the operational codes, of law. This is why it remains powerful even though it is easy to see how it "abstracts" from legal realities. At the normative level, law institutionalises many different types of discrimination, i.e. differential treatment involving privileges and exclusions, locking different groups into hierarchy of status: women, foreigners, workers, civil servants, soldiers, businessmen, etc. Even more intense is the discriminative-inegalitarian function of law at the level of application, where the criteria are essentially those of class. Nevertheless, this does not change the structure of law, which continues to be based on the subject and on freedom and equality. This, in any case, is why groups suffering negative discrimination struggle for its abolition, invoking the basic principle of capitalist civil law: individual human rights.

28. Also see Balibar 1993: 67 ff.

29. In the present section, the quotations cited by page number alone come from Balibar 1976. Balibar's positions were recently reintroduced into the debate by Tuckfeld 1997: 43-46.

30. In the present section, the quotations cited by page number alone come from Althusser 1994.

31. The reference here is principally to the detailed study by J. Rancière, published for the first time in the collective volume *Reading Capital*, edited by Althusser, but also to the analyses of Balibar (1976).
32. The title of the extract is "Problems of culture. Fetishism" (Gramsci 1977: 1769-1771).
33. The quotes are Gramsci's.
34. The quotes are Gramsci's.
35. In the CMP, the capitalist is the producer of commodities (he who decides what is to be produced and how, and who owns the resulting product). Commodity production is of course carried out by means of the labour-power of others (and not that of the capitalist himself), which the producer-capitalist has also purchased as a *commodity*.
36. "Capitalism is not a society of independent producers who exchange their products in accordance with the social-average labour time incorporated in them: it is a surplus-value producing economy engaged in the competitive pursuit of capital. Labour-power is a commodity" (Mattick 1969: 38). For what follows also see Chapters 1-3.
37. See Chapter 1, Section 3, esp. Note 6 of the present book.
38. "Capital is not a thing, it is a definite social relation of production pertaining to a particular historical social formation" (Marx 1991: 953).
39. As Renault aptly observes, Marx detected the more general ideological consequences of the depoliticisation of Political Economy which develops also as a result of fetishism: the class-conditioned character of social relations under capitalism is thus rendered opaque (Renault 1995: 98). The activities of the structurally different productive practices are reduced to human activity in general and Political Economy degenerates into a narrative account of the behaviour of individuals reacting in a rational manner against predetermined situations. As noted, apart from his critique of the view of social relations as relations between things, Marx rejects Political Economy's portrayal of the value form and commodity exchange as natural laws, similarly criticising its refusal to study other modes of production which illustrate the emergence of fetishism in bourgeois society (Tuckfeld 1997: 42-43).
40. Apart from the cases of Lukács and Althusser, also see, for example, from the camp of Soviet Marxism, Klein et. al. 1988: 108-110 and from "Western" Marxism Iacono 1992: 82 ff.
41. For two examples of comprehensive analysis see Godelier 1977, Rancière 1972.
42. To put it differently: Marx started from commodity fetishism by way of introduction to *fetishism of capital*.
43. Labica 1985: 465.
44. For the "two inversions" see Iacono 1992: 83-87.
45. What things? Commodities and money? The concept of money has not been introduced. Nor has the concept of the means of production which functions as fixed capital. And what does labour power consist in? Is not the "reification" of social relations associated with the appearance of the exploitative capitalist community –the capital-wage labour relation– as a community of equality? After Marx had spoken about the capital relation and its forms of appearance, he could explain: "Equality, because each enters into relation with the other, as with a simple owner of commodities, and they exchange equivalent for equivalent (...)" (Marx 1990: 280).
46. "In Marx's view, it is not the price system which 'regulates' the capitalist economy but, rather, unknown yet capitalistically-determined necessities of production *acting through the price mechanism*. (...) The market is the stage on which all competitive

activities are played out. But this stage itself is set up and bound by the class nature of the social structure" (Mattick 1969: 53-54).
47. Godelier 1977: 213/4, Balibar 1993: 60.
48. Balibar 1976: 216 and for details Iacono 1992: 90 ff.
49. A woman may or may not be a feminist, but she cannot cease to recognize herself as a woman (even if she "disagrees" with her role in a system of collective domination of women by men), nor can she cease to perceive the world as divided into sexes. Recognition of their being socially constructed constitutes grounds for struggling to change the situation. But this will come to pass with the abolition of the relevant structures and relations, not with individual change of consciousness. A particular society regards an individual "exit" from integration into the dualistic schema of sexes (as with other constructed identities) as a fatal deviation, i.e. as madness.
50. See e.g. Jensen 1994 for a wealth of references.
51. "The analysis of fetishism confirms that the mystification consists in mystification of the structure, that it is itself the existence of the structure" (Rancière 1972: 122).
52. This is made clear in the statements of both Marx and Pashukanis, which must be read in a non-reductionist way (see preceding section 2.3.3.2).
53. Balibar 1997: 174-76, Tuckfeld 1997: 42. Our search has shown that the word ideology appears only once in *Capital*, in a context which is inconsequential with respect to the main analysis (Marx 1990: 931).
54. Balibar 1993: 77.
55. Althusser 1977: 108 ff.; Müller et al 1994: 41 ff. What we are undertaking here is a general characterisation of ideology. Its content is a different question. From this viewpoint ideology constitutes a *heterogeneous* totality of practices. In capitalism its basic principles correspond to the universal-emancipatory ideals (freedom, equality, democracy, solidarity, welfare) which ideological institutions subject to appropriate processing so as to neutralise their contentious and/or rebellious content, without depriving them of their capacity to promote social cohesion and legitimation. In the second place, ideological practices express ruling which provide direct legitimation for class differentiation ("meritocracy", individuality, "law and order") and other discriminatory elements (nationalism, racism, sexism). At a more specialised level there are ideological practices limited to particular groups and conjunctures (irrationalism, fascism, technocracy, etc.).
56. Balibar 1994: 9 ff., 55 ff., 110 ff., 126 ff., Haug 1993: 46 ff. For the prerequisites for ideological critique and methods employed see Hauck 1992: 112 ff.

PART III:
THEORY OF VALUE AND PRICES: MARX'S AMBIVALENCE TOWARDS CLASSICAL POLITICAL ECONOMY

5 Social Capital and the General Rate of Profit

1. Individual Capitals and Social Capital

We saw in the previous Chapters that, according to Marx, capital constitutes a historically specific social relation of exploitation and domination. This relation manifests itself in the first instance in the commodity character of the economy, in the general exchangeability (through money) of the products of labour on the market. The capital-wage labour relationship can be first of all analysed at the level of the isolated unit of capitalist production, the enterprise, which Marx calls *individual capital*. But the relationship also, and especially, acts at the level of the capitalist economy as a whole, where the immanent causal regularities ("laws") of the system apply. These immanent causal relationships governing the capitalist economy transform the totality of individual capitals into elements of *social capital*, i.e. they situate them within an *economic system*, which then exercises a conditioning influence on them.

Social capital is thus the concept of capital at the level of the capitalist economy as a whole, i.e. it is the complex concept embracing empirically detectable regularities of a capitalist economy, but also all the "laws" –the hidden causal determinants– of the capitalist system (the capitalist mode of production). At this level of social capital, the individual "capitalist is simply personified capital, functioning in the production process simply as the bearer of capital" (Marx 1991: 958). The causal relations immanent in the system, which govern *social capital* are shaped, and also imposed, on the individual capitals by means of *competition*.

In this Chapter, we will first deal with some parts of Marx's analyses on prices of production and the general rate of profit in the 3rd Volume of *Capital*, which were subjected to revision through the introduction of the notion "monopoly capitalism" by Rudolf Hilferding's *Finance Capital* (1910) and the subsequently formulated theories of Imperialism. Thereafter, we are going to discuss the "problem of transformation of values into prices of production", which not only has become the point of departure for the formulation of a scorning critique to what is considered to be Marx's theory of value, but also continues until now to be a subject of dispute among Marxist economists. According to our opinion, these disputes are rooted in a characteristic inconsistency which permeates through Marx's mature economic writings, and especially through Volume 3 of *Capital*.

2. Prices of Production, Competition, Average Profit and Monopoly

As already argued, competition ensures the reciprocal engagement, peculiar to the capitalist system, of institutionally independent production units, imposing on the respective capitals the laws of capitalist production. Competition makes it possible for the separate capitalist enterprises, the individual capitals, to constitute themselves and function as social capital. Through their structural interdependence, that is to say their organisation as social capital, the individual capitals proclaim themselves a *social class*: they function as a uniform social force which counterposes itself to, and dominates, labour.

As individual capitals, enterprises are intended to maximise their profit. This tendency is however, through competition, subordinated to the laws, which are inherent in the concept of social capital, and more specifically to the process of equalisation of the rate of profit and the formation of a tendentially average profit. The tendency towards equalisation of the rate of profit is thus a structural characteristic of the capitalist relation as such.

This tendency is related to two processes:

a) Competition *within each branch* or sector of production, which in principle ensures for each commodity the "establishment of a uniform market value and market price", despite the differences in productivity and organic composition of the individual capitals which produce this commodity, despite –that is– the different "individual values" of the different varieties of the commodity (Marx 1991: 281). Competition within each branch of production therefore tends in every instance to impose on all the individual capitals the more productive manufacturing techniques and in this way to equalise the rate of profit within each branch.

b) Competition *at the level of overall capitalist production*, which ensures such mobility of capital from one branch to another that a uniform rate of profit tends to emerge for the entire capitalist economy (the general rate of profit). The shaping of the uniform (in respect of this tendency)

Social Capital and the General Rate of Profit 113

general rate of profit is achieved on the basis of *production prices*. We are speaking, in other words, of precisely those prices for the product of each individual capital that guarantee it a rate of profit (= ratio of the total profit for a certain period of production to the total capital advanced) equal to (tending towards equality with) the general rate of profit in the economy.

According to Marx, distorted forms of appearance of economic relationships do not merely reflect mistaken impressions at the level of consciousness. They have to do with a reality, they comprise a framework of "necessary practices and ideas" (see Chapter 4). In this context, labour power appears to be incorporated into capital, as variable capital. The products of labour appear to be products of capital, and indeed of capital in general (constant and variable). With all the other factors constant, the result is the formation of *production prices*, so that the profit of all the individual capitals will tend towards the general average profit, i.e. correspond in each case to the cost multiplied by the average rate of profit in the economy (see relation 5 below).

Given that different individual capitals generally contain different proportions of constant (C) and variable (v) capital, the relative production prices of the commodities that they produce are different from what their corresponding relative values would be (if the values were calculable, i.e. if at the level of "abstract labour" workers in the same skill category realised equal quantities of abstract labour in the same time). As indicated above, for Marx the "centre of gravity" of prices (or the "natural prices" around which they fluctuate under the influence of changes in supply and demand) are production prices, not values. On the basis of this approach, Marx solved the problem which plagued Ricardo and his School.[1]

"Freedom of capital", its concentration and centralisation and its capacity to move from one sphere of production to another –mobility necessitated by competition, because every individual capital seeks employment where it can achieve the highest rate of profit– are the terms which secure the predominance of the tendency towards equalisation of the rate of profit. The different rates of profit which initially emerge in the various branches and sectors of production in the end tend to even out in an average general rate of profit.

Of course the fact that there is a tendency towards equalisation of the rate of profit that causes the individual capitals to constitute themselves as social capital does not mean that at any given moment, in any capitalist social formation, the rates of profit of the different capitals in isolation will automatically be equal. Here too, exactly as in the case of competition, the possibility may be perceived of some inequalities in the rate of profit being reproduced, albeit within the context of the tendency toward equalisation of the rate of profit, not invalidating such a tendency.[2]

Extra (above average) *profit* is therefore possible within the capitalist mode of production. It is an *immanent potential of the tendency* towards equalisation of the rate of profit, created precisely within – and parallel to – that tendency, which naturally continues to remain the predominant one. This matter demands closer attention, because in response to the emergence of gigantic corporations, views were formulated in the early years of the twentieth century according to which the tendency towards formation of a general rate of profit constituted a "law" whose validity applied only for an earlier historical period of capitalist development, the period of "competitive capitalism". According to this school of thought, on the basis of which the "Soviet Marxist" current was established from the first decades of the twentieth century, free competition gave way to the "domination of the monopolies". The capitalist system entered its "monopoly stage".

It was Rudolf Hilferding (1877-1941) in his *Finance Capital*, who (transcribing and further developing in a Marxist way the basic ideas of Hobson's *Imperialism*, 1902), introduced the notion of a 'latest *phase*' of capitalism, which is characterised by the following features (Milios 1999, 2001): the formation of monopolistic enterprises (which put aside capitalist competition); the fusion of bank and industrial capital (leading thus to the formation of finance capital, which is considered to be the ultimate form of capital); the subordination of the state to monopolies and the finance capital; finally, the formation of an expansionist policy of colonial annexations and war.[3]

The idea of a "latest", monopolistic-imperialist stage of capitalism, possessing the above described features was adopted by Bukharin, Lenin, Kautsky and others, (despite the disputes among them, in relation to specific features of this approach or its political consequences), shaping thus what is called the Marxist theories of monopoly capitalism, that dominated, until recently, most Marxist streams of thought, and especially Soviet Marxism (see Abalkin et al 1983, Brewer 1980, Milios 1988).

However, this positing of a supposed antithesis between free competition and monopoly, the central tenet of all theories of "monopoly capitalism", is based on an arbitrary ideological displacement and as such must be rejected. Specifically, it evokes an empirically verifiable phenomenon, the tendency towards concentration and centralisation of capital and the establishment of very large corporations, but gives no sign of being able to comprehend this phenomenon. It does not take into account that while monopoly pertains to the theoretical category of individual capital –denoting an individual capital which on account of its peculiar position in the capitalist production process earns higher-than-average profit– free competition by contrast relates exclusively to the category of social capital and is the pre-eminent condition for integration of the individual capitals into social capital. As Marx puts it:

> *Free competition* is the relation of capital to itself as another capital, i.e. the real conduct of capital as capital. The inner laws of capital – which appear merely as tendencies in the preliminary historic stages of its development – are for the first time posited as laws; production founded on capital for the first time posits itself in the forms adequate to it only in so far as and to the extent that free competition develops, for it is the free development of the mode of production founded on capital; the free development of its conditions and of itself as the process which constantly reproduces these conditions. It is not individuals who are set free by free competition; it is, rather, capital which is set free. (...) Free competition is the real development of capital. *By* its means, what corresponds to the nature of capital is posited as external necessity for the individual capital; what corresponds to the concept of capital, is posited as external necessity for the mode of production founded on capital (...) is the *free,* at the same time the *real* development of wealth as capital. (...) The predominance of capital is the presupposition of free competition, just as the despotism of the Roman Caesars was the presupposition of the free Roman 'private law' (Marx 1993: 650-1).

Marxist theory therefore proceeds on the assumption that free competition is a structural feature of the capital relation, which clearly cannot be abolished. The development of capitalism can be associated only with the evolution, not with the abolition, of free competition.

Monopoly is accordingly not the polar opposite of free competition. It is a *form of individual capital,* which is created precisely within the framework of free competition: not outside of and/or alongside free competition but through free competition and as one of its constituent elements. Monopoly is thus defined in Marxist theory as individual capital which systematically earns an above-average rate of profit (and not as a company which monopolises the market, as in Neoclassical theory).

Marx in his *Capital* draws a distinction between three types of monopoly: *natural, artificial and accidental monopolies* (also see Altvater 1975, Varga 1974: 117 ff.).

Natural monopolies arise from monopolistic possession of the elements of production in their natural form, which leads to increased productivity (in relation to the social average) and increased (monopoly) profit.[4]

Artificial monopolies also establish their monopoly status on the basis of conditions of labour productivity higher than the social average within a certain branch of production. However, in this case the higher-than-average productivity derives not from monopolisation of a natural resource but from the technological superiority of the specific individual capital in relation to average conditions in its own specialised branch of production. This technological superiority is reflected in higher surplus value and higher profits.[5]

The extra-profit enjoyed by artificial monopolies "acting as a coercive law of competition, forces his competitors to adopt the new method [of production]" (Marx 1990: 436). Artificial monopoly is thus brought into existence through competition and abides in the midst of it, although at the same time its monopoly position is under continual threat from competition. The same is true of natural monopoly, given that its superiority in productivity, which derives from monopolisation of a natural resource by the specific individual capital, may very well be forfeited as a result of technical innovations introduced by its competitors.

According to Marx there is a third type of monopoly which may come into existence, but this time in the sphere not of production but of circulation of commodities (the market). Marx named this type of monopoly the *accidental monopoly*. The term is applied to certain *individual capitals* which are able to secure extra-profit by exploiting conjunctural or more permanent imbalances and fluctuations of supply and demand in the market.[6] This type of monopoly corresponds to some extent to what in Neoclassical theory is described as an oligopoly.

It follows from the above that monopoly profit cannot be the predominant characteristic of the capitalist mode of production. The predominance of the tendency towards equalisation of the general rate of profit is the social condition that ensures the self-organisation of individual capitals into a ruling capitalist class:

> The various different capitals here are in the position of shareholders in a joint-stock company (Marx 1991: 258). This is the form in which capital

Social Capital and the General Rate of Profit 117

becomes conscious of itself as a *social power*, in which every capitalist participates in proportion to his share in the total social capital (Marx 1991: 297).

At this point we can recapitulate: The social capital is not the sum of the individual capitals. It is the social predominance of the capital relation, which is secured and elaborated in its adequate forms by means of the equalising processes imposed by free capitalist competition.[7]

So the claim of the "monopoly capitalism" theories that monopolies suppress the tendency towards equalisation of the general rate of profit in essence distort or even abolish the Marxist category of social capital, i.e. the central tenet of Marxist theory in relation to the CMP.

3. The Reproduction of Social Capital

Marx's theory of the social capital includes an approach to the problem of expanded reproduction of the capitalist economy: In the second volume of *Capital*, Marx formulates in terms of values the conditions for unimpeded reproduction on (a simple and) an expanded scale of a pure capitalist economy comprised of two sectors, one of which (Sector I) produces means of production for the entire economy and the other (Sector II) means of consumption for all workers and capitalists. In other words, the *reproduction schemes* developed by Marx in Volume 2 of *Capital* show under what conditions the circuit of capital, M-C-M′ may function on the level of the whole capitalist economy, i.e. in respect with the social capital.

Let us postulate that Ic+Iv+Is is the output (the gross product) of Sector I, which produces means of production, and IIc+IIv+IIs are the output of Sector II, which produces means of consumption. For the conditions of unimpeded reproduction to be fulfilled, the output in each sector must be equal to the demand in both sectors for the means – of production or consumption – produced in the sector under discussion.

Thus, in the case of Sector I, which produces means of production, its total output must be equal to the demand for means of production in both sectors (for replacement of worn-out components and for accumulation). The value of worn-out means of production is Ic for Sector I and IIc for Sector II, while their demand for additional means of production (constant capital) for the purpose of expanding their productive base (accumulation) is

ΔIc and ΔIIc respectively. Thus, the condition which favours unimpeded reproduction of social capital on an expanded scale is:

$$Ic+Iv+Is = Ic+\Delta Ic+IIc+\Delta IIc \qquad (1)$$

Considering that neither credit relations nor value transfer can exist *between one sector and another* and that accordingly the surplus value appropriated by capitalists in Sector I must secure both satisfaction of the consumer demand of capitalists and satisfaction of their demand for constant and variable capital for accumulation, the following will apply:

$$Is = \Delta Ic+\Delta Iv+Ik \qquad (2)$$

(where the figures $\Delta Ic+\Delta Iv$ denote the aggregate of additional constant and variable capital and Ik personal consumption of Sector I capitalists).

From the combination of relations (1) and (2) we conclude finally that Sector I expenditure on means of consumption must be of the same value as Sector II expenditure on means of production:

$$Ic+Iv+\Delta Ic+\Delta Iv+Ik = Ic+\Delta Ic+IIc+\Delta IIc \Rightarrow Iv+\Delta Iv+Ik = IIc+\Delta IIc \quad (3)$$

We would end up with exactly the same relationship (3) if we commenced from Sector II (which produces means of production) and equalised its output (IIc+IIv+IIs = IIc+IIv+ΔIIc+ΔIIv+IIk) with demand in both sectors for means of consumption (Iv+ΔIv+Ik+IIv+ΔIIv+IIk).

The theory of unimpeded reproduction and the corresponding reproductive schemata of Marx were an object of controversy between Marxists in the first decades of the 20th century and virtually up until the 2nd World War, in relation with the controversies over economic crises (see Chapter 8). After the 2nd World War, Kalecki (having begun his work on these questions from 1933 on) incorporated the Marxist reproductive schemes into his theory of profit and the economic cycle (Kalecki, 1969: Part 2). At the same time Joan Robinson (1966) in her attempt to uncover "the Keynesian element in Marx" also placed emphasis on Marx's reproduction schemes (Robinson 1966: vii).

4. The "Transformation of Values into Production Prices": A Category Confusion

4.1 Marx's Approach and the "Correct Solution" of von Bortkiewicz

Marx's presentation of the theory of value (see Chapters 2 and 3) demonstrated that value and prices are not situated at the same level of analysis. They are not commensurate i.e. qualitatively similar (and so quantitatively comparable) entities. Money is the necessary form of appearance of value (and of capital) in the sense that prices constitute the necessarily "distorted" (and only) form of appearance of the value of commodities. The difference between values and production prices is thus not a quantitative one, assuming that the latter are determined in accordance with the general rate of profit and the consequent "redistribution of the surplus value among capitalists". It is a difference between two non-commensurate and so *non-comparable* quantities, which are, though, intertwined in a notional link, which connects causal determinations (values) and their forms of appearance (prices).

Nevertheless Marx distances himself from this implication of his own theory when in the 3rd volume of *Capital* he draws a quantitative comparison between values and production prices and through mathematical calculations "transforms" the former into the latter. In this way, albeit tacitly, he adopts (he retreats to) the Classic viewpoint that values are entities that are commensurable with prices.

When in the course of his analysis about the average profit Marx reaches the conclusion that, with given the general rate of profit, the mass of profit accruing to each individual enterprise is determined by the total mass of capital advanced by it,[8] and therefore that "the individual capitalist (or alternatively the sum total of capitalists in a particular sphere of production), (...) is right in believing that this profit does not derive just from the labour employed by him or employed in his own branch" (Marx 1991: 270); he should reiterate the conclusions of his former theoretical analysis on the relationship between value and surplus value on the one hand and price and profit on the other: that although labour, productively expended, is the source of all value and surplus value in capitalism (as it was also the source of all wealth and surplus-product in pre-capitalist modes of production), this labour, in its value-producing function, i.e. as *abstract* labour, is not an empirically tangible (i.e. directly measurable) magnitude: Abstract labour

120 *Karl Marx and the Classics*

expended, manifests itself only through the *forms of appearance* of value, the commodity prices (see Part I of this book).

Instead, therefore, of re-affirming his theoretical system, according to which prices are derived from values through an analysis which deciphers how "the *social* character of labour appears as the *money existence* of the commodity" (Marx 1991: 649), Marx retreats to the *empiricism* of the Ricardian theory: He accepts the problematic that two individual capitals utilising the same amount of living labour but different amounts of constant capital produce an output of equal *value* but (given the general profit rate) unequal (production) price. He then claims that in order to justify the theory of value one has to prove that, *on the level of the economy as a whole the sum of values equals the sum of commodity prices, while at the same time the total surplus value should be equal to the total profit*. The "transformation of values into prices of production" was aimed to provide that proof.

For each individual capital, the cost price in value terms (k) is the outlay in constant (c) and variable (v) capital, namely the quantity k=c+v. Assuming a constant rate of exploitation s/v, the amount of value in a commodity will be:

$$w = c+v(1+s/v) \qquad (4)$$

and for a *given cost price* (c+v = constant) it will increase with v (with decreasing c/v).

By contrast, for a given rate of profit, r, and assuming for the sake of mathematical simplicity, that all the constant capital is used up in the course of each production period (i.e. C'=c'), the *production price* of the commodity is:

$$P = (c'+v')(1+r) = k'(1+r) \qquad (5)$$

where c'+v' is the cost price (k') in price terms. It is obvious that, (with r = const.), P remains constant for a given cost price (c'+v'= constant), irrespective of changes in the ratio c'/v'.

In the second section of the 3rd volume of *Capital*, Marx tried to formulate the mathematical relations resulting from the hypothesis that the sum of values equals the sum of production prices. He so calculated the production prices starting from values, and erroneously used the cost price in value terms (k instead of k') and surplus value (s) so as to calculate,

firstly, the rate of profit (r) [positing $r = \Sigma s_i/\Sigma(c_i+v_i)$]. Subsequently, he again employed this mode of expressing the rate of profit and cost price in terms of value (and not production prices, k instead of k′) in order to arrive at production prices (P).
Thus, according to Marx's analysis in the 3rd volume of *Capital*:

$$P_i = [c_i+v_i]\cdot[1 + \Sigma s_i/\Sigma(c_i+v_i)] \quad (6)$$

Apart from the mathematical errors committed here by Marx (since he uses value cost instead of the corresponding figure in production prices), his whole theoretical approach in this section of his work, according to which one could start from the *value of each commodity as such* and through mathematical calculations arrive at its production price, implicitly deviates from his own theoretical system. Specifically, it adopts the viewpoint of the Classical School of Political Economy on value as "labour expended", according to which the value of each commodity is determined independently, and is not qualitatively different from "natural price" (i.e. belongs to the category of *empirically* calculable quantities). Consequently, value can be reduced to production price by means of mathematical calculation.

In this theoretical context, Ladislaus von Bortkiewicz (1907) provided a "mathematically sound" solution to the problem of *transformation* of values into production prices. The author took as his starting point the model of a totally capitalistic economy with three sectors, in which Sector I produces the means of production consumed (productively) by the economy as a whole, Sector II produces the consumption goods consumed by the wage-earners in all three sectors (the wage-purchased commodities of the economy) and Sector III produces the consumption goods consumed by the capitalists in all three sectors (the luxury commodities of the economy). For the sake of simplicity he considered that C=c (absence of fixed capital) and that there is no accumulation (i.e. the system is one of simple and not expanded reproduction). In terms of value, the (gross) product in Sector I is $c_1+v_1+s_1$, in Sector II $c_2+v_2+s_2$, and in Sector III $c_3+v_3+s_3$. The conditions for unimpeded reproduction of the system will be:

Sector I: $\quad c_1+v_1+s_1 = c_1+c_2+c_3 \quad$ (7a)
Sector II: $\quad c_2+v_2+s_2 = v_1+v_2+v_3 \quad$ (7b)
Sector III: $\quad c_3+v_3+s_3 = s_1+s_2+s_3 \quad$ (7c)

For the values in the system to be "transformed" into production prices, von Bortkiewicz introduced three unknown transformation coefficients (x, y, z), which transform the value of the means of production (coefficient x), wage-purchased commodities (coefficient y) and luxury commodities (coefficient z) into the corresponding production prices. The system under examination is now transformed into the following:

Sector I: $(c_1 x + v_1 y)(1 + r) = (c_1+c_2+c_3) x$ (8a)
Sector II: $(c_2 x + v_2 y)(1 + r) = (v_1+v_2+v_3) y$ (8b)
Sector III: $(c_3 x + v_3 y)(1 + r) = (s_1+s_2+s_3) z$ (8c)

There thus emerges a system of three equations with four unknowns (the transformation coefficients x, y and z and the rate of profit r). As a fourth equation one of the two might be chosen which can be inferred from the hypotheses of Marx, namely, a) at the overall level the sum of the production prices is equal to the sum of the values or b), that total surplus value is equal to total profit. On the basis of von Bortkiewicz's system of equations (8a-c) it can be shown that, apart from marginal cases, it is impossible for conditions (a) and (b) both to be satisfied, i.e. that, if for example it be assumed that the total production prices are equal to the total values, then the total surplus value is *not* equal to the total profit and thus the rate of profit in value terms is not equal to the rate of profit in terms of production prices, as Marx had assumed. Von Bortkiewicz's model seems to correct the mathematical errors made by Marx in "transforming" values into production prices, but at the same time *to damage the argument* that for value theory to be sound, value must equal price *and* surplus value profit.

Nevertheless, the essential problem of Marx's "transformation of values into production prices" is not to do with his mathematical errors but, as we said, with the explicit position contained in this section of his work, that values and production prices may be considered commensurate entities, in accordance with the Classical concept of value. Marx's entire argument concerning a "transformation" of values into production prices thus constitutes an empiristic retreat from his own theoretical system in the Critique of Political Economy towards Classical (i.e. Ricardian) Political Economy.

As far as the specifics of his analysis are concerned, what Marx does is to "transform" production prices from a necessarily distorted form of appearance of value into a category or component of value,[9] i.e. a "form" of value, which from the qualitative viewpoint is entirely compatible with value

– and as such can be added to it or multiplied by it, because it is perceived to be qualitatively similar (commensurate) with it.

In other words Marx assumes a) that there exists a unit of measurement of value (e.g. a labour hour) which b) is commensurate with the unit of measurement of prices (dollars or any other currency). The implication of a) is that in practice we are able to measure values independently of (abstracting from) money. The implication of b) – which is merely the other side of the same coin – is that "abstract social labour" (or labour in general) belongs to the world of empirically observable and measurable objects, exactly like money. As Michael Heinrich, who has thoroughly investigated this contradiction in Marx's writings, correctly observes:

> The attempt to effect a quantitative transformation of values into production prices is probably the most important example of the theoretical field of Political Economy acting on the scientific terrain recently opened up by Marx (…) Marx's quantitative analysis of the transformation of values in the third volume of *Capital* represents an attempt to lend greater precision to the analytical schema of Ricardo *within the arena of Classical Political Economy*. Inside that arena (of Classical Political Economy) Marx attempted to find a simple method of conversion from one quantitative system to another, and in so doing left money entirely out of account. (…) In the context of Marx's monetary theory of value there can thus be no question of quantitative conversion of values into production prices (Heinrich, 1999: 278 ff.).

4.2 Neoricardian Linear Production Systems and the Neoricardian Critique of the Marxist Theory of Value

In his book *Production of Commodities by Means of Commodities* (1960), Piero Sraffa presented a model of calculating production prices without any reference to values. In accordance with this model, which was described as the Neoricardian approach, we can stipulate a linear system of n equations, each one of which denotes a particular productive process. Introduced into this process as inputs, (in their natural form), are quantities of all the "commodities" produced by the system.

The Sraffian "production system" of n sectors takes the following form:

$(a_{11}p_1 + a_{12}p_2 + \ldots + a_{1n}p_n)(1+r) + L_1 w = p_1$ \hfill (9a)

$(a_{21}p_1 + a_{22}p_2 + \ldots + a_{2n}p_n)(1+r) + L_2 w = p_2$ \hfill (9b)

....

$(a_{n1}p_1 + a_{n2}p_2 + \ldots + a_{nn}p_n)(1+r) + L_n w = p_n$ \hfill (9n)

where p_i is the price of the "commodity" i, the production of which used up natural quantities from a_{i1} to a_{in} of all the "commodities" in the system and a quantity of labour L_i (in units of time: hours) for which their bearer (the worker) is paid the amount $L_i w$ (w being the nominal hourly wage). The figure r represents the uniform rate of profit in the system, so that the prices p_i resemble Marxian production prices.

The Sraffian system of equations possesses two degrees of freedom (n equations with n+2 unknowns: the n "prices" p_i, the rate of profit r, and the hourly wage w). If the rate of profit r or the nominal hourly wage w[10] are introduced as external factors, then there remains only one degree of freedom, which is covered through the "normalisation of prices", i.e. the hypothesis that a unit of one among the "commodities" serves as money-commodity or *numéraire* which measures the price of all other commodities. Mathematically this means that one of the unknown prices (p_1 to p_n) is set equal to the unit (say, for example $p_1 = 1$).

Sraffa believed that the solution of his system of equations (the relative prices) is independent of the normalisation of prices (i.e. of the choice of the numéraire) which, however, has been proven not to be true in certain cases (see Kliman 1999). Furthermore, the Sraffian approach belongs to what Karl Marx defined as "vulgar Political Economy", as it does not even pose the question of what *are* the commodity prices, or why are use-values in capitalism commensurate (and therefore exchangeable). It simply defines prices (of outputs) through prices (of inputs), in a way of circular tautology which is peculiar to all non-scientific discourses.[11] The mathematical formalisation can hardly disguise this lack of theoretical foundation of the Neoricardian approach (analytically, see Stamatis 1984).

The Neoricardian mathematical formalisation was employed initially as a critique of Neoclassical theory, and in particular its basic finding that compensations to production factors (the nominal hourly wage, w; the rate of profit as monetary payment to one unit of means of production) are linked immanently to the price of the commodity produced, given that each compensation is taken to be the monetary expression of the corresponding marginal product. (For example: wages constitute the monetary value of the marginal product of labour, that is to say the *marginal product of labour* multiplied by the price of one unit of the social product [= a *partial derivative* of the product *in relation to the labour employed*]: w = [∂S/∂A]'p). The Neoricardian system shows that prices are determined independently of the compensations paid to the production factors, and that prior to the *exogenous* determination of the relations of distribution (the exogenous determination, alternatively, either of w or of r) there can be no conclusion as to how much each factor contributes to production (Heinrich 1999: 273).

The Neoricardian formalisation was also employed subsequently for criticism of the Marxist theory of value. Unlike many Marxists, first and foremost Engels, who from Marx's analysis of the "transformation" of values into production prices drew the conclusion that values are the necessary point of departure for calculation of production prices (see Chapter 10 where the Preface by Engels to Volume 2 of *Capital* is discussed), Samuelson (1971) observed that the Sraffian system proves precisely the opposite: production prices, p_i, are determined without there ever having to be any reference to values.

On this basis Steedman (1975, 1977) and others formulated the view that the Marxist theory of value is *redundant* for analysis of the capitalist economy. In fact Steedman (1977: 207) asserted that the Marxist theory of value is "a major fetter on the development of (...) the project of providing a materialist account of capitalist societies", because in certain cases of production of complex commodities (joint production: when two products are manufactured from one productive process) there emerge (for positive prices) negative "labour values".

From the argument that the labour theory of value is superfluous, the *surplus approach* (Steedman 1981) was formulated, according to which the basic production system from which production prices later emerged, together with the relations of distribution, is that which is attributed in *material terms (physical quantities* of means of production and output, and labour time) so that the decisive measure is the *material surplus* which emerges in one production period. These views gave all opponents of Marxist theory, whatever school of economic thought they belonged to, the arguments they needed to support their claim that Marx's theory is theoretically inconsistent and superfluous.

The basic arguments concerning the superfluity of the theory of value and theoretical priority of the material system of physical quantities and material surplus were first formulated in 1900-1901 by Tugan-Baranowsky, who wrote:

> No theory of value is necessary to explain why 15 million tons of grain are 50% more expensive than 10 million tons of the same item or why a person pays 20% more for 220,000 tons of cotton cloth than he does for 200,000 tons of the same product. (...) The social product is assigned a price in the course of the exchange process and that the distribution of the social product between the various social classes is achieved through intervention of the price mechanism. (...) The price determines the part of the social product that is appropriated by each separate individual (...) The community as a whole does not have anyone to share its product with. Consequently, social wealth is independent of prices. It can be expressed only in use values (...) The theory of profit we have developed (...) is independent of every theory of value (Tugan-Baranowsky 1969: 220, 221, 226).

There are very many Marxist economists (for details see Heinrich 1999: 276 ff.) who, in their endeavour to provide answers to the arguments of the Neoricardian critique of Marxist theory of value, have involved themselves in Sraffian mathematical technicism, seeking new solutions in relation to the "transformation coefficients" for converting values into prices, proposing a different "formalisation of prices" to the Neoricardian production system and so implicitly conceiving of values as entities commensurate with production prices. In their effort to defend Marx's analysis on the "transformation of values into prices of production" they essentially erased the Marxist theory of value and of money from their problematic. Thus, even if they formulated a significant critique of certain individual presentations of the Neoricardian theory,[12] they left the theory itself entirely intact, as they did not point out:

a) that what is involved is a mathematical reformulation of the common-sense (from the scientific viewpoint "vulgar") theory of production costs, which fails to comprehend not only the specific characteristics of capitalist economics – it does not ask why products and labour power are commodities – but even of economics generally (it is not capable of asking questions about the commensurability of "economic goods", which it simply takes for granted);

b) that, exactly like Neoclassical theory, Neoricardian theory is situated in the category of pre-monetary approaches, since it takes as its point of departure a system of equilibrium between material quantities (use values) and then introduces "prices". By contrast, Marxist theory perceives that the conditions for reproduction of a capitalist economy are satisfied (when they are satisfied, in a context of economic cycles and crises) with the monetary *price* of each commodity *pre-established*, given that the exchange value of the commodities can be expressed only in mediated form, through money.

The fact that many Marxist economists integrated their analyses into the Neoricardian problematic undoubtedly has to do with the theoretical contradictions of Marx's own analysis and its relapse to the level of Classical Political Economy on the question of "transformation of values into production prices". Like Marx himself, these economists attempted to construct mathematical models in terms of which a redistribution of value and surplus value among capitalists would emerge that would result in a uniform rate of profit and corresponding production prices, with the sum of production *prices being equal to* the sum of *values* and the sum of *profits being equal to* the sum of *surplus values*.[13] It is characteristic that when Marx describes the mechanism for equalising the rate of profit in the various sectors of the capitalist economy by means of competition, he frequently speaks – following the concepts of the Classical system – of the *values* which initially diverge and are then transformed through competition into production prices, instead of the *prices which diverge from the production prices* (and thus entail different rates of profit) but which are finally converted into production prices (which is tantamount to equalisation of the rate of profit):

> This constant migration, the distribution of capital between the different spheres according to where the profit rate is rising and where it is falling, is what produces a relationship between supply and demand such that the average profit is the same in the various different spheres, and *values are therefore transformed into prices of production* (Marx 1991: 297, emphasis added).

However, it is not the case either that values take the form of empirically palpable entities to be transformed through competition into prices, or that the redistribution of values and surplus values among capitalists leads to prices, because value and price are not commensurate. They are concepts existing on different analytical planes, categories between which there is an unbridgeable semantic gulf, so that there is *no way* the one can be "reduced" to the other (just as *concrete labour* can in no way be reduced to *abstract labour* (see Part 1).

Prices represent exclusively *forms of appearance* of value, and production prices represent that price level which secures average profit for all enterprises in – and all sectors of – the economy. Through competition between individual capitals, *prices* converge towards the levels of production prices, or in other words *production prices* constitute the "centre of gravity" for prices.

Values show what prices *are*, without being the factor determining their exact level. Values as such cannot be measured quantitatively, and it is even more impossible to refer to the level of any value at all as such, taken in isolation. Values are expressed through their forms of appearance, prices, i.e. their expression is *mediated* through money.

The significance of the above is that the argument concerning the superfluity of the Marxist theory of value is mistaken: Marx's theory is the only theory which gives an answer to the question: what are *prices*? In other words it is the only monetary theory of value. The concepts of value and surplus-value are a prerequisite for theoretical comprehension of the issue of what (production) prices are. The transition from values to production prices is a *conceptual* and not a quantitative one. So what is superfluous is the conceptual equation of values and production prices (or of abstract labour and money) as commensurate entities, towards which Marx relapses when he formulates the problem of "transformation" of values into production prices. Also superfluous is the Neoricardian reformulation of the scientifically "vulgar" theory of production costs. As noted by M. Heinrich (1999: 280):

"The real contribution of the Neoricardian critique of the theory of value consists in its successfully showing that a *pre-monetary* theory of value is superfluous for determining *non-monetary* production costs".

Notes

1. Marx describes as follows the formation process of production prices and so the tendency towards equalisation of the different rates of profit: "As a result of the differing organic composition of capitals applied in different branches of production, (...) very different amounts of labour are set in motion by capitals of equal size, so too very different amounts of surplus labour are appropriated by these capitals. (...) The rates of profit prevailing in the different branches of production are accordingly originally very different. These different rates of profit are balanced out by competition to give a general rate of profit. (...) The profit that falls to a capital of given size according to this general rate of profit, whatever its organic composition might be, we call the average profit. That price of a commodity which is equal to its cost price, plus

the part of the annual average profit on the capital applied in its production (not simply the capital consumed in its production) that falls to its share according to its conditions of turnover, is its price of production" (Marx 1991: 257-8).
2. "With the whole of capitalist production, it is always only in a very intricate and approximate way, as an average of perpetual fluctuations which can never be firmly fixed, that the general law prevails as the dominant tendency" (Marx 1991: 266).
3. "Finance capital signifies the unification of capital. The previously separate spheres of industrial, commercial and bank capital are brought under the common direction of high finance, in which the masters of industry and of the banks are united in a close personal association. The basis of this association is the elimination of free competition among individual capitalists by the large monopolistic combines. This naturally involves at the same time a change in the relation of the capitalist class to state power" (Hilferding 1981: 301).
4. "Possession of this natural force forms a monopoly in the hands of its owner, a condition of higher productivity for the capital invested, which cannot be produced by capital's own production process; the natural force that can be monopolized in this way is always chained to the earth. (...) The increased productivity of the labour he applies arises neither from the capital and labour themselves nor from the simple application of a natural force (...) that is (...) available to all capital in the same sphere of production. (...) What is used is rather a monopolized natural force which, like waterfall, is available only to those who have at their disposal particular pieces of the earth's surface and their appurtenances" (Marx 1991: 784-5).
5. Artificial monopoly is created when an individual capital is able, through its technological superiority, to keep the "individual value" of the commodities it produces lower than their real value (which is determined as we said at the level of society as a whole): "The individual value of these articles is now below their social value; (...) The real value of a commodity, however, is not its individual, but its social value; (...) [The] capitalist who applies the new method sells his commodity at its social value (...), he sells it (...) above its individual value, and thus he realizes an extra surplus-value" (Marx 1990: 434).
6. "By accidental monopoly, we mean the monopoly that accrues to buyer or seller as a result of the accidental state of supply and demand" (Marx 1991: 279).
7. On this point Marx is unequivocal: "Capital arrives at this equalisation [of the general rate of profit] to a greater or lesser extent, according to how advanced capitalist development is in a given national society: i.e. the more the conditions in the country in question are adapted to the capitalist mode of production" (Marx 1991: 297).
8. "Since the rate of profit is s/C or $s/(c+v)$, it is clear that everything that gives rise o a change in the magnitude of c, and therefore of C, also brings about a change in the profit rate, even if s, v and their reciprocal relationship remain" (Marx 1991: 201).
9. Or, rather, it "transforms" the value into a component of the "normal" price (i guaranteeing the average rate of profit).
10. In a "Marxist" or "Classic" version of this approach it might be considered that the nominal hourly wage w is the price of the (given) real hourly wage, i.e. of the (given) basket of commodities corresponding to the necessary means of subsistence of the worker. It will therefore apply (as one further equation of the system): $w = b_1p_1 + b_2p_2 +....+ b_np_n$, where b_1 to b_n, are the (known) quantities of the "commodities" 1 to n which constitute the real hourly wage.

11. "The vulgar economists (...) assume the value of one commodity (...) in order in turn to use it to determine the values of other commodities" (Marx 1990:174).
12. For example, as Heinrich (1999: 275) points out, Wolfstetter (1976), 'Positive Profits with Negative Surplus Value. A Comment', *The Economic Journal*, Vol. 86: 854-68, has shown that "negative values" emerge in conditions that are entirely lacking in substance from an economic viewpoint: maintenance of two joint production processes which, employing the same quantity of labour, yield two identical products in each case, with the net product (for both goods) of one production process greater than that of the other.
13. Since the early 1980's a number of approaches to the "transformation problem" was formulated, which distanced themselves from the Neoricardian mathematical formalisation and the equilibrium of physical quantities on which it is based (e.g. Duménil 1980, Foley 1982 and 2000, Wolff, Callari and Roberts 1984, Moseley 1993 and 2000, Ramos-Martínez and Rodriguez-Herrera 1996, Freeman 1999). Despite the differences among them, all stressed, in one way or another, the Marxian analysis of the Circuit of Social Capital, which is expressed not in physical quantities but in monetary terms (M-C-M'). However, they all ended in a quantitative "transformation" (correspondence) of the monetary unit to (units of) abstract labour, i.e. they assumed a "value of money" or a "monetary expression of labour-time", which is supposed to be the quantitative "relation between the value and the price, of all commodities taken together" (Freeman 1999). Once more, value and price are treated as commensurable quantities; value is so "transformed" mathematically into price. Through the "value of money", the labour value of aggregates emerges as an empirically tangible quantity.

6 Theory of Value and Ground Rent (Smith-Ricardo-Marx: Converges and Disputes)

1. Introduction

In this chapter our interest will focus on theoretical questions bearing on ground rent. We will accordingly seek to demonstrate through an exposition of Marx's views that although it is generally asserted that in relation to *differential rent* Marx follows Ricardo, in reality it would be equally true to say that he follows Smith. Special attention will be given to the fact that when dealing with the theory of *absolute rent*, Karl Marx "flirts" with the Classical theoretical system in a way which is similar to the one he followed when dealing with the "transformation problem" (see Chapter 5). In other words, he once again abandoned his own system of the Critique of Political Economy, in favour of the Classical concept of value (as an empirically measurable quantity of "labour expended").

Before proceeding we should note that in the first instance when we refer to *ground rent* we mean the rent paid by the occupier of a section of ground and its substratum to the person exercising proprietorship over it in recompense for his occupation of that ground.

Rent, occupier, exercising proprietorship are historical categories, variable both in themselves (in form and content) and in their intercombination, in accordance with the *historical epoch*, that is to say with the prevailing *mode of production* (see Chapter 1, Section 3).

The historical framework to our analytical investigation relates to the historical epoch of the capitalist system (of capitalism), that is to say to the historic system organised under the rule of the capitalist mode of production (CMP).[1]

2. Capitalist Mode of Production and the Content of Rent

As already argued in Chapter 1 of this book, from the structure of the CMP itself two social classes are constituted which are bearers of the relations of the matrix (the inner structure) of this mode of production: the class of the capitalists and the class of the workers. Thus the landowner becomes a third party, outside the mode of production.[2] Landownership itself (as a relation) becomes external to the predominant mode of production, expressing simply a legal relationship and not an economic *production relationship* (Rey 1973: 20, 60, 88, 93. See also Marx 1991: 753-55).

In other words, the class of landowners and ground rent constitute elements of specific capitalist economies, but they do not belong to the structure of the CMP (as the capitalist class and the class of wage-labourers). In any specific capitalist society there are always more classes than those connected to the CMP, as an effect of processes emanating from the historic development of this society (see Milios 2000). One such process is the formation of new classes from transition processes, as some *modes of production dissolve* under the weight of the expanded reproduction of the CMP. The class of landowners in some capitalist countries (e.g. Britain), is a typical example of a class which emerged from the transformation-adjustment of the class of the feudal lords: with the break-up of the feudal mode of production, feudal ownership is transformed into a capitalist type (complete) ownership of land, and the serfs are evicted from the land (which is now fenced off by the land-owners), and are deprived of any of their previous rights to the (use of) land. Within this process, the feudal lords become landowners in the contemporary (capitalist) sense: owners of the land, who (as we have already noted), enjoy as a special form of income, the capitalist land-rent, through the renting of their lands to the capitalist-farmers.

The class of landowners, however, does not constitute an inevitable and necessary result of the prevalence and domination of the CMP. It constitutes a manifestation of a specific *historical variation of this domination.*[3]

Despite the conversion of landownership into "uselessly and absurdly superfluous" (Marx 1991: 755), "superfluous and harmful" (Marx 1991: 760) for the CMP, the relationship of legal proprietorship of land, once historically formed, brings about economic results which are none other than the rent which the capitalist tenant must remit to the landowner who is its legal proprietor.[4]

In order to function as a capitalist, the tenant must derive from the capital he has invested in land the average (or normal) rate of profit. This means that the *capitalist tenant can remit as rent to the landowner who is its legal proprietor only that portion of his profit that exceeds the average (rate of) profit on capital.* So, according to Marx:

Rent "is only the excess portion of this surplus-value which is extracted by him from the agricultural labourer by direct exploitation, by means of his capital, which he turns over to the landlord as rent" (Marx internet: vol. 3 - chapter 47, Marx 1991: 935).

Capital, of course, does not find itself up against the monopoly of land ownership[5] only in the sphere of agricultural production, though in the present analysis we shall confine ourselves to rent from ownership of agricultural land and not to rent from mines and from real estate.

3. So-Called Differential Rent

3.1 On the Definition of Differential Rent

Generalising Marx's viewpoint we can say that what the capitalist gives the landowner in the form of rent is the part of profit that remains above and beyond the average profit on capital and is derived from direct capitalist exploitation of workers.

Taking it for granted that the capitalist tenant in any event will be reaping the average rate of profit, let us investigate exactly what the size of the surplus above and beyond the average rate of profit is dependent on, which is also equal to the size of the rent appropriated by the landowner, and what is its "nature".

The analysis by the Classic theorists of Political Economy (Smith and Ricardo) of the size of the surplus turned on two factors. Firstly on differences in fertility and location between different tracts of land. Secondly on differences in the amount of capital invested in those different tracts.

It is a question of what Marx calls *differential rent*, in two variants: differential rent of the first type and differential rent of the second type respectively. Differential rent is expressed through the conversion into rent of the additional profit that emerges from the *difference between the market price* (determined generally speaking by the production price of the capital invested in the worst land, which is equal to the production cost plus the average profit) *and the "individual" production price of the individual capital that is invested in a piece of land* (Marx 1991: 779-881. See also Smith 1981: I.xi.a.1, Smith 1981: I.xi.a.6 and 8, Ricardo 1992, Ch. II, X, XXIV, XXXII).

In both its expressions, excluding the question of demand fluctuations, differential rent (as a quantity) correlates positively with differences in productivity of labour as between different sections of land (whether attributable to differences in fertility and position of the various locations – type one– or to the differing amounts of capital invested at the different sites –type two) given that the productivity of labour correlates negatively with the production prices of the individual capitals.

In both variants of differential rent it seems, too, that the worst tract of land does not yield differential rent, as we have accepted that the production price of the capital invested in the worst land determines the market price (the price regulating the market). This is not exactly the view of Smith or Marx on the subject. But this point we shall deal with in what follows.

3.2 Market Price, Lower-Quality Land and Differential Rent

We have taken it, in principle, for granted that the market price of the product of land is determined by the production price of the capital invested in the worst land.

But we might well ask: Why is it that the market value (price) of the product of land is not determined by the "average value [price], hence of a value [price] midway between the two extremes" (Marx 1991: 279), as, for example, in industry?

According to the Smithian, Ricardian and Marxian approach with the increase in population, demand for agricultural product tends continually to exceed supply, and in any case exceeds the supply available from the most fertile and favourably-situated lands. The pressure of demand leads to the cultivation on each occasion of the worst land. If the market price did not cover the production price of the worst land, this land would be withdrawn from cultivation. Unsatisfied demand would bring it back by raising the market price to the level of production price on that, the worst, land.

Would it not however be possible to formulate a similar line of argument for the output of a factory (the worst) in a branch of analogous products, such that this would determine the market price?

The answer, for Ricardo, is negative and this has to do with the specific "imperfection" of land "compared with the natural agents by which manufactures are assisted" (Ricardo 1992: 39), given, of course, the heightened "specific weight" of agricultural land in farm production. What is the imperfection? The *relatively limited extent* specifically of fertile agricultural land in the best position and generally of agricultural land (see also Lenin 1986: 23).

However, is the market price of each specific agricultural product determined independently by the production price of the invested capital on the worst land for producing it? Not exactly, at least according to Marx, who follows Smith. We thus find ourselves at this point at one of what Marx called "one of Adam Smith's great services":

> He showed how the ground-rent for capital applied to the production of other agricultural products, e.g. of flax, of dye-stuffs, in the independent stock-raising, etc., is determined by the ground-rent yielded by capital invested in the production of the staple crop. In fact no further progress has been made in this connection since his [Smith's] time (Marx 1991: 752).[6]

Nevertheless, for the chief staple to regulate the rent from land on the capital that is employed in producing other agricultural products, one basic prerequisite is necessary. The tracts of agricultural land that are used in the production of the staple must be such that cultivation can be switched from other crops to it and vice versa (Smith 1981: I.xi.b. 38).

So the lands on which the staple is cultivated generally determine the rent from land yielded by capital which is employed in the production of other agricultural products, in the sense that they *regulate the lower limit of ground rent in terms of the fertility and location of the farming land.* Every use of land other than production of the main staple which does not secure this lower limit will lead to a turn (given the high effective demand for the staple) towards production of the staple.[7]

Thus, according to Smith and Marx, *it is not the worst land which independently determines the market price of any agricultural product apart from the staple.* Irrespective of its production price, the market price of any agricultural product apart from the staple must be such that on the worst agricultural land for the production of that product the capitalist tenant will pay to its landowner proprietor a ground rent at least equal to that from the agricultural land of equivalent fertility and position on which the chief staple is cultivated.

4. So-Called Absolute Rent

4.1 Marx's Definition of Absolute Rent

We shall direct our analysis towards agricultural land and ask the question: Can the worst agricultural land for cultivating, let us say, grain, become the object of capitalist exploitation *only* by the landlord who is its legal proprietor, given that he (or any other legal proprietor) cannot derive the benefit of a rent from it?

Ricardo answers in the affirmative on the basis of the exposition we have offered. But Marx's answer is negative. The first-cultivated land, and also the worst land, can yield rent. Not differential rent but *absolute rent*.

According to Marx absolute rent is created in connection with the monopoly that landownership enjoys over the land. He argues in the following way: Absolute rent is derived from the totality of the land and flows from the *surplus in the value* of agricultural products *over and above their production price*. Once again, Marx considers value to be a measurable quantity, which is perfectly compatible with price (i.e. qualitatively similar), so that one may posit the question of a *difference in magnitude* between both quantities.

But let us follow the course of argument developed by Marx: He claims that a prerequisite for *value* being able to be greater than the production price of agricultural products is the lower average (organic) composition of the capital invested in land than that of average social capital (i.e. the comparatively greater proportion of variable capital in the overall capital or, differently expressed, the comparatively smaller proportion of fixed capital in overall agricultural capital, in relation to the average social capital). This lower composition of agricultural capital leads to more surplus value being produced in the agricultural economy than the corresponding surplus value of capital of the same size with average social organic composition. This amounts to an excess of farm profit over average profit, i.e. the production not just of surplus value but of extra surplus value in the sphere of agricultural production.[8] The monopoly of landownership prevents this excessive surplus value (functioning as a barrier to the diversion of capital from industry into the agricultural economy) from going into a general equalisation of the rate of profit, in this way securing as rent its excess over and above the average profit (Marx 1991: 882-907, Chapter 45).

Theory of Value and Ground Rent 137

4.2 The Analytical Framework of "Absolute Rent"

Here, as we also saw above, a serious theoretical problem arises: the problem of *symmetry of values and production prices*, as already analysed in Chapter 5 in connection with Marx's analysis of "transformation of values into production prices", presupposing the consideration of prices as *figures akin to values, meaning that the latter possess a tangible empirical substance corresponding to prices.* It is what we have already described as an empiricist retreat from the Marxian theoretical system to Classical (i.e. Ricardian) Political Economy.

For the purposes of subjecting it to criticism, we proceed to an exposition of Marx's argumentation, cognisant that it represents a departure from his own theoretical system.

Marx asserts, then, that the composition of capital invested in agriculture is lower than its average social composition. This hypothesis is based on the relative backwardness of agriculture, such that absolute rent, as emerging from the differences between (organic) composition of capitals in the agricultural and non-agricultural sectors, appears –in principle— to be a historically superseded category.[9]

Nevertheless, even if we accept that the composition of capital in agriculture is lower than its average social composition, there is another type of issue, which we shall present through a simple example.

Let us postulate that:
In agriculture: $70c + 30v + 30s = 130$ value.
In industry: $80c + 20v + 40s = 140$ value.

What does our simple example tell us? That even though the organic composition of capital in agriculture is lower than that in industry ($7/3 = 2.3$ as against $8/2 = 4$), for capitals of the same size ($= 100$) the higher rate of surplus value in industry ($40/20 = 200\%$) compared with agriculture (100%) means that the value of the gross industrial product exceeds the value of the gross agricultural product. Is it reasonable for one, without abandoning Marx's argument, to assume that there is a higher rate of surplus value in high (organic) capital composition industry and a lower rate of surplus value in low (organic) capital composition agriculture? We believe that the whole analysis of Marx on the concept of relative surplus value in Volume 1 of *Capital* leaves no doubt that it is.[10]

Marx observes the rise in the productivity of labour accompanying the rise in the organic composition of capital without examining the immediate consequence of this increased productivity: the increase in the rate of surplus value. Thus, substantiation of absolute rent on the basis of differences in the (organic) composition of capital demands a very specific combination of outcomes (compositions of capital and rates of surplus value) making possible an overabundance of surplus-value in the sphere of agricultural production.

So even if we follow the argumentation of Marx, which in relation to this point is based on the Ricardian (non-Marxian) concept of value, once again the conclusion that Marx comes to concerning the origins of absolute rent is anything but a self-evident one.

4.3 Absolute Rent as "Political Rent": The Correlation of Class Forces and Monopoly Pricing

Is it possible for the discussion on absolute rent to be disentangled from the specialised accretions of compositions of capital and rates of surplus value or must one consider absolute rent as a theoretical category from the realm of the chimerical? (Vergopoulos no publication date, Harvey 1982)

Given that in Marx's system any argumentation based on or implying that values and prices are commensurable and as such quantitatively comparable magnitudes would have to be rejected, our view is that the Marxist theory of absolute rent should be accepted only if the category of absolute rent is being interpreted as a "political rent" that is connected with a form of *monopoly pricing*. This notion of "political rent" can be formulated in relation to Marx's notions of class balance of forces on the one hand and value, as the social form of wealth in the CMP, on the other: Due to its limited extent, land, (which cannot be reproduced at any quantity, like any "ordinary" commodity), may under certain political and social conditions be monopolised by a specific class, the landowners:

> Landed property presupposes that certain persons enjoy the monopoly of disposing of particular portion of the globe as exclusive spheres of their private will to the exclusion of all others (Marx 1991: 752).

As a result of this monopoly, in all cases when the relation of class forces permits it (in the historical arena of a given capitalist society and in a specific conjuncture), agricultural products are sold at a *monopoly price*, as

Theory of Value and Ground Rent 139

there is a *rent created by the monopoly of landownership*. Alternatively, rent can generate a monopoly price because of the impediment landownership erects at capital's disposal of land.

Rent of this kind, in contradistinction to differential rent, is purely *"political"*, because it is independent of any differences in fertility, location, labour productivity and capital investment in the land. *"Political" rent is the potential economic outcome of the landowner's legal proprietorship of the land*, under the conditions of bourgeois - landowner class conflict (politically imprinted in the *state policy* on agriculture, see in this connection Emsley 1998).

The above means that it is not the high price (or value) of agricultural products (due to the low organic composition of capital in the agricultural sector or for any other reason) that creates or enables rent, but on the contrary, rent, evoked by landownership, that causes a monopoly-high price of agricultural products. Marx himself adopts at least once this thesis (see also Bensch 2000):

> Even though landed *property can drive the price of agricultural products above their price of production*, it does not depend on this, but rather on the *general state of the market*, how far the market price rises above the price of production (Marx 1991: 898, emphasis added).[11]

However, this "general state of the market" may be regarded as the economic crystallisation of a class relation of forces between the capitalist and the landowner class in a given capitalist society. It is a question of "the market (...) being shaped on the basis of existing class relations" (Vergopoulos 1975: 205).

The market price is determined not by the production price on the worst land but by the production price on the worst land plus the "political" rent. This market price is a monopoly price. Consequently, the best land yields not only differential rent but a rent which is the sum of differential and "political" rent. In short, "political" rent reconstitutes the market price determined on the basis of differential rent, making it a monopoly price.

The theoretical notions formulated by Marx, but not his transient flirting with the Ricardian value theory, make it thus possible for one to conceptualise the economic forms which characterise capitalist agriculture.

5. Conclusion

Marx's analysis on ground rent and especially the part of it on absolute ground rent is one of the weakest points in his whole economic work. Not only it does not definitely surpass the Classical framework that was formulated by Adam Smith and David Ricardo (as in the case of differential rent), but also, when attempting to do so (as in the case of absolute rent), it is trapped in Marx's ambivalences towards Classical Political Economy (the qualitative equation of value and price which evokes quantitative "comparisons" between the two) and falls into unsolvable conceptual contradictions.

However, as we tried to show in Section 4.3 of this Chapter, the Marxian value and class theory, freed from Marx's own mistakes, is the only theoretical system which may allow one to come to grips of the phenomena emerging from the fact that a special class, that of landowners, may monopolise "a particular portion of the globe as exclusive spheres of their private will".

Notes

1. Marx also analysed the pre-capitalist forms of ground rent, which appear as "labour rent", "rent in kind", or "money rent". In the feudal mode of production, "labour rent" and "rent in kind" constituted the "dominant and normal forms (...) of surplus labour and surplus product" (Marx 1991: 930).
2. "With the intervention of the capitalist between landowner and the actual working tiller, all relationships that arose from the former rural mode of production are torn asunder. The farmer becomes the real controller of these agricultural workers and the real exploiter of their surplus labour, whereas the landowner stands in a direct relationship only to this capitalist farmer" (Marx 1991: 935).
3. It is thus understandable how the reduction, or even the disappearance of the class of landowners occurred, in countries where the domination of capitalism led to class relations of power in rural areas which favoured the peasants or the capitalist farmers. The most common historical case is thus the splitting up of the lots, and their acquisition by those who directly cultivate them, a portion of whom are transformed into self-employed producers of simple commodities and another portion into capitalists (who employ wage farm-workers on a permanent or seasonal basis).
4. "At certain specified dates, e.g. annually, this farmer-capitalist pays the landowner (...), a contractually fixed sum of money (...). This sum of money is known as groundrent, irrespective of whether it is paid for agricultural land, building land, mines, fisheries, forests, etc. (...) Ground-rent is thus the form in which landed property is economically realised, valorised" (Marx 1991: 755-6).

Theory of Value and Ground Rent 141

5. This *monopoly of land ownership* is not attributable to the forms of monopoly we discussed in Chapter 5 (natural, artificial and accidental monopolies), as it is connected neither to the exclusive use of a production factor that increases labour productivity (a natural resource or a technological novelty), nor to a favourable position in the market. It refers to the legal monopoly (proprietorship) of land or any other factor and the claim, thereof, to a payment (rent) when this factor is being conveyed by lease, irrespective of the production outcome or even the form of its use (productive or unproductive) by the lessee.
6. According, then, to Smith: "It is in this manner that the rent of the cultivated land, of which the produce is human food, regulates the rent of the greater part of other cultivated land. No particular produce can long afford less; because the land would immediately be turned to another use. And if any particular produce commonly affords more, it is because the quantity of land which can be fitted for it is too small to supply the effectual demand" (Smith 1981: I.xi.b. 34).
7. Marx notes in the *Theories of Surplus Value* (Marx 1971: Part II, Ch. 44) that rice is an exception to this, in the regions where it is the chief staple, because muddy rice-paddies cannot be transformed into grassy meadows, wheatfields, etc. or vice versa.
8. "If the composition of capital in one sphere of production is lower than that of the average social capital (...) the value of its product *must* stand above its price of production" (Marx 1991: 892-93, emphasis added).
9. On this subject Marx writes: "If the average composition of agricultural capital were the same as that of the average social capital (...) the result would be the disappearance of absolute rent" (Marx 1991: 899). And he explains: "Whether the composition of agricultural capital is less than the social average in a particular country is a question which can be settled only by statistical investigation. (...) In any case, it still holds theoretically that it is only on this premise that the value of agricultural products can rise above the price of production" (Marx 1991: 894). Most Marxists took this premise for granted. So, for example, Lenin argued as follows: "There are the peculiarities of agriculture (...) large-scale mechanical production in agriculture will never have *all* the distinctive features that it has in industry" (Lenin 1986: 41).
10. As noted by P. Sweezy, "a rising organic composition of capital goes hand in hand with increasing labour productivity [...] rising productivity tends to bring with it a higher rate of surplus value" (Sweezy 1970: 100-1).
11. Marx was more than once ambivalent towards the possible explanations of absolute rent: "It is necessary to distinguish whether the rent flows from an independent monopoly price (...) or whether the products are sold at a monopoly price because there is a rent" (Marx 1991: 910).

PART IV:
THE CIRCUIT OF SOCIAL CAPITAL, THE PROFIT RATE AND THE ECONOMIC CRISES

7 The "Law of the Falling Tendency in the Rate of Profit"

1. Introduction

In Part IV of the book we are going to deal mainly with questions of instability and economic crises, deriving theoretical arguments and conclusions on the one hand from Marx's concepts and analyses and on the other from the historic Marxist controversies on these subjects. However, before approaching our main theme, we are going to compendiously refer to Marx's "law of the tendential fall in the rate of profit", which for more than a hundred years has become a matter of dispute among Marxist scholars.

The tendency of the rate of profit to fall had become part of the economists' credo since the time of the Classical School of Political Economy. Ricardo tried to interpret it as a symptom of the "law of diminishing returns". The functioning of this "law", bringing about on the one hand an increase in the (real and monetary) returns paid by farmers (capitalist tenants) to landowners, on the other an increase in nominal (monetary) wages, owing to rise in prices for wage commodities, would lead to a corresponding fall in (real and monetary) profits.

Through the law of the *falling tendency* of the rate of profit, Marx attempted to show that technological innovation – which is introduced into production by the individual capitalist in a context of competition and aims at increasing the productivity of labour (and so the rate of surplus value) – could be the cause of such a phenomenon. He based his analysis on the concepts of *technical composition of capital* (which connotes the quantity in material terms of means of production per unit of living labour) and *value (or organic) composition of capital* (the ratio of constant to variable capital, in value terms).

2. Marx's Main Arguments

In Volume 1 of Capital, Marx describes as "specifically capitalistic mode of production" and "specifically capitalistic methods of production" the conditions of increasing technical composition of capital which lead to an increasing value composition of capital and to a falling profit rate.[1] The technical composition of capital increases with accumulation and technological innovation. Marx maintained that that if all other factors remain constant, a fall in the rate of profit may emerge if the value composition of capital increases, due to a more rapid increase in the technical composition than the productivity of labour it creates.

Considering that the rate of profit is a dependent variable (R) we may write:

$$R = \frac{s}{C+v} = \frac{s/v}{[C/v] + 1} \qquad (1)$$

where C symbolizes constant capital, s/v the rate of exploitation (rate of surplus value) and (C/v) the value (organic) composition of capital.

It may be shown that the value composition (C/v) is a positive function of (T/π), where T is the technical composition of capital and π productivity of labour (or conversely of the value of a product unit). Thus, if T increases more rapidly than π, the value composition of capital, C/v, rises. In all cases where this increase is more rapid than the increase in the rate of exploitation (s/v), (an increase following technological progress, as the latter, by increasing labour productivity, lowers the price of the – constant or slightly variable – real wage) the falling tendency in the rate of profit rate prevails over the countervailing tendencies (see Stamatis 1977: 22-110 for a detailed analysis).

Following the logic of Marx's analysis, one may put forward the view that in all cases where technological innovation does not bring higher increases in the technical composition of capital as opposed to increases in the productivity of labour, the rate of profit will tend to rise. There will also be a tendency for the rate of profit to rise when the rate of exploitation (s/v) increases faster than the value (organic) composition of capital, or when the organic composition decreases faster than the rate of exploitation.[2]

From the above it becomes obvious that the "law of the falling tendency" in the rate of profit is characterised by the following elements:

a) It applies under specific historical conditions of production, which Marx called "specifically capitalist methods of production", because he considered that they constituted the principal vehicle for the introduction of technological innovation in his day: more rapid increase in the technical composition of capital in relation to the productivity of labour, and the inability of the increasing rate of exploitation to compensate for the consequences of the increase in the value composition of capital. Nevertheless, the "law" does not exclude the possibility of the non-existence of these conditions and thus the containment or reversal of the falling tendency in the rate of profit.

b) It applies (to the degree that the abovementioned conditions are fulfilled) "all other factors remaining constant". Thus it provides no adequate basis for judgement on the course of evolution of the rate of profit in general, given that this is influenced just as much by "all the other factors" apart from those having to do with technological innovation. Among the other factors are change in the length of the working day and running speed of the machinery, change in raw materials prices (which affects the value composition of capital), a rise in the level of skills of working people (of "the collective worker") in the given production system (and with given technology), etc. (for details see the Chapter 9).

It is worth pointing out that Marx himself noted the "historical character" of the law which he had formulated, attributing its power to the way in which – in his day – new technologies were disseminated. Technologies were introduced which lowered the rate of profit, because their relatively slow proliferation enabled the capitalist who introduced them first to enjoy extra profit for a considerable length of time. Marx wrote:

> No capitalist voluntarily applies a new method of production, no matter how much more productive it may be or how much it might raise the rate of surplus-value, if it reduces the rate of profit. But every new method of production of this kind makes commodities cheaper. At first, therefore, he can sell them above their price of production. (...) He pockets the difference between their costs of production and the market price of the other commodities, which are produced at higher production costs. (...) His production procedure is ahead of the social average. But competition makes the new procedure universal and subjects it to the general law. A fall in the profit rate then ensues (Marx 1991: 373-4).

Nevertheless, very many Marxists interpreted, and continue to interpret, the "law of the falling tendency" of the rate of profit as an inherent and universally valid characteristic of the capitalist mode of production, which applies for as long as capitalism exists. Moreover they have truly seen it as constituting a "*law*" which describes the *real* evolution of the rate of profit, no knowledge being required of "all the other factors" which Marx – in the section of his work mentioning the "law" – considered constant, applying the scientific principle of "ceteris paribus".[3]

3. The "Law of the Falling Tendency in the Profit Rate" Interpreted as *the* Marxian Theory of Crises

The "law of the falling tendency" in the rate of profit has been interpreted by some economists as the "Marxist theory of economic crises". The first theoretician who formulated this interpretation, in the late 1920s and early 1930s at the border of the historic dispute between underconsumption and overaccumulation theories (see the following Chapter), was Henryk Grossmann. According to him, the law of the falling profit rate was the decisive distinguishing characteristic of crises: Crises were the manifestation of the increase in the organic (value) capital composition in the course of capitalist development, at a faster rate than the increase in labour productivity.

When those factors of capitalist economy that counteract the profit rate's tendency to fall are exhausted, the end of capitalism will arrive, according to Grossmann's approach. He wrote:

> The law itself is in reality an obvious consequence of the labour theory of value, in the event that accumulation takes place on the basis of a continuously higher organic composition of capital. (...) Finally, accumulation will become impossible, because the surplus-value mass will not be sufficient to create the necessary increase ratio in the quickly raising constant capital. (...) With a further increase in the organic composition, there must be a time when any continuation of accumulation will be impossible. This is the Marxian law of collapse (Grossmann 1971: 28-29).[4]

The first critique posed to the theory discussed here, is that according to Marx, overproduction crisis constitutes a periodic phenomenon, which cannot therefore be explained in terms of a long-term tendency such as the falling profit rate (Bukharin, in Luxemburg/Bukharin 1972: 204, 262-263).

A much more radical critique of Grossmann's approach was developed in the 1930s by Natalie Moszkowska (1935: 45-59). She claimed that technical innovation of capitalist production after World War I did not increase the value composition of capital faster than the exploitation rate of labour-force (surplus-value rate). On the contrary, it simultaneously a) increased the exploitation rate, and b) increased labour productivity faster than technical composition of capital, thus causing a fall in organic composition of capital. She claimed that under the influence of both factors an upward tendency of the profit rate is established, at least in the long term.

Moszkowska's approach was not based on an empirical analysis of the accumulation process of that period, which would have revealed the actual tendencies of the factors affecting the profit rate. However, it should be regarded as very important because it emphasised the fact that the profit rate is a function of both a) the value composition of capital, and b) the surplus-value rate. Therefore, it can rise not only in the case discussed by Moszkowska, but also either when the rate of surplus value increases more rapidly than the value composition of capital or when it decreases more slowly.

Grossmann's approach gave the Marxian law a "mechanistic-economist" and "determinist" interpretation, converting it into a "theory of collapse" of capitalism. However, the interpretation of crises on the basis of the "law of the falling tendency in the profit rate" was adopted later on by other Marxists, such as Maurice Dobb (1968) and Ernest Mandel (1995) in a non-determinist and non-mechanistic version. They claimed that the Marxian law manifests itself only temporarily (and that is when an economic crisis takes place), being later on overborne by counter-tendencies, which restore the profit rate levels.[5] Dobb, writing in 1937, also established a relationship between profit rate fall, in the sense of the Marxian law, and squeezing of the surplus-value rate due to a temporary diminution or even exhaustion of the "industrial reserve army" in the conjuncture of expansion of capitalist production. The partial stoppage of production which follows an abrupt fall in the profit rate, was regarded as the starting point for an upward reversal in the trend of the profit rate, through closing down of less profitable plants, increasing unemployment and decreasing wages, introduction of new labour-substituting production methods, etc. (see Dobb 1968: 79-126. For Mandel's approach see also Chapter 9).

Even if we take for granted that the Marxian law of falling profit rate occasionally prevails over its counteracting factors, it is not correct, in our opinion, to conceive crisis merely as a result of this Marxian law. The law considers only the effect on organic composition and profit rate of technical innovations, that is of changes (increases) in the technical composition of capital. However, the organic composition of capital, and hence the profit rate, depends also on other factors besides technical change.

4. The Rejection of Marx's "Law"

In Volume 3 of *Capital* Marx studied his "law of the tendency of the profit rate to fall" under the assumption that all constant capital wears out in each production process, or, alternatively, that the constant capital, C, in formula (1) equals the cost in constant capital, c, in the period under examination (C=c). In doing so, Marx practically studied the "cost efficiency" – i.e. the ratio $r = s/(c+v)$, instead of $R = s/(C+v)$ as it should be. He thought that the trend of the "cost efficiency" coincides with that of the profit rate. However, this is not so, as we will argue below. If the trend of both magnitudes were always the same, then it can be shown that under certain reasonable preconditions there should be a *tendency of the profit rate to rise*, instead of the "law of the falling tendency" stated be Marx.

The first theoretician who subjected to criticism the "law of the falling tendency" of the rate of profit was Tugan-Baranowsky (1969 [1901]), to be subsequently followed by other economists, the presently most known being Okishio (1961). These criticisms attempt to substantiate the view that the introduction of technological innovations in every case result in a rise and in no case a fall in the rate of profit, and thus that the Marxist law is logically flawed.

Tugan-Baranowsky's basic assertion is that the replacement of labour by machinery (i.e. the introduction of innovations into production) should in all cases be based on the assumptions of (1) an *undiminished total material output*, (2) an *undiminished material surplus*, and (3) *in the absence of an increase in real wages* (assumptions he perceived as being derived from the capitalist relations of production as analysed by Marx). He then proved that these assumptions necessarily entail that there will be no fall in the "cost efficiency", which he also regarded as an index showing exactly the same trend with the rate of profit (see Tugan-Baranowsky 2000: 81-108).

Tugan-Baranowksy constructed his analysis on the basis of the simple example of an enterprise which produces a *material product* (use values) of magnitude "a" and *value* "b" ($b = v+s$ = quantity [hours] of labour expended), with *rate of surplus value* at 100% ($s/v = 1$), and the use of only variable capital ($C = c = 0$, so $v = s = \frac{1}{2}b$). The real wages are $\frac{1}{2}a$, as is the material surplus. The productivity of labour (units of the product per unit of expended labour) is $\pi = a/b$. In terms of value it is: $(\frac{1}{2}b)v + (\frac{1}{2}b)s = b$, and in material terms: $(\frac{1}{2}a)v + (\frac{1}{2}a)s = a$. The rate of profit (="cost efficiency") will be $r = \frac{s}{v} = 1$.

Tugan-Baranowsky then postulates that the enterprise is in a position to produce *the same quantity* of material product, "a", replacing half of the living wage labour with machines (with constant capital). This postulate is reasonable (there would be no point in a change in the technical composition of capital from which there would emerge a smaller quantity of material product) but marginal, because a change in the technical composition is normally associated with increases in material output. This assumption means that in the new technical conditions the remaining workers, using machines, produce exactly as much additional product as the dismissed workers produced in the old technological environment. The material surplus $(=\frac{1}{2}a)$ remains constant. Given that now half the quantity of labour is expended for producing the same amount of material product, there will be an increase in the productivity of labour, with a simultaneous halving in the value of (= quantity of labour expended in) the product. The replacement of labour by machines does not favour the increase in real salaries, so the assumption is made that they remain stable, i.e. in aggregate they are now a/4, owing to the halving of the number of workers. But their value (the nominal wage), again owing to an increase in the productivity of labour, diminishes, which means that the rate of surplus value will increase. All the constant capital is again used up in the course of one production period (C=c).

Of the total material output "a", the net product (in terms of use value) is:

$(\frac{1}{4}a)v + (\frac{1}{2}a)s = \frac{3}{4}a$. The remainder $(\frac{1}{4}a)$ is destined, as value, to replace the value of the means of production used up. In the new conditions the productivity of labour results from division of the net material product by its value (the total amount of expended labour), i.e. is $\pi = (\frac{3}{4}a):(\frac{1}{2}b) = \frac{3a}{2b}$. The value of variable capital is the quantity of it in material terms divided by the productivity of labour, $v = \frac{1}{4}a : \frac{3a}{2b} = \frac{b}{6}$, and is equal, on the assumptions of the writer, to the value of the means of production used up during this period. The new value (= the total amount of labour expended) is $\frac{1}{2}$ b and if from that we subtract variable capital (v = $\frac{b}{6}$), the resulting exponent for surplus value is s = $\frac{1}{3}$ b. Thus, in value terms we have: $\frac{b}{6}$ c + $\frac{b}{6}$ v + $\frac{b}{3}$ s = 2$\frac{b}{3}$, and the rate of profit (="cost efficiency") is r = $\frac{s}{c+v}$ = 1, that is to say, it remains constant.

The author makes the following comments on the conclusions which emerge from the example we quoted:

> The replacement of manual by mechanical labour, as well as the substitution of variable capital by constant capital must then lead to the following modifications: the surplus-value must fall relatively but, at the same time, the productivity of labour must increase, bringing about, necessarily, a fall in the labour-value of both, the variable and the constant capital. The reduction in the labour-value of variable capital is equivalent to an increase in the rate of surplus-value. All these counteracting factors cancel out their respective effects on the rate of profit, which thereby remains constant. (...) However in our analysis we have made a very important supposition, which certainly does not correspond to reality: namely, we have assumed that the introduction of machines does not increase the mass of social product. Actually, under these conditions, the total mass of product undergoes a strong increase. (...) This implies a modification in our conclusions (...) The rate of profit must increase as a consequence of the relative rise in the constant capital (Tugan-Baranowsky 2000: 95-96).

Marx's "law of the falling tendency in the profit rate" was also criticised in the post World-War II era on the basis of the "Okishio theorem", formulated by in 1961 Nobuo Okishio, who reached similar conclusions as Tugan-Baranowsky. Okishio (1961) made use of an economic model comprising three sectors (producing wage-goods, capital-goods and luxury-goods –consumption-goods of the capitalist class– respectively), in which he calculated the production prices on the *presupposition* that capitalists introduce new labour-substituting techniques, only when *the criterion of diminishing production costs per unit of output* is being fulfilled. Okishio, like Tugan-Baranowsky, saw the real wage as constant, and studied the trend in r (the "cost efficiency") resulting from the introduction of labour-saving *and* cost-reducing techniques. He concluded that r must rise as result of the relative increase in the capital/labour ratio.

As Michael Heinrich (1999: 337-341) has shown, Okishio's arguments can be stated also in value terms, by means of the following simple considerations:

A capitalist enterprise produces in a production period an output of value:

$$w_1 = c_1 + v_1 + s_1 \qquad (2)$$

Before the next production period a labour-substituting innovation is introduced, which increases the constant capital cost of the enterprise to $c_2 = c_1 + \Delta c_1$ and reduces its variable capital cost to $v_2 = v_1 - \Delta v_1$. The innovation is reasonable only if the criterion of cost reduction is fulfilled, meaning that it must be:

$$\Delta c_1 < \Delta v_1 \qquad (3)$$

It is further assumed that, (a) the real wage remains constant, (b) the enterprise produces in the second production period the same material output as in the first one, and (c) the new production technique, which induces an increase in labour productivity, has been generalised in the whole economy at the end of the first period (remaining then constant).[6] The value of the enterprise's output in the second period will be reduced due to the increase in labour productivity. Let "t" be the factor showing this value diminution per unit product in the whole economy, then the value of the enterprise's output in the second period will be:

$$w_2 = c_2 + v_2 + s_2 = t(c_1 + v_1 + s_1) \qquad (4)$$

The value of its constant capital and variable capital inputs will be, respectively:

$$c_2 = t(c_1 + \Delta c_1) \qquad (5)$$
$$v_2 = t(v_1 - \Delta v_1) \qquad (6)$$

Substituting relations (5) and (6) into relation (4) it follows:

$$s_2 = t(s_1 + \Delta v_1 - \Delta c_1) \qquad (7)$$

154 Karl Marx and the Classics

From relations (2) and (5) - (7) it follows that the "cost efficiency" of the enterprise in the first (before the innovation) and in the second (after the innovation has taken place) production period, will be, respectively:

$$r_1 = \frac{s_1}{c_1 + v_1} \qquad (8)$$

$$r_2 = \frac{s_1 + \Delta v_1 - \Delta c_1}{c_1 + v_1 + \Delta c_1 - \Delta v_1} \qquad (9)$$

Taking into consideration the cost-minimising criterion (Relation 3), we may conclude that $r_2 > r_1$, meaning that with increasing value composition of capital the "cost efficiency", r, also increases. Okishio's theorem seems, therefore, to rebut Marx's "law of the falling tendency in the rate of profit".

5. "Cost Efficiency" vs. the Profit Rate. A Note on the Debate on Marx's "Law"

Okishio's theorem has triggered a long lasting debate among Marxists, not only concerning the validity of Marx's theses but also in regard to the significance of the "law" in the overall framework of the Marxist theory. Nearly all possible interpretations were formulated, from approaches in Henryk Grossmann's tradition, according to which the "law" constitutes a keystone in the theoretical edifice of Marxism as a whole,[7] to the thesis that its rejection is a prerequisite for the development of Marxist theory.[8]

The debate has been recently rekindled (see Kliman 1996 and the papers by Laibman, Foley, Kliman and Freeman in Zarembka 1999 and Zarembka 2000), after the exponents of the so-called "Temporal Single System" (TSS) approach refuted the Okishio theorem on the basis of the argument that the fixed capital of any firm keeps its "historical" value (at the time of purchase), not being affected (devaluated) by afterward increases in labour productivity. The argument seems to us of low significance, for reasons clearly stated in the abovementioned debate.[9]

The Okishio theorem is correct (as it is also Tugan-Baranowsky's analysis, sixty years earlier), given the assumptions on which it is founded. As Stamatis has shown, if one does not adhere to the assumption of a non-increasing real wage, then with the introduction of cost reducing technologies the "cost efficiency" may either increase, remain constant or fall, that is to say it does not necessarily rise as required by Okishio's theorem (Stamatis 1977: 174 ff.). However, the author's major point of critique to the Okishio theorem is that it concerns the "cost efficiency", not the rate of profit. In other words, it reflects the fact that the trend in the "cost efficiency" is not necessarily the same as the trend in the rate of profit. So even on the presupposition of stable real wages, although it is true that the "cost efficiency" necessarily rises in every case of the introduction of technologies which lower costs, the rate of profit may still −depending on circumstances− either rise, remain constant or fall. Because if $C \neq c$, then Relation (5) is transformed to:

$$C_2 = t(C_1 + \Delta C_1) \qquad (5')$$

with $\Delta C_1 \neq \Delta c_1$, which means that Relation (7) shall also be modified. As Stamatis (1977: 149 ff.) has shown, under Okishio's assumptions (stable real wage, cost reducing innovations −always leading to an increasing "cost efficiency"), the rate of profit may fall when the following condition is fulfilled:

$$\frac{C_1}{v_1 + s_1} < \frac{C_2}{v_2 + s_2} \qquad (10)$$

Alternatively, the adequate condition for a fall in the profit rate can be written as follows:

$$\frac{d[s/v]}{dt} \cdot \frac{d[C/v]}{dt} = \frac{[s/v]'}{[C/v]'} < \frac{C}{C+v} \qquad (11)^{10}$$

Marx's main mistake in Volume 3 of *Capital* as regards the falling profit rate is that he considered the trends in the "cost efficiency" and in the profit rate to be identical, and that he so worked at "cost efficiency" calculations in order to prove the possibility of a fall in the profit rate due to technical change. Exactly as in the case of the "transformation problem", the attempt of some Marxists to prove that Marx did not make even a single mistake does not contribute to the theoretical power or reputation of Marxist theory.[11]

Closing this chapter let us remind the reader once more that the Marxist "law of the falling tendency" in the rate of profit, although logically sound, is not a theoretical reflection of the actual trend of the rate of profit. As argued above, it applies under certain conditions (which Marx called the "specifically capitalist methods of production") that may very well not exist in a given capitalist society. Furthermore, it influences the rate of profit along with a variety of other factors not directly associated with technological innovation, factors which Marx considered to remain constant when presenting his "law".[12] This means that a falling profit rate in a given capitalist economy over a time period, which may be established on the basis of a concrete empirical analysis, can be due to factors other than those related with technical innovation and the "law of the falling tendency", which means that a further investigation will be necessary, if one wants to locate the exact causes of the profit rate's course. What is more important, an analysis of the circuit of social capital, economic instability and crises has to take into consideration all of these factors, as Marx himself did in the chapters of Volume 3 of *Capital* which precede the formulation of the "law".

This totality of economic parameters and social contradictions influencing the profit rate will be the object of our theoretical analysis in the two Chapters that follow.

Notes

1. "With the accumulation of capital, therefore, the specifically capitalistic mode of production develops, and with the capitalist mode of production the accumulation of capital. These economic factors bring about, in the compound ratio of the impulses they give to each other, that change in the technical composition of capital by which the variable component becomes smaller and smaller as compared with the constant component" (Marx 1990: 776).
2. Marx himself writes: "Viewed abstractly, the rate of profit might remain the same despite a fall in the price of the individual commodity as a result of increased productivity, and hence despite a simultaneous increase in the number of these cheaper commodities (...) The rate of profit could even rise, if a rise in the rate of surplus-value was coupled with a significant reduction in the value of the elements of constant capital, and fixed capital in particular" (Marx 1991: 336-37).
3. It is characteristic that even Engels felt obliged to supplement (or "correct") Marx's phrase: "The rate of profit could even rise (...)", quoted immediately above (Note 2), with the following affirmation, which is not present in Marx's original manuscripts for the 3rd volume of *Capital* (MEGA II, 4.2: 319): "In practice, however, the rate of profit will fall in the long run, as we have already seen" (Marx 1991: 337).
4. Grossmann's earlier writings supported a different Marxist interpretation of economic crises, namely the version of overproduction theory formulated by Tugan-Baranowsky in 1901 (see Chapter 8). In 1919, summarising his arguments of that time, he wrote:

"A crisis is the result of planless accumulation" (Grossman 2000: 176). On Grossmann's political engagement and theoretical work see Kuhn 2000.
5. To the same tradition belong, among others, Yaffe (1973), Bullock and Yaffe (1975), Callinicos (1987).
6. This means on the one hand that there cannot be any extra-surplus-value effects favouring the enterprise in question and on the other that the constant capital and labour power unit inputs (unit costs) of the enterprise go through the same value diminution as its unit output.
7. "The debate over the tendency for the rate of profit to fall relates directly to key questions of political strategy (...) the overthrow of capitalism and the construction of socialism", John Weeks (1982), "Equilibrium, Uneven Development and the Tendency of the Profit Rate to Fall", *Capital and Class* 16: 62-77, cited in Cullenberg 1997: 60.
8. "The dogmatism that has been associated with the theory of the 'rising organic composition of capital' has been one of the heaviest palls on the development of a creative Marxian project to study the laws of motion of modern capitalist society" John Roemer (1981), *Analytical Foundations of Marxian Economic Theory*, Cambridge: CUP, cited in Cullenberg 1997: 1.
9. "When productivity increases cheapen the replacement for an existing machine that was purchased earlier for more money, that machine is subject to Marx's 'moral depreciation'; in his terms, constant capital is cheapened. (...) The *potential* profit rate has *risen*, and if one capitalist does not get that rate, its competitors will. This is simply an application of the proposition that it is the social, not the individual, situation that determines value" (Laibman 1999: 223).
10. This Relation was first formulated by Tsuru (1951).
11. As Foley correctly noted: "The power and usefulness of Marx's analysis of exploitation as the central social relation of capitalist society does not stand or fall on technical details of matrix algebra or difference equations. The notion that technical gaps in Marx's discussion of the transformation problem undermine his theory of exploitation is a line of argument largely advanced by Ricardian and marginalist critics of Marx whose motivation is to discredit rather than to clarify its contribution" (Foley 1999: 233).
12. "The beginning of true wisdom about technical change (...) is that ultimately, all benchmarks not withstanding, there is no reason to believe that *any* parameter (...) will remain constant. A change in technique alters all of the relationships in the workplace, both explicit and implicit. Productivity norms for each operation must be redrawn, and will be the object of struggle. Lines of authority must be redirected; some centers of power within the workplaces may be eroded by the introduction of a new technique, and others strengthened (...)" (Laibman 1997: 49).

8 The Historic Marxist Controversy on Economic Crises and its Theoretical Significance

1. On the Status of Marx's "Theory of Crises"

Economic crises of capitalism constitute an immediately conceivable reality, with typical characteristics. This explains why Marx and Engels repeatedly referred to economic crises many years before Marx developed the theoretical system of the *Critique of Political Economy*.[1] Until the publication of Volume 1 of *Capital*, in 1867, Marx had referred to the economic crises in a descriptive rather than a theoretical manner (Heinrich 1995).

However, even in Marx's mature economic writings, one finds only fragments of a crisis theory, which are developed along with other theoretical argumentations. A Marxian crisis theory shall therefore be "discovered" and reconstructed/developed only as a result of a systematic theoretical analysis.

In the third Volume of *Capital* Marx names economic crises "crises of overproduction". Furthermore he states that crises block the reproduction of the capital relation per se:

> Overproduction of capital and not of individual commodities – though this overproduction of capital always involves overproduction of commodities – is nothing more than overaccumulation of capital (Marx 1991: 359). Periodically too much is produced in the way of means of labour and means of subsistence, too much to function *as means for exploiting the workers at a given rate of profit* (Marx 1991: 367, emphasis added).

However, crises are only a temporary shaking or destabilisation of the capitalist expanding reproduction process and simultaneously a mechanism for re-establishing balance and restoring the profit rate level.[2] This means that crises do not constitute a permanent feature of the capitalist mode of production but one (potential) outcome of the economic conjuncture, which – it is worth noting – arises *as the result of immanent structural contradictions characterising the capitalist mode of production*. Having, in *Capital*, chosen the capitalist mode of production in general as his object of analysis, Marx concerns himself primarily with these immanent structural contradictions, i.e. with the permanent structural characteristics (the "laws") of the mode of production, and secondarily with their conjunctural crystallisations (phases of the economic cycle, crises, etc.). The fragmentary character of the theory of crises in Marx's work may thus be partly attributable to this fact.

Summarising we may say that according to Marx crises are characterised by a "plethora of capital" (Marx 1991: 359), an overproduction of capital, both in the form of (invested) means of production and in the form of unsold (consumption and investment) commodities. This overproduction is never absolute –referring to social needs– but relative, determined by the social character of the capitalist mode of production. It always refers to the consumption capacity (of means of private consumption and means of production) of a specific capitalist society. In crises, the realisation of commodities cannot ensure that level of the *rate of profit* which corresponds to "the 'healthy' and 'normal' development of the capitalist production process" (Marx 1991: 364).

Overproduction of capital (over-accumulation) has counterparts in the *retardation of capable to pay demand* relative to production (*underconsumption*) and the *fall in the profit rate*. All these concepts aided Marx in describing the interrelated forms of manifestation of economic crisis. The crucial task is to distinguish which of these concepts constitutes the main, decisive, structural relation of capitalist economic crisis. According to the answers given to this question, Marxist theorists were divided into distinct theoretical streams. The theory of economic crisis became therefore an open question for Marxist theory. Even more so, Marx's theoretical work on economic crises cannot any longer be read in isolation from the historical Marxist discussion of crises, precisely because that discussion was carried out on the basis of theoretical concepts and categories developed by Marx: The different Marxist theoretical approaches were in general formulated as interpretations of Marxian positions and theoretical elaborations. As Natalie Moskowska observed in 1935, in reference to Marxist economists: "In no field of Political Economy is there to be found such a great gap between the different viewpoints as in the investigation of economic crises" (Moszkowska 1935: 37. See also Clarke 1994).

Even before Marx's death, the underconsumptionist interpretations of his above stated theses on economic crises had become dominant, in both parts of the globe where Marxist ideas were influencing a considerable part of the intelligentsia and the labour movement: Russia and Germany-Austria. However, these approaches were soon disputed by an analysis deriving from Marx's theory of the expanded reproduction of the social capital, which was introduced in both Russia and Germany by Mikhail von Tugan-Baranowsky.[3] The theoretical controversy that was so initiated lasted for almost four decades, and the most prominent Marxist theorists of the first half of the twentieth century (among others, Lenin, Bukharin, Hilferding, Rosa Luxemburg, Otto Bauer) took part in it. To this day it constitutes the theoretical locus of nearly all Marxist approaches.

In this Chapter, we will critically discuss this historical Marxist controversy over economic crises in an effort to draw some theoretical conclusions that will allow us to reconstruct (in the next Chapter) a Marxist theory of economic instability and crises in relation with the expanded reproduction of social capital. Our point of departure will be the Non-Marxist conceptualisations of underconsuption, which preceded all relevant Marxist approaches and presumably helped shaping the Marxist analyses.

2. Crises as Imbalances Between Supply and Demand: Non-Marxist Underconsumption Approaches as Critique of Classical Theory

As mentioned in Chapter 3 of this work, both Classical and Neoclassical economic theories exclude the possibility of economic crises as generalised situations of imbalance between overall supply and overall demand in the economy. These are pre-monetary theories, which assert that the monetary sphere of the economy is simply a reflection of the "real" economy (the economy of commodities or "goods"), in which production creates a corresponding and equal level of demand or that the (related) prices are formed by definition as the "equilibrium prices" between supply and demand.

"Say's Law", which is accepted by both these schools of economic thought, enables us to reflect on the existence of merely a combination of these (sectoral) mutually invalidating imbalances, arguing as it does that "a product is no sooner created, than it, from that instant, affords a market for other products to the full extent of its own value" (J. -B. Say, *Treatise on Political Economy*, quoted by Rubin 1989: 337).[4] Every growth in production would create by itself an equal augmentation in demand, as products are paid for with other products. Therefore, if certain products rested unsold, it was because other products had not yet been produced. This means that the consumption power will necessarily be increased with every increase in productive power and thus overproduction would have emerged only if under-production had emerged before.[5]

Simonde de Sismondi (1773-1842) and Thomas Robert Malthus (1776-1834) were the first ones who questioned Say's law, and the pioneers of the theories of underconsumption. At this point we are going to focus on the main arguments introduced by these two theorists.

Underconsumption designates the insufficient demand, compared to a product supply, under given prices. Underconsumption means, therefore, relative *overproduction* of commodities *due to a retarded capable-to-pay-demand*. Considering that consumption is not necessarily the logical consequence of production, both theorists criticised the main postulate of Say's law, that products are paid for with other products, which means that money circulation is disregarded and commodity circulation is seen as an uninterrupted process on the base of barter. But as money comes in between buying and selling, the possibility of an overproduction cannot be excluded, since the seller, having the discretion to keep his wealth in money form, is not obliged to buy or to hire additional workers.

The underconsumption theories, as they were developed by Sismondi and Malthus, can be reduced to the following propositions: *First*, that within the capitalist economy it is located an inherent tendency towards economic crises of generalised overproduction, due to the lack of capable to pay demand, compared with production. *Second*, that, when aggregate demand is below supply, there is no endogenous dynamic process towards full employment equilibrium, because demand has the priority over supply; it is demand which triggers off and regulates production and not the opposite, as Say's law presupposes.

However, between Sismondi and Malthus there is differentiation related with the research into the causes of the supposed insufficient demand and into the means for rendering it. Posing the criterion of the main cause, the underconsumption theory can be thus classified (schematically) in two approaches:

The first approach regards *over-saving of capitalists for the purpose of expanding production* as the main cause of crises (and unemployment) and was formulated by Malthus.[6] Malthus argued that the increase in invested savings augments aggregate product disproportionately to the augmentation of the society's consumption power and maintained that the problem of underconsumption by the principal classes of the economy (workers and capitalists) can be dealt with through *expanding the consumption* of landowners, aristocrats and other *non productive classes* (civil servants, clerics, etc.), who will thus absorb the surplus capitalist production.[7]

The second approach, formulated by Sismondi (1815) includes the views which consider that (given the increase in labour productivity and therefore the increase of the aggregate product), the main cause of crises and unemployment is the labourers' inability to consume the product which they have produced, due to the low wages. Sismondi's criticism was informed by his conviction that capitalism (replacing workers with machines and in this way inexorably driving down wage incomes and so popular consumption) would ineluctably take on the appearance of a social pestilence, rendering impossible its own further development. He thus considered that the economic crisis would after a certain point become a permanent characteristic of capitalism. He accordingly dedicated himself to propagating an economy of self-employed producers and petty capitalists.

3. Marxist Versions of Underconsumption Theory I: The Russian Scene 1880-1905

As a result of the social transformation of Russia that got under way in the wake of the Crimean War in conjunction with the Agrarian Reform of 1861 (rise of capitalist social and economic forces, reform of Tsarist absolutism), the intellectual scene in the country came under the domination of the Left.

The predominant current on the Russian Left in the 1865-1905 period is now known as Narodniks (populists), because of their links at that time to the organisation "Narodnaya Volya" ("People's Will"). However, the Narodniks formulated their theoretical arguments exclusively as an interpretation of Marxist analyses; they drew no conclusions from other theories. The Narodnik Taktsov had as early as 1865 translated Marx's *Introduction to a Critique of Political Economy* into Russian. The leading figure in the Narodniks since the 1880s, N. Danielson, (who wrote under the name of Nikolai-on and N-on: 1844-1917) corresponded with Marx and Engels from 1871 to their deaths (see MEW Vols. 33-39. Apart from Marx and Engels, Eleanor Marx and P. Lafargue also corresponded with Danielson). Danielson translated all three volumes of *Capital* into Russian, in each case shortly after the publication of the corresponding German edition (Vol. I 1872, Vol. III 1896).[8]

The Narodniks considered that the reform of the 1860s, i.e. the abolition of serfdom, had in principle created the prerequisites for a "popular," non-capitalist course of development in Russia, based chiefly on the peasantry. The basis for this course of development would be the peasant commune, which was ardently championed by the Narodniks. (They rejected all thought of privatisation of common lands which would lead to the break-up of the communes). In brief, the peasant commune was the structure "in which they wanted to see the rudiments of Communism" (Lenin 1977 Vol. 1: 276).[9]

The whole theoretical edifice was based on an underconsumptionist analysis that was crowned by the conviction that the limitations of the domestic market (precisely because of the poverty of the popular masses in Russia but also because of the perceived tendency of capitalism to depress the living standards of the masses) constituted a formidable impediment, or even rendered impossible, the development of capitalism in Russia.[10]

The first author in the Narodnik current to make "the problem of the home market" into the chief subject of a monograph was probably V. Vorontsov (V.V.), who as early as 1882 published the book *The Destiny of Capitalism in Russia*. V.V. maintained that crises are caused by production of surplus value, which becomes the real purpose of economy under capitalist relations. The "problem of the home-market" and crises (i.e. the excess of production over consumption) are manifestations of the fact that the capitalist class is not in the position of being able to consume the entirety of the surplus value produced:

> The Achilles heel of capitalist industrial organisation thus lies in the incapacity of the entrepreneurs to consume the whole of their income. [...] The immediate cause of the above phenomena (over-production, unemployment, etc.) is not that the working classes receive too small a share of the national income, but that the capitalist class cannot possibly consume all the products which every year fall to their share (in Luxemburg 1971: 281-2).

The striving to increase surplus value brings with it a redistribution of value produced to the disadvantage of labour and so leads to a realisation problem.[11] The only way out of the "problem of the market" that V.V. could see was through the presence of an external market which as a "third factor" apart from the worker and the capitalist could absorb the surplus product.

> Since there is no one inside the country on whom the capitalists could foist this remnant, it must be exported aboard, and that is why foreign markets are indispensable to countries embarking on the capitalist venture (in Luxemburg 1971: 278).[12]

Vorontsov had therefore worked out a Marxist version of the underconsumption approach which converged with that introduced by Malthus: Crises emanate from "over-saving", or, in Marxist terms, from the inability of the capitalist to consume surplus value.

The views of the other Marxist theoreticians of the Narodnik current, and first and foremost *Danielson*, who in 1891 presented his theses in comprehensive form in his *Outlines of our Social Economy after the Reform*, converged with the basic conclusions of Vorontsov's analysis (inability to absorb the product generated owing to capitalism's inherent tendency to increase production beyond society's ability to consume: the external market and "third persons" operate as a *deus ex machina* but Russian capitalism has difficulties making use of this outlet because of its low level of development). Within this framework of analysis Danielson is nevertheless to be distinguished from Vorontsov in respect of the factors to which he traces the underconsumption – he attributes it to contraction in the purchasing power of the popular masses (and not to inability of capitalists to consume the surplus value). Danielson's analysis therefore falls into the school of underconsumption theory initiated by Sismondi.

According to Danielson, capitalist development reduces the number of workers (formerly self-employed craftsmen, small manufacturers, farmers or even labourers – through rapid increase in productivity, which leads to an ever smaller number of workers handling an ever larger mass of means of production) and accordingly also the number of mass consumers, since it marginalizes all those who are being pushed into the industrial reserve army, depriving society of their purchasing power. Crises therefore emerge as a result of *contraction* of the internal market and of *popular consumption*. The only possible solution is non-encouragement of the development of capitalism in Russia. Also in his (immediate) political goals Danielson is therefore close to the positions of Sismondi.[13]

What Danielson was endeavouring to do with his analysis of contraction of popular consumption was above all to link his theory of crises ("underconsumption") with the "theory of pauperisation", i.e. of deterioration in workers' economic position under capitalism. In this context he adopted one version of the "absolute immiseration" thesis (deterioration of the standard of living of the working class).

Danielson's whole analysis appears to ignore or underrate the expansion of productive consumption linked to accumulation and the spread of production of the means of production, as a mechanism for expanding the internal market. Nevertheless, even if the accumulation of capital is taken into account, the problem remains. The question arises as to whether this expansion can be so rapid as to absorb the increase in production, given on the one hand the downward pressure on wages and on the other the relative decline in the working population (per unit of accumulated capital).

The ideological hegemony of Marxist-inspired underconsumption theory in the era we are investigating becomes apparent by the fact that a version of it was also used – by Pyotr Struve – even as a critical tool against the views of the Narodniks. Struve, whose chief work was his *Critical Observations on the Question of Economic Development in Russia* (1894), was at that time a member of the "legal Marxists". This group was critical of N-on and the other Narodniks, putting forward the view that the development of capitalism in Russia was inevitable or at any rate possible.

Struve maintained that the capitalist mode of production does not diminish but in fact expands the home market, incorporating into it all the populations (and the consumption processes) that were formerly activated outside money-mediated relations, in the framework of the "natural economy". Nevertheless he subsequently accepted the basic underconsumptionist thesis that whatever expansion of the market occurred, it would not be sufficient to absorb the increase in capitalist production if the community consisted only of workers and capitalists. He therefore endorsed the conclusions of N-on and Vorontsov concerning "third persons" and the inherent tendency towards underconsumption in capitalism, given that the analysis pertained to the "pure" model of capitalist society. In real capitalist societies however there are always (and will continue to be) a plethora of "third persons", who safeguard capitalist development by absorbing the surplus part of capitalist production. This then was a kind of development based on the internal market, without there needing to be any resort to the international market. Struve in fact asserts that in countries with little capitalist development and a large population, such as Russia, prospects for development are even greater, because there are more "third persons" both relatively (as a percentage of the population, owing to the low level of capitalist development) and absolutely (owing to the large population).[14]

4. Versions of Underconsumption Theory II: The Marxist Theoretical Scene in the German-speaking Lands (1895-1902)

After the deaths of Marx and Engels the "orthodox Marxists" of the German-speaking lands had formulated a similar theory of crisis to that of the Russian Marxists of the Narodnik current. The German Marxists had in fact reformulated the purely descriptive (i.e. not heuristic) view that *in the periodic economic crises* production expands beyond paying consumption[15] into an assertion that under capitalism production *always* increases faster than society's ability to consume. Expansion of the market for commodities by means of "third persons" from non-capitalist modes of production now remained sole (albeit temporary) solution to the immanent realisation problem.[16] The following quotation by Kautsky, from an article of his on economic crises (published in the socialist journal *Die Neue Zeit*, No 3 [29], in 1902) is characteristic of the opinions shared by them:

> Although capitalists increase their wealth and the number of exploited workers grows, they cannot themselves form a sufficient market for capitalist produced commodities, as accumulation of capital and productivity grow even faster. They must find a market in those strata and nations which are still non-capitalist. They find this market, and expand it, but still not fast enough, since this additional market hardly has the flexibility and ability to expand of the capitalist process of production. Once capitalist production has developed large-scale industry, as was already the case in England in the nineteenth century, it has the possibility of expanding by such leaps and bounds that it soon overtakes any expansion of the market. Thus, any prosperity which results from a substantial expansion in the market is doomed from the beginning to a short life, and will necessarily end in a crisis (quoted by Luxemburg, in Luxemburg/Bukharin 1972: 79).

The above quotations of Kautsky's article are of great interest because they summarise the basic postulates of the underconsumptionist Marxist approach to economic crisis: The underconsumption of the working class builds not only the cause,[17] but also the decisive characteristic of the complex structure of economic crisis. Economic crisis reveals the inherent (constantly acting) retardation of real wages (of the consumption ability of the working class) in respect to the productivity of labour (and hence the volume of the capitalist produced commodities). Crisis is the result of a continuously decreasing labour-force value and labour share in the net product.

According to the main postulate of the theory discussed here,[18] an abstract ("pure") capitalist society cannot exist and reproduce itself on an expanding scale. On the contrary, it will suffer a permanent underconsumption-overproduction crisis. The only way out of crisis for capitalism is the creation of an "external" market (in respect to the pure capitalist economy, i.e. the capitalists and their workers), which is formed, according to Kautsky, by "those strata and nations which are still non-capitalist". The notion of the market "external" to the process of capitalist production is typical for all versions of the underconsumptionist approach.

5. Tugan-Baranowsky's Theoretical Intervention

5.1 A Historical Notice

From the beginning of the 1890s Tugan-Baranowsky (T-B) expounded a radical critique of the underconsumption theory then predominant among Russian (and German) Marxists, employing the argument that Marx in Volume 2 of *Capital* had elaborated reproduction schemes for a *pure capitalist society*.[19] In 1894 he published in Russian his book *Studies on the Theory and History of Trade Crises in England*, in which he gave an extensive theoretically and empirically grounded presentation of his arguments. In 1900 he published a second revised edition of the *Studies*, which he then, the following year, translated into German and published. In 1905 he published, in German, *The Theoretical Foundations of Marxism*.

5.2 Tugan-Baranowsky's Principal Theses

Tugan-Baranowsky's critique can be summarized in two main arguments:
 a) With the undeconsumptionist approach, Marxists abandon Marx's theory, which proves, on the basis of the reproduction schemes in Volume 2 of *Capital*, that the expanded reproduction of a "pure" capitalist economy is

possible, while the existence of any non-capitalist "third persons" is unnecessary.

b) The increase in labour productivity and in the profit share (due to the faster increase in the volume of capitalist produced commodities than in real wages) does not mean that the consumption capacity of the internal market lags behind production. A restructuring of the market takes place instead – the sector of the economy producing means of production (sector I) grows at a higher rate than the sector producing consumer goods (sector II) and the internal market for means of production grows faster than the means of consumption market.

With his first thesis T-B raised for Marxists the important issue of the compatibility of their analyses with the analyses in *Capital*. With his second thesis he sought to give a response simultaneously to underconsumption theories of the Vorontsov type (inability of the capitalists to "use up" surplus value) and to underconsumption theories of the Danielson type (inability to absorb surplus value owing to contraction of workers' level of consumption).

What is important for us to observe is that in this endeavour simultaneously to criticise two versions of the underconsumption theory, the position of "absolute immiseration" (absolute contraction of the standard of living of the working class) is not abandoned but on the contrary is reasserted. T-B writes: "it is possible for overall volume of social consumption to contract and simultaneously for overall social demand for commodities to increase" (Tugan-Baranowsky 1969: 25). This position will turn out to be a significant source of contradictions in his analysis, since it is only within the framework of the theory of underconsumption that the "absolute impoverishment" hypothesis has any place.

The only prerequisite, according to T-B for unimpeded expansion of production is that the "right" proportion be maintained between production in the two basic sectors (production of means of production and production of consumption goods), which are described in the reproduction schemes of Vol. 2 of Capital. *Disproportion*, therefore, between production in these two sectors is the cause of crises. Baranowsky summarises his analysis as follows:

> The general view, which to a certain extent was also shared by Marx, that the poverty of the workers, i.e. of the great majority of the population, makes it impossible to realise the products of an ever expanding capitalist production, since it causes a decline in demand, is mistaken. (...) Capitalist

production creates its own market - consumption being only one of the moments of capitalist production. In a planned social production if the leaders of production were equipped with all information about the demand and with the power to transfer labour and capital freely from one branch of production to another, then, however low the level of social consumption, the supply of commodities would not exceed the demand (Tugan-Baranowsky, 1969: 33. Poorly translated in Luxemburg 1971: 312).

Writing in an era of total predominance of the underconsumption viewpoint, T-B for a start accepts, as indicated, that there were a contraction in popular consumption. However he also postulates that – in accordance with its reproduction schemes – accumulation could be expanded independently of popular consumption. To provide a grounding for his view concerning the independence of accumulation and individual consumption, T-B starts from the following postulate: Let us imagine a planned economy, that is to say a community without crises. Then let us ask ourselves how production might be increased. The answer given to this question is as follows: As much means of production and as many consumer goods will be produced as will correspond to planned individual and investment demand, and this planned demand cannot not but correspond to Marx's projections.[20] By contrast, in a capitalist economy:

> Increase in the income of the capitalists may coincide with a contraction in national income. From the viewpoint of the capitalist business, salary – i.e. the income of the great majority of the population – constitutes not income but an element in capital expenditure. For this reason it is possible in a capitalist economy for there to be a simultaneous fall in national income and increase in capitalist income and national wealth – without any kind of disturbance of the equilibrium between production and consumption (op. cit: 167).

Nevertheless, in accordance with the reproduction schemes developed by Marx in Vol. 2 of *Capital*, the values (or, correspondingly, the prices) of consumer commodities which enter into the personal consumption of the capitalists and the workers (already employed or newly employed as a result of the expansion of production) of Sector I of the economy (which produces means of production) must amount to the values (prices) of those (a) used up (during the production period) and (b) *accumulated* means of production from Sector II (which produces consumer goods). Assuming a *constant production technique*, the accumulation of capital thus also signifies

170 *Karl Marx and the Classics*

increase in the volume of consumer goods produced and consumed and so an increase in the value of goods consumed by the totality of workers (increased overall nominal salary).

However, even if we abandon the hypothesis of an unchanging technical level (replacement of labour by mechanised systems), we will be obliged to reject T-B's thesis on diminished popular consumption and lower national income, and so on contraction of Sector II with the result that all economic growth is derived from expansion of Sector I (production and mutual exchange of capital goods). Because, quite simply, the assumption of a Sector II declining and contracting and a Sector I growing in leaps and bounds is not compatible with the existence of a *uniform rate of profit* for the entire economy. *It becomes obvious that no linkage is feasible between the theory of expanded reproduction and the theory of "absolute immiseration"*.[21]

Irrespective of the contradictions in T-B's contributions to the debate, the questions he raises in relation to the link between the Marxist theory of reproduction and the theory of crises were of particular importance and remained in the forefront of discussion between Marxists for more than three decades.[22] Stating that crises are caused by the disproportion between the production of the two sectors of the economy, he situated the mechanism generating the crisis *in the sphere of production and not of consumption*. In other words, the *essential aspect*, of crises is *overproduction* and not underconsumption.

6. Theoretical Repercussions of Tugan-Baranowsky's Intervention

6.1 A Protracted Controversy

T-B's theoretical intervention set the parameters for Marxist literature on the problem of economic crises right up to World War II.[23]

After the appearance of the *Studies* ... the Marxists of Russia and Germany-Austria reacted in three different ways to the question of whether, and if so how, the Marxist theory of expanded reproduction was compatible with the predominant underconsumption approach to the question of crises:

a) Many theoreticians accepted a variant of the theory of crises introduced by T-B from out of the context of the reproduction schemes, rejecting the underconsumption approach, as e.g. in the case of Lenin, Bulgakov, Otto Bauer, Hilferding and others. These Marxists were obliged then to take a position on a second question: *How are the reproduction schemes to be made compatible with the immiseration thesis, i.e. with the predominant view that the position of the workers deteriorates under capitalism?*

b) Others ignored T-B's problematic, insisting on the traditional underconsumption theory (Kautsky, Moszkowska).

c) A third group, around Rosa Luxemburg and later Fritz Sternberg, defended the underconsumption theory against the problematic of the Marxian reproduction schemes.

6.2 Transformation of the Russian Theoretical Scene

T-B's analyses had influenced not only the Russian "legal Marxists" but also the Marxist circles of the Social-democratic Party of Russia around G. Plekhanov (but not Plekhanov himself, see Rosdolsky 1969: 558) and V. I. Lenin (as already mentioned).

Lenin, who had dedicated his writings of the 1893-1899 period to the possibility and potential dynamic of capitalist development in Russia, based his theoretical arguments on the problematic of Marx's reproduction schemes of the social capital, so as to criticise the view that capitalist development ran up against the obstacle of an inadequate internal market. Lenin, exactly like T-B, regarded the expanding capitalist production of production and consumption goods as the "independent variable" in capitalist development and paying demand as the "dependent variable".

> The degree of the development of the home market is the degree of development of capitalism in the country. To raise the question of the limits of the home market separately from that of the degree of the development of capitalism (as the Narodnik economists do) is wrong (Lenin 1977 Vol. 3: 69).[24]

Since the object of Lenin's analyses was the question of capitalist development and not the theory of crisis, he was able to bring his theses into accord with the immiseration thesis. The Russian "third persons" of non-capitalist means of production were regarded not as potential consumers of the surplus product but as a reserve army and as potential workers in the expanding process of capitalist production. The overall volume of working class consumption grows with the inclusion of additional workers. This process does not preclude absolute immiseration of the working population.[25]

The immiseration question in (pure) capitalism has to the best of our knowledge been subjected to critical analysis only by the "legal Marxist" S. Bulgakov. In his book, published in 1897: *On the Markets of Capitalist Production. A Study in Theory* he puts forward the theory that immiseration is to be understood not in an absolute but in a *relative* sense:

> In certain conditions, capitalism may exist solely by virtue of an internal market. It is not an inherent necessity peculiar to the capitalist mode of production that the outside market be able to absorb the surplus of capitalist production. (...) The majority of economists before Marx solved the problem by saying that some sort of 'third person' is needed, as a *deus ex machina*, to cut the Gordian knot, i.e. to consume the surplus value. This part is played by luxury-loving landowners (as with Malthus), or by indulgent capitalists, or yet by militarism and the like. There can be no demand for the surplus value without some such extraordinary mediators; a deadlock will be reached on the markets and the result will be over-production and crises. (...) But if this great public is essentially characterised as consuming the surplus value, *whence does it obtain the means to buy?* (...) Capitalist production knows no other than effective consumption, but only such persons who draw either surplus value or labour wages can be effective consumers, and their purchasing power strictly corresponds to the amount of those revenues. Yet (...) the fundamental evolutionary laws of capitalist production tend, *despite to the absolute increase, to diminish the relative size of variable capital* as well as of the capitalists' consumption fund. (...) Since the normal conditions of capitalist production presuppose that the capitalists' consumption fund is only a part of the surplus value, and the smaller part at that, the larger being set aside for the expansion of production, it is obvious that the difficulties imagined by this (the *populist*) school do not really exist (in Luxemburg 1971: 299, 298, 304, 303, emphasis added).[26]

Bulgakov also addressed another important question concerning reproduction schemes, namely the question of "where the money comes from" which is necessary for the expansion of capitalist production: given that Marxist analysis cannot postulate any direct exchange of goods, capitalists in both sectors must be in a position, for purposes of expansion of their production, to possess the money needed to buy the elements of both constant (c + Δc) and variable (v + Δv) capital for this expansion of their production before they have made any sales (i.e. before they have realised their own output). The presumption of money reserves in the hands of the capitalists cannot solve the problem, because such reserves in a closed capitalist economy, reproduced on an ever-wider scale, soon become exhausted. If one remains with the two-sectoral analysis of Marx (i.e. does not bring in any third sector of "gold production") one must include credit as an immanent moment of the capitalist system, since its function consists precisely in multiplying monetary resources and enabling purchases to be rendered independent of prior sales: *"Credit ... is the necessary complement of a developing economy of exchange which would otherwise soon find itself hampered by a lack of coined money"* (Bulgakov in Luxemburg 1971: 302).

Following on the political and ideological decadence of the Narodniks that ensued in the wake of the 1905 Revolution, the underconsumption approach was suppressed from the crisis and/or development theory that the Socialdemocrats and/or Russian "legal Marxists" had elaborated out of the context of Marxian reproduction schemes.

6.3 The New German-Austrian Orthodoxy

The publication of T-B's *Studies ...* also provoked a split over theory among German-speaking Marxists. However, this time Marxian reproduction schemes were also targeted for criticism by supporters of underconsumption theory (Rosa Luxemburg and her theoretical school: Fritz Sternberg, De Vries[27] et al.).

The most prominent German-speaking Marxist to adopt the T-B problematic as basis for criticism of the underconsumption hypothesis and development of an alternative theory of crises was Rudolf Hilferding (R.H.). In Part Four, and in particular in Chapter 16, of his *Finance Capital* (Hilferding 1981: 239-266), published in 1910, Hilferding formulated his views, the most important point of which was the relativisation of the concept of disproportionality as the cause of crises. According to R.H. disproportionality could arise from any one of a number of possible causes: a rapid increase in consumption, or production of means of production (overinvestment) or, by contrast, a contraction in the abovementioned forms of social product and/or social demand. Disruption of proportionality for R.H. meant disruption in the price mechanism regulating expanded reproduction in the capitalist economy. It also meant that it would not be possible to manufacture products at prices and in quantities that would satisfy paying demand to the extent necessitated for expanded reproduction of the economy at a given profit rate. Disruption of the regulatory price mechanism thus coincided with a fall in the rate of profit.

Despite his purely phenomenological and often contradictory account of the factors inducing such disruption of economic proportionality, in his enumeration of them (as he sought to show how each individual factor, all things being equal, could lead to disruption of proportionality and to crisis) his analysis did introduce new points to the critique of underconsumption theory elaborated out of the context of Marxian reproduction schemes: crisis was to be studied in conjunction with the factors influencing price formation and evolution of the rate of profit. These points were later to be developed further by Bukharin.

6.4 The "Counter-Attack" by the Upholders of Underconsumption Theory. Rosa Luxemburg

As previously indicated, Rosa Luxemburg (R.L.) in her chief work (Luxemburg 1971), published in 1913, carried out a radical critique of the new orthodoxy that had emerged from the context of the Marxian reproduction schemes, also formulating a defence of the underconsumption hypothesis.

R.L.'s key argument is as follows: Since, on the one hand, Marxian reproduction schemes presuppose an expansion not only of the production of means of production but also of consumer goods (Luxemburg 1971: 127 ff.), while on the other hand such an expansion of personal consumption is impossible without involvement of "third persons" (the principal thesis of all underconsumption theories and/or theories of absolute immiseration) the conclusion is that "on the question of accumulation, mathematical problems can prove absolutely nothing, since their historical premise is untenable" (Luxemburg, in Luxemburg/ Bukharin 1972: 65). Expanded reproduction in a pure capitalist economy is according to Rosa Luxemburg impossible.

R.L.'s consistent defence of the underconsumption hypothesis leads to a theory of capitalist collapse: if the reserve of "third persons" with the development of capitalism becomes exhausted, the capitalist system will succumb to its immanent tendency towards underconsumption: reproduction comes to a halt. The socialist revolution in this context must be understood as totally determined by the tendency to collapse.[28]

Many underconsumptionist approaches, especially those formulated after the death of Rosa Luxemburg (with the exception of the work of "Luxemburgists" like Sternberg, who's book *Der Imperialismus* was published in 1926 – Sternberg 1971), try to locate the necessary "third persons" alien to the capitalist mode of production, inside the structure of really existing capitalist social formations (countries). Following Kautsky's notion about "those strata which are still non-capitalist", they claim that capitalist expanded reproduction is made possible in two ways: firstly by increasing the number of people belonging to the "new middle strata" of wage earners in trade, advertising, marketing etc., who are considered to be unproductive workers (they "do not increase economy's values", Moszkowska 1935: 97), while "their consumption vitalises the market" (op. cit.), or secondly by the massive state consumption of capitalist produced commodities (military and welfare expenditures of the state, etc.). In this way, expanded reproduction of capital is conceived as being assured by a non-economic (political) "regulation", aiming at the absorption of capitalist produced values (militarism and territorial expansion alongside the increasing military expenditures, an increasing state apparatus alongside an increasing "non-productive" sales and advertising apparatus of corporations, Moszkowska 1935: 91-104, see also Baran/Sweezy 1973).[29] However, since the consumption capacity of "third persons" and of the state is not inexhaustible, the inherent disequilibrium between production and consumption in capitalism must finally lead to the system's collapse.

Luxemburg's book drew criticism from many Socialdemocrat theoreticians, such as Bauer, Pannekoek and Hilferding. (See Luxembourg, in Luxembourg/Bukharin 1972: 47 ff.). Other Marxists embraced R.L.'s theory. Many others attempted to correct the "weaknesses" of the Marxian schemes R.L. had investigated (i.e. their incompatibility with the pauperisation thesis).[30]

In 1914 Bukharin wrote a polemic against Luxemburg, the revised version of which was nevertheless published only in 1925, under the title *Imperialism and the Accumulation of Capital*. Bukharin's 1925 polemic was probably aimed more at August Thalheimer than at the supporters of Luxemburg (see Hedeler, 2000). Irrespective of any political aims Bukharin may have had, his analysis, which also takes as its starting point the logic of Marx's reproductive schemes, is an exceptionally important study of imperialism and crises, exercising criticism of the theory of absolute immiseration, of collapse-mongering and of economism, i.e. of the (bourgeois) ideological configurations which prevailed only a few years later within so-called "Soviet Marxism". It is for these reasons that we shall concern ourselves more systematically with Bukharin's intervention in the section of this chapter immediately following.

7. Nikolai Bukharin's Polemic Against Rosa Luxemburg: Periodic Crises of Overproduction Arising out of Class Struggle

7.1 The Theoretical Specificity of Bukharin's Analysis

In his polemical pamphlet (Bukharin in Luxemburg/Bukharin 1972) published in 1925, Nikolai Bukharin sought to reject the "consistent" underconsumption theory formulated by Rosa Luxemburg: this meant defending the thesis that according to Marxist theory expanded reproduction of pure capitalism was possible and that crises were only temporary suspensions of this process, rejecting the hypothesis of collapse and/or the view that the economy is in a state of continual disequilibrium between production and paying demand, which without the presence of "third persons" would bring capitalist development and expanded reproduction to a halt.

Bukharin made use of the arguments of Bulgakov, Lenin, Hilferding and others, reformulating them with the aim of showing that the distinguishing feature of crises is overproduction of capital (overaccumulation) and not the immanent underconsumption of the workers. Nevertheless, the drift of his arguments enables us to extract from them a critique of the immiseration thesis that underlay all underconsumption theories. Moreover, his critique of Luxemburg's theories of collapse led him to a corresponding *critique on the one hand of teleological views* in respect of the "purpose" of capitalism and on the other of the *"monistic" views in relation to the origins of crises*. Class struggle emerges from both directions of argumentation as the process in the last instance driving all economic development and also determining the outbreak of economic crises.

7.2 The Expansion of Private Consumption as Prerequisite for Expanded Capitalist Reproduction

In order to contest the taboo-sanctioned position of the Socialist movement that no expansion of private consumption by the masses is possible under capitalism (absolute immiseration of the working class), Bukharin directed his polemical arguments against Tugan-Baranowsky's view that "it is possible for overall volume of social consumption to contract and simultaneously for overall social demand for commodities to increase" (Tugan-Baranowsky 1969: 25). Bukharin wrote:

(1) The increase in means of production calls forth a growth in the amount of means of consumption; (2) simultaneously, this increase creates a new demand for these means of consumption and as a result (3) a specific level of the production of means of production corresponds to a quite specific level of the production of means of consumption; in other words, the market of means of production is connected with the market of means of consumption. Thus, in the last analysis, we arrive at the opposite of that Mr. Tugan claims (Bukharin, in Luxemburg/Bukharin 1972: 210).[31]

His key point is that mass consumption can grow to the extent that it is determined by the dynamic of expanded reproduction of social capital (level of the rate of profit, sectoral restructuring of the economy):

> However large they may be in themselves, the branches producing means of production appear as *preliminary stages of the production of means of consumption*. (...) Thus, in respect to its *value* the share of means of production manifests a relative increase. What does that mean? It means that –expressed in *products*– there is a huge increase in *means of consumption*. The higher the organic composition of capital and the productivity of social labour, the greater is the amount of consumption products which are placed upon the market (Bukharin, in Luxemburg/Bukharin 1972: 208, 209).[32]

Bukharin's analysis showed that the thesis of absolute immiseration (long-term fixing of workers' living standards to a minimum, or even steady erosion of these standards) can be defended only on the basis of underconsumption theory. Tugan-Baranowsky's (and Otto Bauer's) attempt to combine this thesis with a critique of underconsumption theory led to unresolved theoretical contradictions.[33]

7.3 "Permanent Crises Do Not Exist"[34]

Analysis of the character of crises of overproduction presupposes understanding of the origins of economic crises. Tugan-Baranowsky had cited as a cause of crises a disproportionality between production spheres that ran contrary to the prescriptions of the Marxian reproduction scheme. In response to this, Bukharin adopted Hilferding's thesis that although crises appear as a result of the disproportionality between production spheres, "the factor of consumption forms a component part of this disproportionality. (...) A correct proportion between the workers' means of consumption and the other parts of the total social product is an essential requirement for the smooth running of social reproduction" (Bukharin, in Luxemburg/Bukharin 1972: 225, 231-32, 230).[35]

Bukharin nevertheless expanded the content of the abovementioned assertion, in the sense that he perceived the various forms of disproportionality as manifestations of the more generally contradictory character or a capitalist society, i.e. as a result of the historically concrete class antagonisms of a specific conjuncture, setting the parameters for capitalist development and/or expanded reproduction in a given capitalist economy.

In this way, Bukharin's approach acknowledges the total contradictions of the capitalist system as "causes" of crisis. As Bukharin points out:

> Capitalist society is a 'unity of contradictions'. The process of movement of capitalist society is a process of the continual reproduction of the capitalist contradictions. The process of expanded reproduction is a process of the expanded reproduction of these contradictions. If this is so, it is clear that these contradictions will blow up the entire capitalist system as a whole (Bucharin 1970: 98. Poorly translated in Luxemburg/Bukharin 1972: 264-5).

Contrary to underconsumption theory, Bukharin's approach does not end in a collapse thesis. It claims that the overthrow of capitalism will be the outcome of a conjuncture of sharpening of its overall contradictions: "The limit is given by the tension of capitalist contradictions to a certain degree" (Bucharin 1970: 98. Poorly translated in Luxemburg/Bukharin 1972: 264-65).

It follows from this that the crisis will be regarded as a historical conjuncture embodying all the contradictions arising from the class struggle in a *concrete capitalist society* (or group of societies interlinked economically), not as the effect of a single cause *permanently operative in every capitalist society*, which, as with underconsumption theory, "negates" the existence of capitalism through an automatic economic mechanism. On a theoretical plane one may speak of this totality of class antagonisms only as the *absent cause* of the crises. One cannot without concrete analysis determine the possible forms of intensification of the contradictions, leading to generalised overproduction.[36]

Bukharin's theoretical model, according to which the capitalist system must be grasped as a unity of contradictions, has not only philosophical but also theoretical consequences vis-à-vis the theory of crises: According to Bukharin the crisis signifies not only market disequilibrium or a mistaken investment decision but a disturbance of the *overall process of capitalist production*, affecting the production and circulation of all commodities, including labour power.

> We have seen that the production of means of consumption for the workers is the *indirect* production of labour-power or, to be more exact, the precondition of this production. (...) It follows without further ado that the disproportionality between production and consumption also represents a disproportionality of production in a more direct and exact form, namely, in the form of a disproportionality *between the production of means of consumption and the production of labour-power* (Bukharin, in Luxemburg/Bukharin 1972: 233-234).[37]

7.4 A Concluding Note on the Significance of Bukharin's Approach

Summarising the above analysis, we may say that the differentiation between underconsumption theory and overaccumulation theory (Bukharin) does not refer only to the decisive feature of the complex structure of economic crisis, but also to the way each theory conceives the process of capitalist expanded reproduction to be.

Underconsumption theory conceives crisis as being the expression of the immanent disequilibrium of capitalist expanded reproduction ("consumption is inevitably retarded in relation to production"). Expanded reproduction is assured only temporarily through a "third party" of consumers, alien to capitalists and workers. It thus formulates a "law of crisis", which is the inherent retardation of consumption compared to production.

In contrast, according to overaccumulation approach crises occur due to determinations external to the capital relation which, though, affect (overdetermine) the capital relation, since they act through it. Tugan-Baranowsky considers a single such determination, which constitutes the cause of crises: disproportionality between production sectors. In Bukharin's approach, the causes of crises are "absent", i.e. not predictable, as the author considers the causes to be the totality of contradictions characterising a capitalist society. Crisis is, therefore, an outcome of class struggle.

Both approaches are theoretically incompatible among themselves, although they are indeed Marxist approaches to the question of economic crises. Marxism was never a monolithic theoretical approach but was always characterised by internal conflicts, by the emergence of objects of dispute and contradictory currents within itself (also see Milios 1995). What is foreign to Marxist theory is by contrast the superficial approach which, without comprehending the conceptual content of any of them, attempts to fuse together both the Marxist currents we have examined here into a uniform "Marxist interpretation" of crises, without perceiving the impropriety of this amalgam (as a characteristic example of such atheoretical and empty would-be analysis see Lipietz 1985).

In any case, the existence of different Marxist approaches does not signify anything more than a need to more the analysis forward, to embark on theoretical disputation with one's chosen view and attempt to achieve clarification through confrontation with contending approaches. That is precisely what we shall attempt to do in the next Chapter.

8. Regression: A Reproduction Scheme With "Third Persons"

Before closing our account of the notion of underconsumption, it is worth pointing out that the basic question on which this theory is unable to make any pronouncement is how and why the "third party" (e.g. Luxemburg's "third persons of the colonies") are to buy up the surplus capitalist production. The only possible answer to the question is that this "third party" acquire income from production of non-capitalist commodities, which are then sold so that capitalist commodities can (also) be purchased. It is therefore a question of transactions between the capitalist and the non-capitalist economies (or "milieus"). However, because what is involved is by definition an exchange of equivalents, the capitalist economy unloads (disposes of) the same amount of value as it takes on (is supplied with). Marx's reproduction schemes are modified, but the supposed "problem" with them, as the underconsumptionist theoreticians identified it, does not go away.

Let us undertake such a modification, postulating a simplified version where we suppose that there are four sectors: two capitalist and two non-capitalist. Specifically:

Capitalist sector I, production of means of production.
Capitalist sector II, production of means of subsistence.
Non-capitalist sector III, production of raw materials (means of production).
Non-capitalist sector IV, agricultural production (means of subsistence).

The Historic Marxist Controversy on Economic Crises 181

We also postulate that production in the non-capitalist sectors is simple reproduction of the producers as autonomous non-capitalist producers: the purpose is not profit but subsistence. Outside labour power is not used for production, which involves simple reproduction of the non-capitalist sectors. The non-capitalist producers are satisfied with the equivalent of a workman's wage ($\Rightarrow$ surplus product = 0).

We thus have:

Sector I: $Ic + Iv + Is$.
Sector II: $IIc + IIv + IIs$.
Sector III: $IIIc + IIIvi$.
Sector IV: $IVc + IVvi$.

(where vi = is the equivalent of the working wage of an independent producer).

If we are to have unimpeded reproduction, supply must equal demand. That is to say:

Supply of means of production = demand for means of production (to replace worn-out means and for accumulation in the capitalist sectors):

$$Ic + Iv + Is + IIIc + IIIvi = Ic + \Delta Ic + IIc + \Delta IIc + IIIc + IVc \quad (1)$$

Supply of means of consumption = demand for means of consumption:

$$IIc + IIv + IIs + IVc + IVvi =$$
$$Iv + Ik + \Delta Iv + IIv + IIk + \Delta IIv + IIIvi + IVvi \quad (2),$$

where Ik, IIk denote individual consumption by capitalists in sectors I and II.

We accept the hypothesis that overall demand in every sector for means of production and consumption is equal to the value of the gross product of that sector:

$Ic + \Delta Ic + Iv + Ik + \Delta Iv = Ic + Iv + Is$ (3),
$IIc + \Delta IIc + IIv + IIk + \Delta IIv = IIc + IIv + IIs$ (4),
$IIIc + IIIvi = IIIc + IIIvi$ (5),
$IVc + IVvi = IVc + IVvi$ (6).
From (3) $\Rightarrow Ik + \Delta Ic + \Delta Iv = Is$ (3i).
From (4) $\Rightarrow IIk + \Delta IIc + \Delta IIv = IIs$ (4i).

Given (3i), (4i) [(5) and (6)], (1) and (2) become:
Ic + Iv + Ik + ΔIc + ΔIv + IIIc + IIIvi =
Ic + ΔIc + IIc + ΔIIc + IIIc + IVc (1i),
IIc + IIv + IIk + ΔIIc + ΔIIv + IVc + IVvi =
Iv + Ik + ΔIv + IIv + IIk + ΔIIv + IIIvi + IVvi (2i).
From (1i) and (2i) ⇒ *Iv* + *Ik* + *ΔIv* + *IIIvi* = *IIc* + *ΔIIc* + *IVc*   (7).

Relation (7) is a (modified) condition for unimpeded reproduction. Its similarities are obvious with the condition for unimpeded reproduction of a pure capitalist economy (see relationship 3 of Chapter 5).

It is again a condition which shows under what prerequisites expanded reproduction of the capitalist sectors is possible in the case of simple reproduction of the non-capitalist.

When this condition is fulfilled, reproduction of the system is unimpeded. Accordingly, when it is not fulfilled, its reproduction encounters an obstacle.

9. Conclusions

The problematic introduced by Tugan-Baranowsky, which used the reproduction schemes formulated by Marx in Vol. 2 of *Capital* to frame a critique of underconsumption theory, contributed (despite the contradictions in some of the ways it was elaborated) to the formation of a specifically Marxist interpretation of economic crises, some elements of which are theses such as the following:

1) The new problematic had reversed the pointer of causality between reproduction and mass consumption. It had thus defended the validity of the Marxian thesis that "the rate of accumulation is the independent variable; the rate of wages is the dependent not the independent variable" (Marx 1990: 770). Marxian criticism of Say's Law does not, as the theoreticians of underconsumption had assumed, depend on there always being excess demand under pure capitalism but on there not always being an equilibrium between supply and demand. Crises testify to this tendency towards disequilibrium. But there are no permanent crises.

2) Crises are conjunctural suspensions of the conditions for unimpeded reproduction of total social capital. They constitute transitory manifestations of the internal contradictions of capitalism and not permanently operative causal relationships inherently governing capitalist relations (a permanent

deficiency in consuming power as against production, or the ever acting "law of the falling tendency in the profit rate").

3) Production relations and not circulation is at the heart of crises.

4) Demand as *motive power of capitalist production* is a concept to be rejected.

5) The disequilibrium between supply and demand is not the cause or the essential content of the crisis, but a superficial manifestation of it – its form of appearance.

6) The essential content of the crisis has to do with overproduction of capital and the fall in the rate of profit that is associated with this phenomenon.

7) Expanding reproduction of social capital presupposes the existence of the credit system.

Notes

1. In the *Communist Manifesto* [1848] Marx and Engels wrote: "In these crises, there breaks out an epidemic that, in all earlier epochs, would have seemed an absurdity – the epidemic of over-production. Society suddenly finds itself put back into a state of momentary barbarism; it appears as if a famine, a universal war of devastation, had cut off the supply of every means of subsistence; industry and commerce seem to be destroyed. And why? Because there is too much civilization, too much means of subsistence, too much industry, too much commerce. The productive forces at the disposal of society no longer tend to further the development of the conditions of bourgeois property; on the contrary, they have become too powerful for these conditions, by which they are fettered, and so soon as they overcome these fetters, they bring disorder into the whole of bourgeois society, endanger the existence of bourgeois property. The conditions of bourgeois society are too narrow to comprise the wealth created by them. And how does the bourgeoisie get over these crises? One the one hand, by enforced destruction of a mass of productive forces; on the other, by the conquest of new markets, and by the more thorough exploitation of the old ones. That is to say, by paving the way for more extensive and more destructive crises, and by diminishing the means whereby crises are prevented" (Marx-Engels 1985: 86).
2. "Crises are never more than momentary, violent solutions for the existing contradictions, violent eruptions that re-establish the disturbed balance for the time being" (Marx 1991: 357).
3. For the interpretation of crises in accordance with the "law of the falling tendency in the rate of profit", an approach which was developed at the border of the Marxist controversy to be discussed in this Chapter, see Chapter 7, Section 3.
4. In the words of Ricardo (1992: 192) "demand is only limited by production". For presentation and criticism of Say's Law, see Rubin 1989: 335 ff. In the Neoclassical ideological framework, the empirically discernible reality of economic cycles and crises

is explainable only as a malfunction, attributable to "monopolies" or non-economic factors. Jevons' attempt to interpret fluctuations of the economic conjuncture and crises on the basis of supposed natural fluctuations in the annual cycle of agricultural production is entirely typical (Roll 1989: 376 ff.) By contrast Keynes sees the cyclical fluctuation of economic conjuncture as being attributable to "cyclical variations of the marginal productivity of capital". However, marginal productivity of capital is defined by Keynes as the "relationship between the expected return from the use of an additional unit (...) of capital and the production cost of that unit" (Keynes 1993: 135), that is to say he defines that quantity "in terms of investors' expectation of returns" (Keynes 1993: 136). As a result, the contradictions (and fluctuations) that arise from the structural characteristics of the capitalist mode of production disappear from view and it is considered that the productivity of capital (and so the economic conjuncture) "is determined by the personal judgement of ignorant financial speculators" (Keynes 1993: 324), without the requisite emphasis being placed on the economic relationships that are the causal determinants behind the "psychology" and the practices of these financial speculators.

5. On the base of the above argument, Neoclassical economics indicate that the cause of unemployment is not insufficient demand for goods (and so undercosumption) but rather quite the opposite, excess demand for goods: Supporting that the equilibrium condition is given by: $(Y^d - Y^s) + (N^d - N^s) = 0$, then if $N^d < N^s$ it is because $Y^d > Y^s$ (where Y^d stands for aggregate demand, Y^s for aggregate supply, N^d for labour demand and N^s for labour supply). However, in the long run, given the funds, a perfectly free competition determines the equilibrium prices (the real wages as well) in such levels, that the excess demand disappears and all markets (the labour market as well) will be led to a state of equilibrium; there is no possibility for permanent involuntary unemployment by Say's law.

6. In a similar but not identical line of argument John Maynard Keynes had argued in his *General Theory* that the planned savings, increasing faster than the planned investments, reduce the aggregate demand.

7. "The population necessary to furnish clothing for such a society by the help of machines would be reduced to a trifling number, and would absorb but a small part of the excess of a rich and well cultivated territory. There would evidently be a general falling off in the demand, either for productions or population. And whilst it is certain that a proper passion for consumption (unproductive) would preserve a just proportion between the supply and demand, whatever may be the power of production, it does not appear less clear that an inclination to save must inevitably lead to a production of commodities exceeding what the organisation and habits of such a society would permit them to consume" (Malthus, Th. [1820], *Principles of Political Economy*: 365, cited in Say 1821).

8. Most writers who refer to the period we are examining draw a distinction between Narodniks and Marxists and, influenced by Soviet historiography, consider that it was Plekhanov who introduced Marxism into Russia when in 1883 he founded the "Emancipation of Labour" group (see the non-Marxist Isaiah Berlin's [1978: 210 ff.] characteristic analysis). In reality even their theoretical and political opponents within the Left such as Lenin regarded them at that time as vehicles for "mistaken interpretations" of Marxist theory. Lenin wrote characteristically of Danielson: "'Genuine' Marxism consists in learning *Capital* by heart and quoting passages from

it, in season and out ... à la Mr. Nikolai-on" ("Uncritical criticism", Lenin 1977 Vol. 3: 615). As Luxemburg (1971: 274) pointed out, in the Russian controversy over capitalist development and economic crises "for the first time, the argument centred purely in the reproduction of capital as a whole, in accumulation, (...) the issue was no longer between laissez-faire and social reform, but between two varieties of socialism". Riazanov was the only Russian bolshevist who acknowledged the Narodniki's devotion to Marx and his theory: "Marx was already able to read the Russian translation of his *Capital*. His popularity in Russia was steadily on the increase, even after the Hague Congress. As the critic of bourgeois political economy he was regarded as a great authority and his influence, direct and indirect, was felt in most of the economic and political writings in Russia. (...) Marx and Engels valued greatly the movement known by the name of Narodnaya Volya (the People's Will)" (Riazanov 1937, Chapter IX). See also Milios 1999-a.

9. As Marx and Engels pointed out in the 1882 Preface to the Russian Edition of the *Communist Manifesto*, the Narodniks were convinced that the Russian community could "pass directly to the higher form of communist common property" (Marx-Engels 1985: 56).

10. The Narodniks repeatedly submitted these positions to the judgement of Marx and Engels. One of the most important texts criticising the Narodniks was written by Engels as early as 1875 and published in the newspaper *Der Volksstaat*, Nr. 45, 21.4.1875 (MEW Vol. 18: 562-67).

11. "If the working part of the population consumes what enters into the costs of production in form of the wages for labour, the capitalists themselves must destroy the surplus value, excepting that part of it which the market requires for expansion. If the capitalists are in position to do so and act accordingly, there can be no commodity surplus; if not, over-production, industrial crises, displacement of the workers form the factories and other evils will result" (in Luxemburg 1971: 281). "Yet eat, drink and dance as much as they like – they will not be able to squander the whole of the surplus value" (in Luxemburg 1971: 278). V.V's analysis is, however, contradictory, as he also states that: "The simplest solution of this problem will be an appropriate change in the distribution of the aggregate income among those who take part in production. If the entrepreneurs would remain for themselves only so much of all increase of the national income as they need to satisfy all their whims and fancies, leaving the remainder to the working class, the mass of the people, then the régime of capitalism would be assured for a long time to come" (in Luxemburg 1971: 282).

12. But Russia could not make use of this outlet because, according to V.V. and the other Narodniks, it was not in a position to compete successfully with the other capitalist countries on the international market. Russian capitalism could not therefore overcome the "problem of the markets", with the result that its level of development remained low.

13. On the dispute between Danielson and Engels see Rosdolsky, 1969: 542-43 and also MEW Vol. 38: 469, Vol. 39: 38. Nearly four decades after Danielson, in 1934, M. Gandhi was portraying machinery as a "sin": "Machinery has begun to desolate Europe. Ruination is now knocking at the English gates. Machinery is the chief symbol of modern civilisation. It represents a great sin. (...) It is necessary to realise that machinery is bad. We shall then be able to do away with it. (...) I have no partiality for return to the primitive method of grinding and husking for the sake of them. I suggest

the return because there is no other way of giving employment to the millions of villagers who are living in id lenses" (Cited in Gasgupta, 1996: 68, 71).
14. The categories of "third persons" Struve identifies are self-employed people, civil servants, "non-productive" employees in the private sector etc., essentially reproducing the model of Malthus, according to which landlords and other non-productive categories in the population function as consumers of surplus production.
15. "The expansion of the markets cannot keep pace with the expansion of production. A collision becomes unavoidable, and because it cannot generate any solution, as long as it does not explode the capitalist mode of production itself, it becomes periodic" (Engels, *Anti-Dühring*, in MEW, Vol. 20: 257).
16. Henryk Grossmann mentions that the view of the "external market" or "third persons" (in relation to the capitalist mode of production) as an interpretation of capitalism's ability to recover from crises was introduced into German-language Marxist discussion by Cunow, who wrote in 1898 that without continual expansion of its external markets England "would long ago have experienced a clash between the ability to consume of its internal and external markets and the gigantic increase in capitalist accumulation" (Cunow, "Die Zusammenbruchstheorie", in *Die Neue Zeit*, XVIII, 1898, quoted in Grossmann, 1971: 162).
17. "According to our theory under-consumption is the ultimate cause of crises" (Kautsky, quoted by Luxemburg, in Luxemburg/Bukharin 1972: 79).
18. The postulate, namely, that the growth rate of real wages must lag behind the growth rate of the labour productivity and of the volume of the capitalist produced consumer goods.
19. In 1893 in his essay "On the so-called Question of Markets", Lenin discussed a paper by G.B. Krassin, under the title "The Question of Markets", which reproduced the positions of Tugan-Baranowsky. See Lenin 1977 Vol. 1: 75-125.
20. "What would workers produce (...) if production were organised in the same way? Obviously, the goods that they themselves would consume, and the means of production. What purpose would these means of production serve? That of expanding production over the ensuing period. Producing what goods? Once again, means of production and consumer goods for the workers – and so on and so forth ad infinitum. (...) As a consequence of our abstract analysis of the process of reproduction of social capital, we come to the conclusion that there cannot be a surplus social product in the event of proportional distribution of social capital" (Tugan-Baranowsky 1969: 191, 34).
21. As early as 1893 Lenin criticised this notion of expanded reproduction independent of consumption by workers and also of individual consumption by the whole of society. In the article to which we have already referred (Note 19) he noted the mutual dependence between the accumulation process and both sectors of the economy: "Of course, it is wrong to speak of accumulation being 'independent' of the production of articles of consumption, if only because the expansion of production calls for new variable capital and, consequently, articles of consumption; evidently by using that term, the author [G. B. Krasin] merely wanted to stress the specific feature of the scheme, namely, that the reproduction of Ic –constant capital in department I– takes place without exchanges with department II, i.e., every year a certain quantity of, say, coal is produced in society for the purpose of producing coal" (Lenin 1977 Vol. 1: 84). A similar criticism of T-B was later formulated by Kautsky (who noted that it did not correspond with Marxian reproduction schemes to imagine there could be

accumulation of capital even in the event of a diminution in the volume of commodities consumed by the working class) and also by Rosa Luxemburg, in their endeavour to defend underconsumption theory: "The accumulation of Department II is completely determined and dominated by the accumulation of Department I (...) accumulation must proceed simultaneously in both departments, and it can do so only on condition that the provisions-department increases its constant capital by the precise amount by which the capitalists of the means-of-production-department increase both their variable capital and their fund for personal consumption" (Luxemburg 1971: 127).

22. Above and beyond the Marxists, the work of Tugan-Baranowsky was also of interest to certain non-Marxist writers. Even though his work was not translated into English (a French version of the *Studies*, revised by the author himself, came out in 1913 under the title of *Les Crises Industrielles en Angleterre* – M. Giard and É. Brière, Paris), praising references to certain aspects of his analyses were made by J.-M. Keynes (in his, 1930, *A Treatise on Money, Vol. II, The Applied Theory of Money*, Macmillan, London: 100 ff.) and by Alvin Hansen (in his, 1964, *Business Cycles and National Income*. W.W. Norton, New York: 281). See Ramos-Martínez 2001.

23. The following quotation from an article of Henryk Grossmann published in 1932 sheds much light on the importance of the theory of crisis developed by T-B from out of the context of Marxian reproduction schemes: "On the other hand Hilferding was quite justified in referring to the 'neglected (prior to the appearance of Tugan-Baranowsky's book in 1901) analyses of the second volume' (*Finance Capital*, Vienna, 1910, p. 303), subsequently adding that: 'Tugan-Baranowsky in his well-known *Studies* performed the service of demonstrating the significance of these investigations for the problem of crises. What is most remarkable is that such a demonstration was required in the first place' (ibid, p. 304). With the turn that set in after the appearance of T-B's book, things went to the opposite extreme" (Grossmann, 1971: 62). For the significance of Baranowsky's intervention see also Luxemburg, in Luxemburg/Bukharin 1972: 77-78).

24. In the Second Edition (1872) of Volume 1 of *Capital* Marx writes: "To put it mathematically: the rate of accumulation is the independent variable; the rate of wages is the dependent not the independent variable" (Marx 1990: 770).

25. "The decline in the well-being of the patriarchal peasant, who formerly conducted a mainly natural economy, is quite compatible with an increase in the amount of money in his possession, for the more such a peasant is ruined, the more he is compelled to resort to the sale of his labour-power, and the greater is the share of his (albeit scantier) means of subsistence that he must acquire in the market" (Lenin 1977, Vol 3: 42).

26. "It follows therefore that in proportion as capital accumulates, the situation of the worker, be his payment high or low, must grow worse" (Marx 1990: 799).

27. See in this connection Fritz Sternberg 1971 [1926]; *Dokumente zur Imperialismustheorie* Nr. II, 1971.

28. "The rebellion of the workers, their class struggle –and that is exactly where upon the surety of their victorial power is based– is only the ideological reflection of the objective historical necessity of socialism, resulting from the objective economic impossibility of capitalism at a certain level of its development" (Luxemburg 1966: 410. Poorly translated in Luxemburg/Bucharin 1972: 76). Collapse, or breakdown, theory is apparent in nearly all underconsumptionist writings, since it practically constitutes the ultimate logical consequence of this approach. However, it is explicitly

formulated only in some of these writings, especially those produced at times of severe economic crisis (e.g. Moszkowska 1935: 101 and 102). In others, especially those written in boom phases of capital accumulation, it is modified to a "stagnation theory" of capitalism (e.g. Sweezy 1970: 217): "Since the tendency to underconsumption is inherent in capitalism (...) it may be said that stagnation is the norm towards which capitalist production is always tending".

29. So, the "third persons" of the colonies by Rosa Luxemburg and her followers (Sternberg), become the "non productive new middle-class" or state-expenditures asserting the absorption of "economic surplus" in Moszkowska (1935: 96-7). Moszkowska (1935) claims that the growing middle-class of "non-productive" workers is a side effect of underconsumption itself: The falling sales force enterprises to spend an ever increasing amount of money in sales' promotion, advertizing, etc. As Karl Schoer (1976: 95) notes correctly, (referring to Moszkowska's book *Das Marxsche System*, Berlin 1929), "incidentally in this book and in her second important work on *The Dynamics of Late Capitalism* (*Die Dynamik des Spaetkapitalismus*) she developed many of the basic theses later to be adopted by Baran and Sweezy".

30. Otto Bauer regarded the Marxian schemes as "arbitrary and not without contradictions" and attempted to formulate sound reproduction schemes of his own. His main thesis was that "*in the capitalist mode of production there is a tendency towards accommodation of capital accumulation to population growth*" (cited in Luxemburg/Bukharin 1972: 81-2. Also see Grossmann 1971: 69 ff.).

31. Bukharin also wrote: "The 'limits of consumption' are expanded by production itself, which increases (1) the income of the capitalists, (2) the income of the working class (additional workers) and (3) the constant capital of society (means of production functioning as capital)" (Bukharin, in Luxemburg/Bukharin 1972: 204).

32. Following this argument, Bukharin states that crisis starts as overproduction of means of production, but manifests itself also as overproduction of means of consumption, which is the directly perceivable "form of appearance" of crisis (Bukharin, in Luxemburg/Bukharin 1972: 208, 227-28).

33. Moreover economic development in the twentieth century in all capitalist countries, particularly after the Second World War, has vindicated Bukharin's positions on the association between expanded reproduction and "massive proliferation of *consumer goods*".

34. Bukharin, in Luxemburg/Bukharin 1972: 204.

35. Bukharin inferred from this thesis that crises share in the features of generalised overproduction, and he criticised Tugan-Baranowsky for having proposed a non-Marxist model of partial overproduction. (Bukharin, in Luxemburg/Bukharin 1972: 221 ff.).

36. Contrary to this approach, Rosa Luxemburg (and, generally, underconsumption theory), "seeks for superficial, formally logical contradictions in capitalism, which are not dynamic, do not adjust to each other, are not elements of a contradictory unity, but patently deny this unity. But in reality we find dialectic contradictions of a whole, periodically adjusting to each other, constantly reproducing, to blow up the entire capitalist system at a certain stage of development" (Bukharin, in Luxemburg/Bukharin 1972: 237).

37. It is of some theoretical interest to note that this concept of expanded capitalist reproduction enabled Bukharin to question the notion of a "purpose" (external to the

process) of expanded reproduction, something which Rosa Luxemburg had laboured to identify. To her criticism that Marx's reproduction schemes constituted a "never-ending roundabout in the void" because they did not answer the question of "for whom" accumulation took place, Bukharin made the following comment: "Is there any justification for posing the question from the point of view of subjective *aim* (even if it is the subjective aim of a class)? What is such *teleology* doing in social science? It is clear that even the formulation of the question is methodologically incorrect, in as much as we are dealing with a formulation that is to be taken seriously and not with a sort of metaphorical cliché" (Bukharin, in Luxemburg/Bukharin 1972: 163-64). On the same subject see also the notion "Process without a Subject or Goal(s)", in Althusser 1984: 133-39.

9 Defining a Marxist Theory of "Overaccumulation Crises"

1. Introduction

From the critical presentation of the historic Marxist controversy on economic crises in Chapter 8, it became apparent that we support that version of the overaccumulation approach which conceives economic crises as a conjunctural overproduction of capital due to "absent causes". In other words, crises shall be identified neither with the "law of the tendential fall in the profit rate", nor with some supposedly intrinsic underconsumption of the labouring classes. Instead, a crisis shall be comprehended as a conjunctural production of commodities (means of production and means of consumption) in such quantities and prices, that the accumulation process and the circuit of social capital is temporarily retarded, as the rate of profit is being suppressed. Moreover, this overaccumulation is not seen as the result of a single –and therefore manageable– cause (e.g. the disproportionality between sectors of production), but as the (periodically recurring) outcome of the circuit of total social capital in the course of capitalist expanded reproduction, emanating from a fusion of the totality of social and economic contradictions which "overdetermine"[1] the capitalist relation. In the last instance, all categories of factors affecting the value composition of capital and the profit rate are influenced by class struggle, the main object of which is the (level of) exploitation of the labour power.

In this chapter we are going to argue that the above stated thesis can also be formulated by means of a systematic reading of Marx's work: We refer to a reading of Marx which clearly distinguishes itself from all approaches of his work that are based on citation of isolated passages, but attempts to discover and develop the inner logic of the Marxian argument and to examine also its theoretical coherence.[2] The notion of *capital overaccumulation*, as constructed by Marx in Volume 3 of *Capital* – in

Defining a Marxist Theory of "Overaccumulation Crises" 191

relation to his "preliminary definition" of "absolute overproduction"– will be our point of departure. Before doing so, a comment on the distinction between internal-necessary and external determinations in Marx's work will be necessary.

2. Internal-Necessary and External Determinations

On comprehending Marx's approach to capitalist crises and the notion of capital overproduction, one is forced in one way or another, to examine the logic of *Capital*; that is the internal coherence and the organisation rules of the Marxian logical constructions.

Marx's analyses of the capitalist socio-economic relations, (in *Capital*, as well as in his other 1857-67 writings), are logically based upon the distinction between "internal" and "external" determinations. One understands *internal determinations* of (every) capitalist production process as the necessary relations, which remain unchanged and are constantly present, regardless of all the changes in historical development. The internal determinations refer thus to relations belonging to the structural elements of the capitalist mode of production (see Chapter 1). These relations are present even though they remain hidden beneath the surface of everyday events and the changes of economic, political or ideological conjuncture. On the contrary, the *external determinations* of capitalist relations of production constitute the variety of relations and events which do not originate from the unchanged structural characteristics of the given type of society (mode of production), but from the *changing mutual strengths* in the class struggle of the antagonistic classes, within one and the same type of class power. For example, capitalist exploitation and surplus value extraction is an internal determination of social relations in every capitalist society. The fact that we are dealing with a capitalist society though, does not indicate that the working day will be 12, 10 or 7 hours, that the welfare services will be more or less extended, or that the workers' trade unions will be strong or weak, etc. These last relations belong to the variety of external determinations (external to the structural connections that constitute the capitalist mode of production), which can take on many different forms in different countries, or in the different historical phases of a capitalist society (Duménil 1978, Althusser/Balibar 1997).

What is most important in Marx's elaboration, is his analysis of the way these two forms of social relations articulate with each other. He clearly showed that the external determinations do not constitute any violation of the economic laws arising from the internal determinations, nor are they acting restrictively or in contradiction to these laws. On the contrary, the external determinations act and produce results only *through* immanent and necessary relationships. Their activity is thus mediated through economic laws. For example, in determining the value of labour power, what happens is not that two separate independent factors insinuate themselves into the equation, on the one hand the socially necessary labour time for producing the means of subsistence and reproduction of labour power and on the other the trade-union, political and ideological power of the working class, i.e. factors each of which for its part yields separate results which could be added together or subtracted one from the other, or could cancel each other out. The change in the value of labour power, in other words, would not emerge as the aggregate (a) of the alteration brought about in it by the class struggle of the workers and (b) the alteration brought about in it by reduction in socially necessary labour time – as a result of increase in the productivity of labour – for production of the commodities which constitute the real wage. But the external factor from the structural viewpoint (i.e. the balance of class forces) operates through the internally necessary relationship: strengthening of the working class elicits, ceteris paribus, an increase in real wages, and so in socially necessary labour time for the production of the means of subsistence and reproduction of this class, and by means of this alteration brings about an increase in the value of labour power (Ioakimoglou and Milios 1993).

The concept of economic law[3] enables us to comprehend what we find in Marx's work in relation to economic crises: necessary connections between things, from which the character of crises may be inferred as inherent *tendencies* in the capitalist mode of production, which *make their appearance conjuncturally under certain external determinations.*

3. The Concept of *Absolute Overproduction* and the Profit Rate

Marx refers extensively to economic crises of capitalism in the third section of Volume 3 of *Capital* (Part 3, Chapters 13-16), which bears the general title "The Law of the Tendential Fall in the Rate of Profit". A special emphasis on the subject is given in the section of Chapter 15 (Volume 3) which was labelled by Engels "Surplus Capital Alongside Surplus

Population" (Marx 1991: 359-368. See also the original manuscript of Marx, MEGA II, 4.2: 324-333).

The crucial point of Marx's analysis of *capital overproduction* is the definition of the "absolute overproduction". It can be regarded as a kind of preliminary definition which then leads to the definition of the "relative overproduction". The absolute overproduction refers to a boundary situation, which allows Marx to formulate a clear and comprehensible definition.[4] We now follow Marx's definition:

> There would be an absolute overproduction of capital as soon as no further additional capital could be employed for the purpose of capitalist production. But the purpose of capitalist production is the valorisation of capital, i.e. appropriation of surplus labour, production of surplus-value, of profit. Thus as soon as the capital has grown in such proportion to the working population that neither the labour-time that this working population supplies nor its relative surplus labour-value can be extended (the latter would not be possible in any case in a situation where the demand for labour was so strong, and there was thus a tendency for wages to rise); where, therefore, the expanded capital produces only the same mass of surplus-value as before, there will be an absolute overproduction of capital; i.e. the expanded C+ΔC will not produce any more profit, or will even produce less profit, than the capital C did before its increase by ΔC. In both cases there would even be a sharper and more sudden fall in the general rate of profit, but this time on account of a change in the composition of capital which would not be due to a development in productivity, but rather to a rise in the money value of the variable capital on account of higher wages and to a corresponding decline in the proportion of surplus labour to necessary labour (Marx 1991: 360).

Firstly, there is a distinction to be made in the above definition. In the case of absolute capital overproduction, the fall in the profit rate is *not the result of a development in the labour-power's productive capacity* (with a subsequent increase in the organic composition of capital – at a higher rate than the increase in the surplus-value rate). This argumentation is related to the fact that in previous sections of the third volume of *Capital*, (Marx 1991: 317-359), Marx had already formulated and analysed the law of the tendential fall in the rate of profit as a ceteris-paribus outcome resulting from a development of the productive capacity of the labour-power – under the presupposition that the technical composition of capital increases faster than the productivity of labour.

In the definition of absolute overproduction Marx makes it clear, therefore, that he refers to a fall in the profit rate determined by factors other than in the case of the law of the tendential fall. In the case of absolute overproduction, it is "the decline in the proportion of surplus labour to necessary labour" (op. cit.). In other words, the determining factor in the fall of the profit rate is now the *decrease in the surplus-value rate*.

For reasons arising from the history of the labour and communist movement, this Marxian argumentation has not been seriously considered by Marxists, who tend to think that almost every fall in the profit rate is a result of an increase in the value (organic) composition of capital. Furthermore, as already argued in Chapter 7, many Marxists consider every increase in the value (organic) composition of capital to be an outcome of the increase in labour productivity due to technical change (law of the tendential fall). However, Marx considers the value (organic) composition of capital to depend also on other factors ("economy in the use of constant Capital", "Fluctuations in the price of raw material" –Marx 1991, Ch. 5 and 6: 170-234, see below).[5]

In any case it is apparent that the profit rate depends on two "variables": the surplus-value rate on the one hand, and the value composition of capital on the other. One should note at this point, that the definition of Marx quoted above, seems to take into consideration only the surplus-value rate, that is the relation between surplus labour and necessary labour. However, this "one-sided" analysis is not due to an omission or a theoretical mistake: Marx uses here the "ceteris paribus" method, i.e. he studies the change of a specific quantity (the profit rate) under the influence of the change of another quantity (the surplus-value rate), under the assumption that all other factors remain constant.

The question that now arises is in what way does Marx study the *combined effect of value (organic) composition* –which does not depend only on the increase in labour productivity due to technological change– *and surplus-value rate* on the profit rate? Considering the profit rate to be the dependent variable (R), then the exploitation rate (s/v) and the value (organic) composition of capital (C/v) will be the independent variables, according to the known relation (see Chapter 7):

$$R = \frac{s}{C+v} = \frac{s/v}{[C/v] + 1} \qquad (1)$$

where s stands for surplus value, v for the variable part of capital (value of labour-power), and C for constant capital (value of the means of production); s/v is then the exploitation rate (surplus-value rate).

As mentioned, Marx studies the influence of (s/v) on R by considering (C/v) as a constant quantity (in section 3, chapter 15 of Volume 3of *Capital*), where he defines overaccumulation. On the contrary, when he studies the "nature of the law" of the tendential fall in the profit rate (Chapter 13 of Volume 3), he initially considers (s/v) as a constant quantity. Therefore, *it seems* that he successively studies the influence of the independent variables on the dependent one, in an effort to cover all possible cases and factors that determine the change of the dependent variable.

However, in the last case (the "nature of the law" of the tendential fall in the profit rate), he only considers changes in C/v due to technological change. In addition, his first assumption, that an increasing labour demand due to the capital accumulation ("as soon as capital has grown in such proportion to the working population that ...", op. cit.) will lead to a falling rate of surplus-value and subsequently to a fall in the profit rate and to (absolute) capital over-accumulation, is also *one-sided*: His argumentation with regard to changes in the surplus-value rate, is that this is due to the lack of additional workers (very low unemployment rate) and to subsequent increases of real wages. However, the surplus value rate depends also on *other factors*, which Marx does not seem to feel obliged to explain. The *absolute labour time*, on the one hand, does not depend exclusively on the number of workers, but also on the length of the working day. On the other hand, the *relative labour time* (i.e. the rate of exploitation) does not only depend on the wages, but also on the increase in labour productivity. These "omissions" by Karl Marx concerning the definition of capital over-accumulation can be explained as follows:

- The length of the working day is purely an external relation with regard to the examined internal economic determinations, as explained above.
- The labour productivity is regarded as an unchangeable factor, exactly like the value (organic) composition of capital.

Therefore we are not dealing with omissions in Marx's analysis, but with his scientific method of abstraction. The economic law does not refer to the concrete capitalist relations in a given society. It refers to their "kernel", or their inherent elements of their specific structure, having excluded:

a) all the multiple external determinations, which occur in one form or another, and, depending on the changing economic, social and political conjuncture in a given society, may not even exist.

b) all determinations which are considered *temporarily* constant, so that the effects of each "independent variable" on the "dependent variable" become separately apparent.

It is obvious, for instance, that in the case of a concrete analysis of a concrete society, the assumptions of a constant labour productivity or organic composition of capital shall be abandoned. This means that when the decrease in the exploitation rate is being compensated for by an even higher decrease in the value composition of capital, the profit rate will rise instead of fall.

The following question shall be now posed: Under what circumstances does a change in the rate of exploitation, (as Marx described it in section 3, Chapter 15, Volume 3 of *Capital*) lead to a decrease in the profit rate and to an economic crisis? Marx deals with this problem in a section of Volume 3 of *Capital* which precedes the formulation of the law of the tendential fall in the profit rate.

4. Factors Affecting the Value (Organic) Composition of Capital

Let us follow then the methodology of Karl Marx. This time we will consider the surplus value rate (s/v) as a constant quantity and deal with the relation between the value composition (C/v) of capital and the profit rate (R). One could argue that this problem is treated by Marx principally in Part 3 of Volume 3, and more precisely in Chapter 13 (the law of the tendential fall in the profit rate). However, the value composition of capital depends not only on technological change (as in the case of the "law") but also on a series of other factors, which are considered here (part 3 of Volume 3) as constant quantities. For this reason, our analysis shall focus its attention on Part 1 –Chapters 1-7– of Volume 3 of *Capital*.

Let the following relation guide us:

$$\frac{C}{v} = \frac{C}{Y} \cdot \frac{Y}{v} = \frac{C}{Y} \cdot \frac{(s+v)}{v} = \frac{C}{Y} \cdot [\frac{s}{v}+1] \qquad (2)$$

which means that:

$$R = \frac{\frac{s}{v}}{\frac{C}{Y} \cdot [\frac{s}{v}+1] + 1} \qquad (3)$$

where Y is the net product, that is the sum of surplus-value and value of labour force (variable capital).

The above relation (2) shows that the factors influencing the value (organic) composition of capital (C/v) can be analysed to the factors that influence the surplus-value rate (s/v), on the one hand, and those that influence the quantity (C/Y), on the other.[6]

This last quantity expresses the value of constant capital which is necessary for the production of one unit of product. The increase or decrease of this quantity illustrates, therefore, the ability of capitalists to spare or economise on constant capital (or to purchase it in favourable prices). Marx himself devoted a significant part of his analysis to this subject (Chapters 5 and 6 of Volume 3).[7] In this part of Marx's text we find the enumeration of all factors related to the ability of capitalists to economise on constant capital, or to lower its price.

Once again, Karl Marx follows the method we described above. He considers that the surplus-value rate is "given"[8] (i.e. constant), which "is a necessary assumption, if we are to investigate the situation in its pure form" (Marx 1991: 200). He then describes the factors which ensure or restrict economy in the use of constant capital.

More precisely, the factors affecting the value composition of capital can be sorted in the following categories:

A) Those factors which are related to the time and intensity of the means of production utilisation, *under a given technology of production and technical composition of capital*:
 – *Lengthening of the workday or workyear*.[9]
 – *Economy on the conditions of work at the expense of the workers*.[10]

B) Those factors which are related to the skills and the concentration of the collective worker, or, in other words, to the possibility of increasing labour productivity *without any change in the technical composition of capital* – or the technological status of the production process:
 – *Socially combined labour (concentration and cooperation of workers, social character of labour)*.[11]

- *Economy designated by the experience of the collective worker.*[12]
- *Economy as a result of the appropriate education of the collective worker and his subordination to the factory despotism.*[13]

C) Those factors, which are connected with an *increase in labour productivity due to technical innovation* and/or increase in the technical composition of capital. Only in this case we are dealing with forms of "economy in the use of constant capital" also affecting the profit rate in ways studied by Marx in his law of the tendential fall in the profit rate:
- *"The concentration of means of production and their employment on a massive scale"*, (Marx 1991: 172-175).
- *Economies that arise from the continuous improvement of machinery"*:
  a) "the reduction of wastage" (Marx 1991: 195-199);
  b) productivity increase in sector I, (which produces means of production).

What shall be reminded here, is that Marx considers the possibility of *technical changes* in the production process, which cause opposite effects to the value composition of capital and the profit rate, as those considered in his famous "law of the tendential fall". In other words, Marx abandons here the assumption that the technical composition of capital changes faster than labour productivity (see Chapter 7 of this book), as he was aware of the fact, that there could exist forms of technological innovation and of subsequent increases in labour productivity, which reduce the value composition of capital and, therefore, *increase the profit rate*:

> Here it is the development of labour productivity in its external department, the department that provides him with means of production, which causes the value of the constant capital applied by the capitalist to fall relatively and the profit rate therefore to rise (Marx 1991: 175).

D) All factors causing an *appreciation* or *depreciation* of the components of constant capital, which are *not* related to economy in the use of constant capital or technological change, i.e. they are not the outcome of changes in the production process, but stem from changes in prices, and more precisely from the fluctuations in the price of raw material (Marx 1991: 200-234).[14]

Marx directly combines these price fluctuations with the outbreak of economic crises: "Violent fluctuations in price thus lead to interruptions,

Defining a Marxist Theory of "Overaccumulation Crises" 199

major upsets and even catastrophes in the reproduction process" (Marx 1991: 201-202). He summarises his analysis as follows:

> Here too, as in the previous case, it should be noted that, like those variations that result from economy in the use of constant capital, variations resulting from fluctuations in the price of raw material also always affect the rate of profit, even if they leave wages, and thus the rate and mass of surplus-value, completely undisturbed (Marx 1991: 200).

It is obvious from the above presentation that Marx considers the value composition of capital (and consequently the profit rate –the fall of which designates a conjuncture of crisis) to depend on a wide variety of factors.[15] Which of these factors determine the outburst of each *specific* crisis is not a matter of theoretical anticipation but of concrete analysis of the circuit of social capital in a capitalist economy, i.e. of the factors influencing the immanent tendencies of the capital relation. That is why Marx, after stating that "to understand what this over-accumulation is, we have only to take it as an absolute" (Marx 1991: 359), he postulates that *"the closer analysis* of crises *belongs to the study of the appearing movement of capital"*, a thesis which has been excluded by Engels from the text of Volume 3 of *Capital*.[16]

The "appearing movement of capital" takes the form of an overaccumulation crisis in all cases that the totality of the external determinations influence the value composition of capital and the rate of exploitation in ways resulting in the decline of the general profit rate.

5. Capitalist Expanded Reproduction and its Overdetermination by Class Struggle

The factors affecting the value composition of capital, and consequently the profit rate, belong to the external determinations of the capitalist production process (length of the working day, concentration, education and experience of the collective worker, factory despotism, forms of political coercion of the working classes, type of technical progress inflicted through capitalist competition or class-struggle,[17] etc.). The same is true for the factors affecting the rate of exploitation.

In order to study a conjuncture of crisis, all factors affecting the profit rate shall be taken into account. For instance, an increase in the prices of raw materials is transformed into a fall in the profit rate only in the case that it is not compensated for by economies in the use of constant capital or a rise in the exploitation rate.[18] On the contrary, a large increase in the factor illustrating the use of constant capital (factor C/Y) over a certain time period (i.e. a fall in the "constant capital efficiency" Y/C) may lead to a fall in the profit rate and an overaccumulation crisis, even in the instance of a constant or increasing exploitation rate.[19]

In order to investigate the causes or the determining factors of crises some authors have employed the circuit of social capital:

M—C–[→P→]C′—M′ (see also Chapter 3).

Since crises constitute interruptions or retardations of the circuit of social capital, they investigate under what conditions each separate phase of the circuit (e.g. the phase M—C or C′—M′) could be interrupted.[20] These approaches resemble to that of Rudolf Hilferding, discussed in Chapter 8, according to which each specific "disproportionality" in the reproduction process of social capital (including that between supply and capable to pay demand[21]) may be the cause of crisis. However, as argued above (see also Chapter 8) the discussed "disproportionalities" (or disruptions of the circuit of social capital) are rather the forms of appearance, not the "cause" of crises.[22] In reality, no phase in the circuit of social capital can be isolated and identified as the "starting point" or the "cause" of crisis or of any other "appearing movement of capital". In the words of Chris Arthur (1998: 107): "Capital itself is an emergent form that cannot be reduced to a particular inner moment or phase of its cycle of activity".

Crises constitute a fusion-condensation of all forms of contradictions induced by the totality of concrete "external" relations dynamically articulated with the capital relation, in a way that a fall in the rate of profit and a holdback or even a halt of the capitalist expanded reproduction process occurs. All these contradictions, even those possessing an apparently "technical" character are in the last instance determined by the class relation of forces in a given capitalist society, i.e. with the ability of capital to exploit the labouring class at a given rate of profit. They appear as an outcome of the totality of contradictions characterising capitalist expanded reproduction (see Bukharin's analysis as presented in Chapter 8), *at a given conjuncture of class struggle*. It is this plurality of contradictions overdeterminating the capital relation, which allows us to speak of *class struggle as the "absent cause" of crisis*; a "cause" which cannot be "isolated" and "eliminated".

Once a crisis breaks out, it develops its own dynamics on nearly every aspect of social life. For instance, as we argued in Chapter 8 and also in previous sections of this Chapter, and as it becomes clear by the fact that in many cases consumption increases during the whole period preceding the outbreak of the crisis, underconsumption of workers shall not be considered as the cause of economic crises. It constitutes, however, one of its major effects, which then produces its own effects in respect to the profit rate. The whole process takes on the form of a "vicious cycle": As the crisis itself unavoidably results in a fall or deceleration in demand, it thereby leads to an increase in the unemployed production capacity, that is an increase of the so-called capital intensity (C/N) of the capitalist economy. The crisis aggravates also the contradictions between industrial and financial capital over financial policy and the level of the interest rate, as already discussed in Chapter 3 (Section 5) of this book (see also Fine and Harris 1979: 87 f., Itoh 1980).

The point that we would like to stress here, as a conclusion of the whole analysis, is that *all forms* of external relations affecting the profit rate (i.e. not only those directly affecting the rate of surplus value) are overdetermined by class struggle, the main object of which is the production of profit through the exploitation of the labour power.

That is why Marx introduces the concept of *overproduction* (overaccumulation) *crisis* by referring to a fall in the exploitation rate (see the definition of "absolute overproduction", Marx 1991: 359), and explains that crises indicate the (temporary) inability of the capitalist class to exploit labour "at a given level of exploitation" (Marx 1991: 364).[23]

Converging with the above stated interpretation of Marx's crisis theory are the analyses to the same subject by Resnick and Wolff (1978) and by Fine and Harris (1979). The latter authors summarise their conclusions as follows:

> The cycle and crisis are therefore the products of the capital/labour antagonism which manifests itself in production and in exchange and in distribution. (...) Crises occur when these contradictions exist in particular relation to each other when, in terms of Althusser's concept, there is an overdetermination of contradictions. Thus, crises are not produced by exchange contradictions (market wages or profits, or by production contradictions (law of the tendency of the profit rate to fall) but by this in a particular relation to each other (Fine and Harris 1979: 88).[24]

However, as it also can be concluded from the above cited passage, the authors reduce all contradictions in the sphere of capitalist production to the "law of the falling tendency in the rate of profit" and its "countertendencies", thus underestimating parameters like organisational restructuring of the labouring process within a given technological environment and economy in the use of constant capital (see above). That is why they often adopt formulations in favour of an interpretation of Marx's crisis theory in accordance with the "law of the falling tendency": "Marx sees crises as resolving the contradictions between the law of the tendency of the profit rate to fall and the counteracting tendencies" (Fine and Harris, 1979: 81).[25]

Following the trend of our analysis, we must add that according to Marx the ability of the capitalist class to economise on constant capital is not a "technical aspect" of the production process, but an outcome of the social relation of forces, that is a result of class struggle. Increasing economy in the use of constant capital presupposes an increasing power of the capitalist class over the production process itself. It is often connected with a deterioration of the workers' economic and social status, as Marx showed. He repeatedly denoted that the ability of capitalists to economise on constant capital (thus reducing the value composition of capital and raising the profit rate), depends mainly on the skills and attitudes (towards capitalist exploitation) of the collective worker. He wrote:

> For all economies of this kind it is largely true once again that this is possible only for the combined worker and can often be realised only by work on a still larger scale. (...) This development in productivity can always be reduced in the last analysis to the social character of the labour that is set to work, to the division of labour in society, and to the development of intellectual labour, in particular of the natural sciences (Marx 1991: 174-5).

If ensuring of the "normal" levels of capital profitability can always be reduced in the last analysis to promoting capitalist exploitation and discipline, it is comprehensible why the capitalist way out of economic crises is always connected with the declaration of a class-war against the working class, its collective forms of organisation, its social rights (and not with policies of "social consensus" and "vitalising of popular demand", as a Keynesian point of view would tend to think). The analysis of Marx reveals the objective background of bourgeoisie political strategies.

Notes

1. For the concept of "overdetermination" see Althusser 1990-a: 87-128.
2. It is clear, that, due to the status of Marx's texts on economic crises (see Chapter 8), the "citation method" can be used to "prove" or "reject" any crisis theory. For example, one can isolate passages both in favour and against the undercosumption approach: "The ultimate reason for all real crises always remains the poverty and restricted consumption of the masses, in the face of the drive of capitalist production to develop the productive forces as if only the absolute consumption capacity of society set a limit to them" (Marx 1991: 615). However, "it is a pure tautology to say that crises are provoked by a lack of effective demand or effective consumption. The capitalist system does not recognise any forms of consumer other than those who can pay. (...) That fact that commodities are unsaleable means no more than that no effective buyers have been found for them, i.e., no consumers. (...) If the attempt is made to give this tautology the semblance of greater profundity, by the statement that the working class receives too small a portion of its own product, and the evil would be remedied if it received a bigger share, i.e. if its wages rose, we need only note that crises are always prepared by a period in which wages generally rise, and the working class actually does receive a greater share in the part of the annual product destined for consumption. From the standpoint of these advocates of sound and 'simple' (!) common sense, such periods should rather avert the crisis. It thus appears that capitalist production involves certain conditions independent of people's good or bad intension, which permit the relative prosperity of the working class only temporarily, and moreover always as a harbinger of crisis" (Marx 1992: 486-7).
3. "The law" – says Karl Marx – is the "inner and necessary connection between two apparently contradictory phenomena" (Marx 1981: 331).
4. "Now the real overproduction of capital is never identical with the one we consider here but, compared with it, it is only a relative one" ["Die wirkliche Ueberproduction von Capital nun ist nie identisch mit der hier betrachteten, sondern ist gegen sie betrachtet nur eine relative"] (MEGA, II, 4.2: 329). At this point, Marx adopts a methodology which is common in the natural sciences, e.g. the "boundary definition" of the "ideal gases", and which later on has been adopted also by Sociology through the notion of the "ideal type" – utilised to highlight the characteristics of a social phenomenon in its pure form, which therefore is "exaggerated" as to the actual situation being studied.
5. The case of Ernest Mandel (1995) is very characteristic, for the way that the author incorporates the "law of the tendential fall in the profit rate", (see also Chapter 7 of this book), in his theory of "long waves". According to him, capitalist development is characterised by phases of long-term fluctuation in the rate of profit, extending over two or three decades, with each phase characterised by a high rate of profit (and consequent high rate of accumulation and growth of the national product), succeeded by a phase – approximately equal in duration – of low levels of profit, slow rates of accumulation and growth, and high unemployment. Mandel links the rising long waves with a host of "exogenous" economic and social parameters which stem from the class relation of forces (and allow for a restructuring of production, the contraction of all forms of costs, etc.) as a result of which there emerges the rising tendency in the rate of profit. But he posits a one-way connection between the descending phase in the rate of profits and the tendency – seen as endogenous in capitalism – towards increase in the organic composition of capital in consequence of technological innovation, i.e. in consequence

of the "law of the falling tendency" in the rate of profit. The whole scheme presupposes: i) that technical innovations (if not counterbalanced by "exogenous" factors) must always tend to increase the organic composition of capital, at least after they have been generalised in the economy; ii) that this long-term trend in the organic composition of capital is strongly influenced by "other factors" (except profit-squeezing technical change) only when the "distress signal" of low profitability and crisis starts flying. By contrast, in this chapter, we are going to argue that, according to Marx, the profit rate shall be *always* considered as a "multi-variable function", in the sense that it is *always* determined by a sum of factors (influencing labour productivity and the organic composition of capital) besides technical change.

6. A change in factor C/Y can be the result of either a change in (Y/N) or/and in (C/N), since: C/Y = (C/N)•(N/Y), where N is the number of workers, (Y/N) is the "apparent labour productivity", assuming that the length of the work year is constant, and (C/N) is the "capital intensity" (constant capital per worker).

7. "Economy in the use of constant capital" and "The effect of changes in price" (Marx 1991: 170-234).

8. "In our present investigation, (…) we proceed from the assumption that the rate and mass of surplus-value are given – in order to avoid needless complications" (Marx 1991: 171).

9. "The volume of fixed capital (factory buildings, machinery, etc.) remains the same, whether work continues for 16 hours or for 12. The extension of the working day requires no new expenditure on this, the most expensive portion of the constant capital" (Marx 1991: 170).

10. "The contradictory and antithetical character of the capitalist mode of production leads it to count the squandering of the life and health of the worker, and the depression of his conditions of existence, as itself an economy in the use of constant capital, and hence a means for raising the rate of profit" (Marx 1991: 179).

11. "By the concentration of workers and their cooperation on a large scale, constant capital is spared. The same buildings, heating and lighting equipment, etc. cost relatively less for production on a large scale than on a small scale. The same holds for power and working machines. Even if its value rises absolutely, it falls relatively, in relation to the increasing extension of production and to the size of the variable capital or the mass of labour-power that is set in motion. The economy that a capital makes in its own branch of production consists firstly and most directly in economising on labour, i.e. in reducing the paid labour of its own workers; the economy previously mentioned, however, consists in the greatest possible appropriation of unpaid alien labour in the most economical fashion; i.e. in operating at the given scale of production with the lowest possible costs" (Marx 1991: 175).

12. "Finally, however, it is only the experience of the combined worker that discovers and demonstrates how inventions already made can most simply be developed, how to overcome the practical frictions that arise in putting the theory into practice -its application to the production process, and so on" (Marx 1991: 198-199).

13. "If nothing is to be lost or wasted, if the means of production are to be used only in the manner required by production itself, then this depends partly on the workers' training and skill and partly on the discipline that the capitalist exerts over the combined workers" (Marx 1991: 176).

14. Marx writes: "As long as other circumstances are equal, the rate of profit falls or rises in the opposite direction to the price of raw material. (…) We can thus understand how

important for industry is the abolition or reduction of import duties on raw materials" (Marx 1991: 201-202).
15. To these factors Marx adds also the feedback effects created by the credit system, which "lead to a regular plethora of money capital at certain phases of the cycle. (...) At the same time as this, there develops the need to pursue the production process beyond its capitalist barriers: too much trade, too much production, too much credit" (Marx 1991: 640).
16. "Um zu verstehn, was diese Ueberproduction ist (die nähere Untersuchung darüber gehört in die Betrachtung der *erscheinenden Bewegung des Capitals*, wo Zinscapital etc. Credit etc. weiter entwickelt) hat man sie nur *absolut* zu setzen" (MEGA II, 4.2: 325). For the differences between Marx's manuscript and Volume 3 of *Capital* as edited by Engels see Jungnickel (1991), Heinrich (1995), Heinrich (1996-97).
17. "It would be possible to write a whole history of the inventions made since 1830 for the sole purpose of providing capital with weapons against working-class revolt" (Marx 1990: 563).
18. This is, for example, the case of the first "oil shock", in 1973, which aggravated the overaccumulation crisis building up in most of the developed capitalist countries. (See Ioakimoglou – Milios 1993).
19. This is the case in most capitalist countries during the 1980s and 1990s.
20. For a compendious presentation of these approaches see O'Hara 1999, and the Literature discussed in it.
21. "Proportionality may also be disrupted by a change in the relation between production and consumption" (Hilferding 1981: 266).
22. As Fine and Harris (1979: 89) correctly argue, "underconsumptionist theories confuse the form of crises with their cause".
23. "Overproduction of capital never means anything other than overproduction of means of production – means of labour and means of subsistence – that can function as capital, i.e. can be applied to exploiting labour at a given level of exploitation; a given level, because a fall in the level of exploitation below a certain point produces disruption and stagnation in the capitalist production process, crisis and the destruction of capital" (Marx 1991: 364. MEGA II, 4.2: 330).
24. Compare also the following intruding comments by Resnick and Wolff (1978: 51, 48): "For Marx all crises are constituted by collapsing effective demand, and hence suddenly accelerated drops in realized rates of profit, rising unemployment, reduced investment, and business failures. None of these features *explain* the crisis; they *are* the crisis and thus need to be explained as consequences, recurrent in nature, of the 'normal' accumulation process. (...) Thus it misconstrues Marxism to search for causes of crisis in either production *or* circulation, in the of surplus value *or* its realization". For a review of the Marxist controversy on economic crises until the early 1990s see Norton (1992).
25. "Marx's theory of the inevitability of crises depends upon his law of the tendency of the rate of profit to fall" (Fine 1989: 54).

10 Epilogue: On the Character of Marxian Theory, "Ricardian Marxism" and the Role of F. Engels

Exposition of the basic points of the Marxist theory of value and its ideological implications, of money (Parts I and II), of social capital and of crises (Parts III and IV) makes it clear that the theoretical analysis (the system of concepts and their logical implications) in question is not compatible with other currents in Political Economy. Marx's *Critique of Political Economy* constitutes, to our opinion, the only scientific (and, for that reason, critical) discourse of the capitalist relations of production: Starting from the forms of appearance of these relations, deciphers their causal determinants.

However, as argued mainly in Part III, Marx's theoretical system evolved neither uniformly nor without contradictions in Marx's writings:

- First of all one has to bear in mind that the major tenets of this economic theory had not been developed by Marx until the writing of the *Grundrisse* (1857), which means that one shall not identify all of Marx's economic writings (e.g. sections of *The Poverty of Philosophy*, 1847) with his theoretical system of the *Critique of Political Economy*.
- Most importantly, this new theoretical "domain" was explored and developed by Marx in a not straightforward way: In parts of his 1961-65 writings, Marx flirted with or even retreated back to the value theory of Classical (Ricardian) Political Economy (as we noted in relation to the "problem of transformation" of values into production prices and in

relation to the theory of ground rent – see Part III). This consists the main theoretical discontinuity in Marx's mature economic writings.[1]

The above stated critique to Marx does not aim at his theory, the *Critique of Political Economy*, but quite the opposite: Our main argument is that Marx was mistaken as to his own theory, *when* he adopted (or retreated to) the theses of Political Economy, exactly because he distanced himself from his own theoretical system, the *Critique of Political Economy*.

The question is now raised, of what may be the possible causes of Marx's ambivalences towards Classical Political Economy. Answering in a general way, one may say that the issue simply reflects the contradictions of Marx's break with Ricardian theory, contradictions which are immanent in every theoretical rupture of the kind, i.e. in every attempt to create a new theoretical discipline on the basis of the critique of an established system of thought.

In this context we shall notice that what we have identified as Marx's ambivalences towards Classical Political Economy appear in his (unpublished during his lifetime) Manuscripts 1861-65, especially in the Manuscript 1864-65, which was edited by Engels and published as Volume 3 of *Capital*. In other words, they appear at a time period when Marx was re-examining and revising the work plan of his great theoretical project.

We are referring to the fact that during the course of writing his great opus, Marx altered his work plan. While in 1857-9 he planned to write six books (Capital, Landed Property, Wage Labour, The State, Foreign Trade, The World Market and Crises) later on he worked out the plan for the three books of *Capital*, whereby capital, wage labour and rent are dealt with simultaneously in the analysis of the capitalist production and circulation process. This change of plan is due primarily to a modification of concepts: Initially Marx reflected on the distinction between causal determinants and forms of appearance on the basis of the concept of "capital in general", as opposed to the "competition of many capitals" (whereby the latter became comprehensible as the form of appearance of the former). However, his analysis of the formation of the general rate of profit led him to an understanding of competition also as an immanent determining factor of capitalist relations. Thus, in *Capital* he abandoned the notion of "capital in general" and formulated the concepts of *social capital* (involving all causalities of the capital relation on the level of the whole economy, but having also empirical articulations, i.e. dimensions referring to empirical regularities – e.g. the "production prices") on the one hand, and *individual capital* on the other.[2] This change of plan and the modification of concepts may have temporarily influenced Marx's lines of argumentation in a way that allowed the incorporation into his writings, of positions stemming from Classical Political Economy. The further investigation on this subject exceeds, however, the scope of the present book.

In this epilogue we would like to stress the thesis, that Marxian theory is attenuated when Marxists do not comprehend Marx's ambivalences towards Political Economy, i.e. the existence of conceptual contradictions and, much more important, of a second, non-Marxist, discourse in his writings. Every "sanctifying" attitude towards Marx, presenting him, as the inculpable master who never made a single false step, practically blurs the scientific and heuristic kernel of Marx's analysis, as it identifies it with the Ricardian element, present in some of his elaborations. This "sanctifying" approach to Marx's work is though as old as Marxism itself: It starts with Friedrich Engels, Marx's closest collaborator and also co-author of many texts, who edited the 1863-65 Manuscripts of Marx and published them as Volumes 2 and 3 of *Capital*.

Engels was until recently considered, not to have played any significant role in the economic writings of Marx, apart from the necessary editorial work on Marx's drafts. However, the recently (1992) published original Manuscript of Volume 3 of *Capital* (MEGA II, 4.2) has made clear that:

> Engels made significant modifications to the manuscript, despite his own claim that he had restricted his role to one of faithfully presenting Marx's work. Changes to Marx's text include design of headings, insertion of sub-headings, and textual transpositions, omissions and insertions. The changes have real impacts on the text, especially in the area of crisis theory, the theory of credit, and the relation between capitalism and commodity production (Heinrich 1996-97: 452).

If one excluded the insertions made by Engels, the German version of the 3rd Volume would be "shrunk" to 580 from 860 pages! (Hecker 1998) Some probably less important, but in any case substantive changes of Marx's text were made by Engels also in the Manuscript of Volume 2 of *Capital* (Arthur 1998: 124-5).

It would be though not correct to consider that Engels misquoted Marx's notions or his development of arguments. From a detailed comparison of the original Manuscript of Volume 3 of *Capital* on the one hand and of the well known text of Volume 3 as edited by Engels on the other, we may conclude that nearly all textual interventions (text additions, transpositions, omissions, completion of phrases or arguments etc.) aimed at a unification of Marx's

Epilogue: On the Character of Marxian Theory 209

discourse, and at giving Marx's draft the shape of a complete work: *the* third Volume of *Capital*, "which concludes the theoretical part" of Marx's work (Engels, in Marx 1991: 91).³

However, by doing so, Engels not only identified the Ricardian element in Marx's writings with the actual Marxian theoretical system of the Critique of Political Economy, but also highlighted this element and thus gave it the status of Marx's theoretical novelty per se: To name the most important example, he presented Marx's "transformation of values into process of production" as the ultimate solution to the problem that has been known as the dead end of Classical Political Economy.⁴ Furthermore, Engels treated Marx's work as the complete unfailing opus of Marxian theory.⁵ This sanctifying stance towards Marx's writings was later to be adopted by the leaders of both the 2ⁿᵈ International (Kautsky etc.) and by Soviet Marxists, especially after Stalin's rise to power.

We believe that the way Engels (and later on most political and theoretical leaders of the socialist and communist movement) treated the theoretical writings of Marx was mainly politically motivated. As Marxism is closely related with the labour movement and the strategy of socialist transformation of capitalist societies, Engels and the other Marxist leaders seem to have believed that they needed to show in every direction that their political course derives from a more or less complete, fully fledged and totally cohesive scientific theory, and that Marx's texts contain this theory.⁶

To make this point clear, we must insist: Marxism is constructed not simply as a theoretical system, but also as an ideology of the masses, as an ideology which determines the political action of organisations and movements of the working classes. As Gérard Bensussan correctly noted:

> Marxism cannot be deduced only to Marxist theory, even if it is the theory of Marx himself. 'It meets' the masses, it intertwines with a history, it participates in social practices: It is then, simultaneously, also an ideology (perhaps more than one). Its crises are crises of this problematic condition (Bensussan 1985: 267).

However, Marxism-as-an-ideology-of-the-masses is not Marxist theory itself. It is certain of the conclusions of Marxist theory, which can function as "battle positions" and principles of political strategy for the worker, and wider people's movement: The class-exploitative character of capitalism, the unity of production-distribution and the detachment of surplus value from the worker to the benefit of capital, the innate conflicting of capital-labour, the concealed class character of the state and of its formally neutral – civil equality – apparatuses, the overturning of this capitalist political power as the precondition of socialism, etc., are conclusions of Marxist theory which in several historical circumstances comprised the basis of Marxism-as-an-ideology-of-the-masses (mass Marxism). We speak about a practical ideology[7] of the workers' movement. Certain of its elements also existed in pre-Marxist critiques of capitalism, while within the daily political and syndicalist struggle, the working class almost spontaneously may approach certain positions of this Marxist ideology (usually in their reformist version), independently of any knowledge of Marxist writings.

In contrast, theoretical analyses like the ones discussed in this book, for example, those that are contained in the writings of Marx in relation to the value form and money, or the expanded reproduction of the social capital, or prices of production and the equalisation of the general profit rate, etc., comprise the component elements of Marxist theory, which as a rule, precisely due to their theoretical character, are not contained in what we have named Marxism-as-an-ideology-of-the-masses. They are part of Marxism-as-a-theoretical-system.

Here we should note that Marxism-as-a-theoretical-system does not constitute "academic Marxism", in the sense of a theoretical system detached from the political and social class struggle. On the contrary Marxism-as-an-ideology-of-the-masses can only then escape from dogmatism and reformism, when it is fuelled and enriched by Marxism-as-a-theoretical-system. In fact, in this case, Marxism-as-a-theoretical-system can extract objects of analysis (as well as conclusions) which are connected directly to the conjuncture of class struggle.[8] This is the way that we comprehend the relation of "internality" between Marxist theory and the labour movement[9] (see also Milios 1995).

The position of the dual substance of Marxism (theoretical system – ideology of the masses) is especially significant in order to comprehend what may have forced Engels (and a whole tradition of Marxists after him) to repel any argument or indication that even Marx's works may not be free of contradictions: The picture of an infallible Marx, laying down by means of "scientific socialism" the victorious future of the working classes, may have been regarded as a useful "weapon" in the process of shaping a socialist political strategy inspired by Marxism. It seems also that Engels, at least from the time on of his permanent habitation in London (September 1870), had devoted himself to this task of proving the labour movement and the left political leaders of the time with those Marxist arguments, which could help reshaping the socialist strategy.[10]

It may be true that strengthening of Marxism-as-a-mass-ideology constitutes a major precondition even for the development of Marxism-as-a-theoretical-system: Marxism having to struggle against the dominant bourgeois ideology, the systematisation of which and its promulgation, is supported in the suffocating supremacy of the ideological state apparatuses (education, family, media, church, etc.), has only one advantage: Its capacity to intertwine with the condition of the struggle of the working classes; in other words, its ability to penetrate the working class, its ability to be reproduced as an ideology of the masses (see also Althusser 1977).

However, if the arguments formulated in the present book are correct, a sanctifying stance towards Marx's writings, which leaves uncriticised the Ricardian elements that have slipped into Marx's analyses (what we have described as Marx's ambivalence towards Classical Political Economy), obscures the scientific substance of Marx's Critique of Political Economy. It thus fetches up a "Ricardian Marxism", which means nothing less than the displacement of Marxist theory by alien to it theoretical discourses (Classical Political Economy or other forms of bourgeoisie theoretical discourse).[11] In this case, Marxism is weakened not only as a theoretical system in its confrontation with theoretical constructs deriving from the Keynesian or the Neoclassical theory but also as an ideology of the labouring classes, as it cannot vindicate its internal consistency or bring forward its ability to decipher the existing economic and social reality.

Notes

1. There are also some other discontinuities in Marx's works, which we regard of minor significance. The most characteristic example has to do with whether capital (exploiting labour) in the circulation process should be regarded as productive or unproductive, a subject on which Marx adopts mutually contradictory theses. In the *Grundrisse* (as well as in Volume One of *Capital*), Marx correctly considers all capital forms equally productive (i.e. producing surplus-value): "Insofar as circulation itself creates costs, itself requires surplus labour, it appears as itself included within the production process. (...) Circulation can *create value* insofar as it requires fresh employment (...) in addition to that directly consumed in the production process" (Marx 1993: 524, 547). However, in Volume Three of *Capital*, Marx regarded capital in the circulation process as unproductive: "Commercial capital (...) creates neither value nor surplus-value" (Marx 1991: 395). These discontinuities or contradictions in the work of Karl Marx have only a minor effect on his theory, as they remain marginal and do not overshadow the consistency of the major analyses on which it is built.
2. For a detailed analysis on the subject see Heinrich 1986 and 1989. Marx's change of plan had been thoroughly discussed by Henryk Grossmann in the early 1930s

(Grossmann 1971). However, most Marxists do not perceive this modification of ideas, and thus consider that the notion "capital in general" is implicitly contained in *Capital*, or that it is identified with total-social capital. For example, Moseley (1997: 12) claims that "the real subject of Volume 1 is this total capital or capital in general". See also his critique to Heinrich (Moseley 1995).

3. There are however cases of textual interventions by Engels, which obviously betray a miscomprehension of Marx's analysis. Apart from the examples discussed in Chapters 7 and 9 with relation to the falling profit rate on the one hand and the character of crisis theory (crises as an outcome of contradictions "external" to the capital relation) on the other, it is worth mentioning that Engels changed the sequence of Marx's draft sheets on the "Trinity Formula" (Volume 3, Chapter 48, according to Engels's edition): He transposed a section of this part of Marx's Manuscript to the beginning of the part (Chapter 48), writing in the place where it belonged "Here a folio sheet of the manuscript is missing – F.E." (Marx 1991: 961). He then divided this section into two subsections, which he labelled "1", "2", and added one more subsection (which he labelled "3") that originally belonged to the section on Absolute Ground-Rent (Marx 1991: 953, 954, 956 MEGA II, 4.2: 720-22). The Chapter, instead of starting with the phrase "We have seen how the capitalist process of production is a historically specific form ..." (Marx 1991: 957), starts now with the subsections "1" – "3", the first two of which actually belonged to the place where the alleged gap in the manuscript was detected, i.e. before the phrase "Differential rent is bound up with the relative fertility of different land ..." (Marx 1991: 961).

4. Already in 1885, in the Preface to Volume 2 of *Capital*, Engels had announced the forthcoming "ultimate solution" of the "transformation problem", in the, at that time still unpublished, Volume 3: "According to the Ricardian law of value, two capitals employing equal quantities of equally paid living labour all other conditions being equal, produce commodities of equal value and likewise surplus-value, or profit, of equal quantity in equal periods of time. But if they employ unequal quantities of living labour, they cannot produce equal surplus-values, or, as the Ricardians say, equal profits. Now in reality the opposite takes place. In actual fact, equal capitals, regardless of how much or how little living labour is employed by them, produce equal average profits in equal times. Here there is therefore a contradiction of the law of value which had been noticed by Ricardo himself, but which his school also was unable to reconcile. (...) Marx had resolved this contradiction already in the manuscript of his *Zur Kritik*. According to the plan of *Capital*, this solution will be provided in Book III. Months will pass before that will be published. Hence those economists who claim to have discovered in Rodbertus the secret source and a superior predecessor of Marx have now an opportunity to demonstrate what the economics of a Rodbertus can accomplish. If they can show in which way an equal average rate of profit *can and must come about, not only without a violation of the law of value, but on the very basis of it, I am willing to discuss the matter further with them*. In the meantime they had better make haste" (Engels in Marx 1992: 101-102). It can be easily concluded from the cited passage, that Engels conceives the "transformation problem" in a Ricardian manner: He does not comprehend the incommensurability between values and production prices, i.e. the incongruity of mathematically transforming the former to the latter. Furthermore, he conceives the *quantitative* deviation of production prices from values as an effect of competition: "Continual deviations of the prices of commodities from

Epilogue: On the Character of Marxian Theory 213

their values are the necessary condition in and through which the value of the commodities as such can come into existence. Only through the fluctuations of competition, and consequently of commodity prices, (...) the determination of the value of the commodity by the socially necessary labour time become a reality" (Preface to Marx's *Poverty of Philosophy*, 1885, internet edition). See also Chapter 5, Section 4.2).

5. From Engels's Preface to the Volume 3, the reader may gain an idea about the status of Marx's text. Referring to Part V of the text ("The Division of Profit into Interest and Profit of Enterprise"), he writes: "I sought at first to complete this Part, as I had done to a certain extent with Part One, by filling in the gaps and expanding upon passages that were only indicated, so that it would at least approximately contain everything the author had intended. I tried this no less than three times, but failed in every attempt, and the time lost in this is one of the chief causes that held up this volume. At last I realised that I was on the wrong track. I should have had to go through the entire voluminous literature in this field, and would in the end have produced something that would nevertheless not have been a book by Marx. I had no other choice but to more or less cut the Gordian knot by confining myself to as orderly an arrangement of available matter as possible, and to making only the most indispensable additions. And so it was that I succeeded in completing the principal labours for this part in the spring of 1893" (Engels, in Marx 1991: 95). However, in the Preface to Volume 2 he had claimed: "The brilliant investigations of the present Volume 2 and their entirely new results in fields that up to now have been almost untrodden are simply premises for the material of Volume 3, in which the final results of Marx's presentation of the process of social reproduction on the capitalist basis are developed. When this Volume 3 appears, little more will be heard of an economist named Rodbertus" (Engels, in Marx 1992: 102).

6. It should be borne in mind, that not all Marxist leaders have followed this stance towards Marx's work. Rosa Luxemburg for example, although being wrong in her theory of underconsumption and capitalist collapse (see Chapter 8), belonged to a different tradition from that of Engels or Kautsky: she was devoted to the thorough examination of Marx's writings, seeking for the further development of Marxist theory, and not to the repetition of "what Marx actually said". She approached, therefore, Marx's arguments from a critical point of view. To the same perspective contributed also the formation in Moscow, with Lenin's approval, of the *Marx-Engels Institute* in July 1922 under the direction of David Riazanov. The Institute's main task was to bring together and to critically edit all the writings of Marx and Engels, a project which gave birth to the first MEGA-Edition (Marx-Engels-Gesamtausgabe). However, this effort was soon proven to constitute a major threat to the supposedly Marxist ruling ideology of the Soviet regime, and so a violent end was put to it. In December 1930 Isaac I. Rubin, who was working for the Institute, was arrested on conspiracy charges. Less than two months later (on February 15, 1931) Riazanov himself was arrested, and was finally executed on January 21, 1938. The same fate shared not only Rubin but also the majority of the Institute's Russian and foreign leading figures, such as Walter Haenisch, Ernst Czóbel, Franz Schiller, Fritz Sauer. For details on the work and life of Riazanov and his colleagues in the Marx-Engels Institute of Moscow, see *Beiträge zur Marx-Engels-Forschung Neue Folge. Sonderband 1*, 1997.

7. "Practical ideologies are complex formations which shape notions-representations-images into behaviour-conduct-attitude-gestures. The ensemble functions as practical

norms that govern the attitude and the concrete positions men adopt towards the real objects and real problems of their social and individual existence, and towards their history" (Althusser 1990: 83).
8. Only under these conditions can we perceive why political leaders of the Left, such as R. Hilferding or R. Luxemburg, authored works which are strictly part of Marxism-as-a-theoretical-system, while at the same time, works of academic Marxists (from Tugan-Baranowsky until Louis Althusser and Nicos Poulantzas) constituted crucial interventions into the ideological conjuncture of the Left, and provoked direct political results (they influenced the ideological fronts and the political correlations of power). In contrast, Marxism-as-a-theoretical-system was omitted by the leadership of the bureaucratic socialist and communist parties, because it constitutes a threat to the infallibility of the specific mass Marxism on the basis of which those parties and those leaderships are composed and reproduced.
9. According to Louis Althusser, this "internality" of Marxism in relation to the labour movement means also something else: For the Marxist intellectual to function really as a Marxist, he/she must first have adopted a revolutionary-proletarian stance within the context of the class struggle. He writes: "This concept is based on the fact that it is absolutely necessary for one to have adopted proletarian class positions, in order, very simply, to see and understand what is happening in a class society. It is based on the simple finding that (...) one cannot see everything from everywhere. One can discern the texture of this reality of conflict only if one adopts within the conflict itself, certain positions and not some other ones, because to passively adopt some other positions means that she/he has caught up in the logic of class illusions, which shall be named ruling ideology. Naturally this pre-condition opposes the entire positivist tradition – through which the bourgeois ideology interprets the practice of natural sciences. (...) Essentially, in the entire work of Marx he says nothing different. When he writes in the Postface of *Capital* that that work 'represents the proletariat', he explains, in the final analysis, that one should adopt the positions of the proletariat in order to comprehend capital" (Althusser 1977: 95).
10. Riazanov describes as follows the situation which Marx and Engels faced at the early 1870s, and the division of roles between them: "Behind Marx and Engels there was only a small group of people, who were acquainted with the *Communist Manifesto* and who understood fully all the teachings of Marx. The publication of *Capital* was in the beginning of very little help. For the vast majority it was in the full sense of the words a granite rock at which they most diligently nibbled; that was all. The writings of the German socialists during the first half of the seventies (...) show the deplorable state in which the study of Marxian theory was at that time. The pages of the central organ of the German party were often filled with the most grotesque mixture of various socialist systems. The method of Marx and Engels, (...) remained a sealed book. (...) Finally, Engels took upon himself the task of defending and disseminating the tenets of Marxism, while Marx, as we have seen, was vainly trying to complete his *Capital*" (Riazanov 1937, Chapter 9).
11. What Louis Althusser (1990: 144) noted for philosophy, applies for theoretical discourse in general: "In philosophy every space is always already occupied. Within it we can only hold a position against the adversary who already holds that position".

Bibliography

1. Works of Marx and Engels

1.1 In English

Marx, K. (internet), *The Poverty of Philosophy*, http://csf.colorado.edu/mirrors/ marxists.org/archive/marx/works/1847-Pov/index.htm.
Marx, K. (internet - Vol. 1), *Capital, Volume one*, http://csf.colorado.edu/mirrors/ marxists.org/archive/marx/works/1867-c1/index.htm.
Marx, K. (internet - Vol. 3), *Capital, Volume three*, http://csf.colorado.edu/ mirrors/marxists.org/archive/marx/works/1894-c3/index.htm.
Marx, K. (1971), *Theories of Surplus Value*, 3 Vols., Progress Publishers, Moscow.
Marx, K. (1981), *A Contribution to the Critique of Political Economy*, Lawrence and Wishart, London.
Marx, K. (1990), *Capital, Volume one*, Penguin Classics, London.
Marx, K. (1991), *Capital, Volume three*, Penguin Classics, London.
Marx, K. (1992), *Capital, Volume two*, Penguin Classics, London.
Marx, K. (1993), *Grundrisse*, Penguin Classics, London.
Marx, K. and F. Engels (1985), *The Communist Manifesto*, Penguin Classics, London.

1.2 In German

Marx, K. (1969), *Resultate des unmittelbaren Produktionsprozesses. Das Kapital. I. Buch. Der Produktionsprozess des Kapitals. VI. Kapitel*, Verlag Neue Kritik, Frankfurt/M.
Marx, K. (1974), *Grundrisse der Kritik der Politischen Ökonomie*, Dietz Verlag, Berlin.
Marx/Engels Gesamtausgabe (MEGA) (1976), *II, 1.1, "Das Kapital" und Vorarbeiten. Manuskripte 1857/1858, Teil 1*, Dietz Verlag, Berlin.
Marx/Engels Gesamtausgabe (MEGA) (1976-a), *II, 3.1, "Das Kapital" und Vorarbeiten, Manuskript 1861-1863. Teil 1*, Dietz Verlag, Berlin.
Marx/Engels Gesamtausgabe (MEGA) (1977), *II, 3.2, "Das Kapital" und Vorarbeiten, Manuskript 1861-1863. Teil 2*, Dietz Verlag, Berlin.

Marx/Engels Gesamtausgabe (MEGA) (1978), *II, 3.3, "Das Kapital" und Vorarbeiten, Manuskript 1861-1863. Teil 3*, Dietz Verlag, Berlin.
Marx/Engels Gesamtausgabe (MEGA) (1978-a), *II, 3.4, "Das Kapital" und Vorarbeiten, Manuskript 1861-1863. Teil 4*, Dietz Verlag, Berlin.
Marx/Engels Gesamtausgabe (MEGA) (1980), *II, 2, "Das Kapital" und Vorarbeiten, Manuskripte und Schriften 1858/1861*. Dietz Verlag, Berlin.
Marx/Engels Gesamtausgabe (MEGA) (1980-a), *II, 3.5, "Das Kapital" und Vorarbeiten, Manuskript 1861-1863. Teil 5*. Dietz Verlag, Berlin.
Marx/Engels Gesamtausgabe (MEGA) (1981), *II, 1.2, "Das Kapital" und Vorarbeiten, Manuskripte 1857/1858, Teil 2*, Dietz Verlag, Berlin.
Marx/Engels Gesamtausgabe (MEGA) (1982), *II, 3.6, "Das Kapital" und Vorarbeiten, Manuskript 1861-1863. Teil 6*, Dietz Verlag, Berlin.
Marx/Engels Gesamtausgabe (MEGA) (1983), *II, 5, "Das Kapital" und Vorarbeiten, Marx, Das Kapital, Erster Band, Hamburg 1867*, Dietz Verlag, Berlin.
Marx/Engels Gesamtausgabe (MEGA) (1988), *II, 4.1, "Das Kapital" und Vorarbeiten, Manuskripte 1863-1867. Teil 1*, Dietz Verlag, Berlin.
Marx/Engels Gesamtausgabe (MEGA) (1992), *II, 4.2, "Das Kapital" und Vorarbeiten, Manuskripte 1863-1867. Teil 2*, Dietz Verlag, Berlin.
Marx-Engels-Werke (MEW), 39 Vols. (1969-1977), Dietz Verlag, Berlin.

2. Works of Other Authors

Abalkin, L., Dzarasov, S., Kulikov, A. (1983), *Political Economy. A Short Course*, Progress Publishers, Moscow.
Althusser, L. (1974), *Philosophie et philosophie spontanée des savants*, Maspero, Paris.
Althusser, L. (1977), *Ideologie und ideologische Staatsapparate*, Argument, Hamburg.
Althusser, L. (1984), 'Reply to John Lewis', in: L. Althusser, *Essays on Ideology*, Verso, London/New York, pp. 61-139.
Althusser, L. (1984-a), 'Freud and Lacan', in: L. Althusser, *Essays on Ideology*, Verso, London/New York, pp. 147-171.
Althusser, L. (1990), *Philosophy and the Spontaneous Philosophy of the Scientists and other Essays*, Verso, London/New York.
Althusser, L. (1990-a), 'Contradiction and Overdetermination', in: L. Althusser *For Marx*, Verso, London/New York pp. 87-128.
Althusser, L. (1994), 'Marx dans ses limites', in: L. Althusser (ed. by F. Mathéron), *Écrits philosophiques et politiques*, v. I, Stock/Imec, Paris, pp. 359-524.
Althusser, L. and E. Balibar (1997), *Reading Capital*, Verso, London/New York.

Altvater, E. (1975), 'Wertgesetz und Monopolmacht', in *Das Argument* AS 6, Theorie des Monopols, Argument, Hamburg, pp. 129-198.
Altvater, E., R. Hecker, M. Heinrich, P. Schaper-Rinkel (1999), *Kapital.doc*, Westfälisches Damfboot, Münster.
Arthur, C. J. (1993), 'Hegel's *Logic* and Marx's *Capital*', in F. Moseley (ed.), *Marx's Method in Capital*, New Jersey: Humanities Press, pp. 53-87.
Arthur, C. J. (1998), 'The Fluidity of Capital and the Logic of the Concept', in: C. J. Arthur and G. Reuten, (eds.), *The Circulation of Capital. Essays on Volume Two of Marx's* Capital, Macmillan, London, pp. 95-128.
Bailey, S. (1825), *A Critical Dissertation on the Nature, Measures, and Causes of Value*, R. Hunter, London.
Balibar, E. (1976), 'Sulla dialettica storica. Note critiche su *Leggere il Capitale*', in E. Balibar, *Cinque studi di materialismo storico*, De Donato, Bari, pp. 207-250.
Balibar, E. (1988), 'De la lutte des classes a la lutte sans classes?', in Balibar, E. and Wallerstein I. (1988) *Race, nation, classe. Les identités ambigües*, La Découverte, Paris, pp. 207-246.
Balibar, E. (1993), *La philosophie de Marx*, La Découverte, Paris.
Balibar, E. (1994), *Lieux et noms de la vérité*, L'Aube, Paris.
Balibar, E. (1997), *La crainte des masses. Politique et philosophie avant et après Marx*, Galilée, Paris.
Baran, P. A. and P. M. Sweezy (1973), *Monopoly Capital*, Penguin, Harmondsworth.
Beiträge zur Marx-Engels-Forschung Neue Folge. Sonderband 1 (1997), *David Borisovic Rjazanov und die erste MEGA*, Argument, Berlin.
Bensch, H.-G. (2000), 'Zur Grundrente. Von Marxschen Anweisungen und Engelsschen Umsetzungen', in *Beiträge zur Marx-Engels-Forschung. Neue Folge* 1999, pp. 212-219.
Bensussan, G. (1985), 'Crises du marxisme', in G. Labica and G. Bensussan (eds.), *Dictionnaire critique du marxisme*, P.U.F., Paris, pp. 259-270.
Bentham, J. (1931), *The Theory of Legislation*, Kegan Paul, Trench, Trubner and Co., London.
Bentham, J. (1948), *The Principles of Morals and Legislation*, Hafner Press, New York.
Berlin, I. (1978), *Russian Thinkers*, Penguin, London.
Bettelheim, Ch. (1974), *Les luttes de classes en URSS. Première période, 1917-1923*, Maspero/Seuil, Paris.
Brewer, A. (1980), *Marxist Theories of Imperialism. A Critical Survey*, Routledge and Kegan Paul, London.
Bucharin, N. (1970), *Der Imperialismus und die Akkumulation des Kapitals*, CARO-Druck, Heidelberg.
Bullock, P. and D. Yaffe, (1975), 'Inflation, Crisis and the Post-War Boom', *Revolutionary Communist*, 3-4, pp. 5-45.

Callinicos, A. (1987), *The Revolutionary Ideas of Marx*, Bookmarks, London.
Carchedi, G. (1977), *On the Economic Identification of Social Classes*, Routledge and Kegan Paul, London.
Catefores, G. (1989), *Introduction to Marxist Economics*, Macmillan, New York.
Clarke, S. (1994), *Marx's Theory of Crisis*, Macmillan, London.
Cole, G. D. H. (1930), 'Introduction', in: K. Marx, *Capital*, Everyman edition, London, pp. i-xxix.
Cullenberg, S. (1997), *The Falling Rate of Profit. Recasting the Marxian Debate*, Pluto Press, London.
Dimoulis, D. (1994), 'Polity, Politics, Class-Politics. Notes and Questions', *Thesseis*, No. 46, pp. 33-62 [in Greek].
Dimoulis, D. (1996), *Die Begnadigung in vergleichender Perspektive. Rechtsphilosophische, verfassungs- und strafrechtliche Probleme*, Duncker and Humblot, Berlin.
Dobb, M. (1968), *Political Economy and Capitalism. Some Essays in Economic Tradition*, Routledge and Kegan Paul, London.
Dobb, M. (1973), *Theories of Value and Distribution Since Adam Smith; Ideology and Economic Theory*, Cambridge University Press, Cambridge.
Dokumente zur Imperialismus-theorie Nr. II (1971) (with texts by De Vries, Herzenstein, Grossmann, Goldstein, Tolonski-Novitzki-Jacobsohn, Varga, Benedict), CARO-Druck, Heidelberg.
Duménil, G. (1978), *Le concept de loi économique dans le Capital*, Maspero, Paris.
Duménil, G. (1980), *De la valeur aux prix de production. Une réinterprétation de la transformation*, Economica, Paris.
Elson, D. (1979), 'The Value Theory of Labour', in: D. Elson (ed.), *Value. The Representation of Labour in Capitalism*, CSE Books, London.
Emsley, S. (1998), *Renewing the case of Marx's Concept of Absolute Rent: Towards an Historical Interpretation*, in *The 1999 Value Theory Mini-Conference: Deepening The Dialogues*, 1999, http://www.greenwich.ac.uk/~fa03/iwgvt/1999/sessions.html.
Engelskirchen, H. (2001), 'Value and contract formation', *The 2001 Value Theory Mini-Conference: Value and the World Economy*, http://www.greenwich.ac.uk/~fa03/iwgvt/2001.html.
Fine, B. (1989), *Marx's Capital*, Macmillan, London.
Fine, B. and L. Harris (1979), *Rereading Capital*, Columbia University Press, New York.
Foley, D. (1982), 'The Value of Money, the Value of Labour Power and the Marxian Transformation Problem', *Review of Radical Political Economics*, 14 (2), pp. 37-47.
Foley, D. K. (1999), 'Response to David Laibman', in P. Zarembka, (ed.) (1999), pp. 229-233.

Foley, D. K. (2000), 'Recent Developments in the Labour Theory of Value', *Review of Radical Political Economics*, 32 (1), pp. 1-39.

Freeman, A. (1999), The Limits of Ricardian Value: Law, Contingency And Motion In *Economics*, paper to *1999 IWGVT mini-conference*, http://www.greenwich.ac.uk/~fa03/iwgvt/1999/sessions.html.

Gasgupta, A. K. (1996), *Ghandi's Economic Thought*, Routledge, London.

Giussani, P. (1999), *Orthodoxy in Marxian Price Theory*, Memo.

Godelier, M. (1977), 'Économie marchande, fétichisme, magie et science selon Marx dans *Le Capital*', in M. Godelier, *Horizon, trajets marxistes en anthropologie*, v. II, Maspero, Paris, pp. 201-224.

Goux, J.-J. (1975), *Freud, Marx. Ökonomie und Symbolik*, Ullstein, Frankfurt/M.

Gramsci, A. (1977), *Quaderni del carcere*, Einaudi, Torino.

Grossmann, H. (1971), *Aufsätze zur Krisentheorie*, Verlag Neue Kritik, Frankfurt/M.

Grossman, H. (2000), 'The Theory of Economic Crisis', in P. Zarembka (ed.) (2000), pp. 171-180.

Harvey, D. (1982), *Limits to Capital*, Basil Blackwell, Oxford.

Hauck, G. (1992), *Einführung in die Ideologiekritik*, Argument, Hamburg.

Haug, W. F. (1993), *Elemente einer Theorie des Ideologischen*, Argument, Hamburg.

Hecker, R. (1998), 'Internationale Marx/Engels-Forschung und Edition', *Z. Zeitschrift marxistische Erneuerung*, No. 33, pp. 8-25.

Hedeler, W. (2000), 'Nikolai Bucharins Studie über die Akkumulation des Kapitals –1914/1925', Memo, Berlin.

Heinrich, M. (1986), 'Hegel, die *Grundrisse* und das *Kapital*. Ein Nachtrag zur Diskussion um das Kapital in den 70er Jahren', in *Prokla*, No. 65, pp. 145-160.

Heinrich, M. (1989), '"Capital in General" and the Structure of Marx's "Capital"', *Capital and Class*, No. 38, pp. 63-79.

Heinrich, M. (1995), 'Gibt es eine Marxsche Krisentheorie? Die Entwicklung der Semantik der 'Krise' in Marx' Entwürfen einer Kritik der politischen Ökonomie', *Beiträge zur Marx-Engels-Forschung, Neue Folge 1995*, pp. 130-150.

Heinrich, M. (1996-1997), 'Engels' Edition of the Third Volume of *Capital* and Marx's Original Manuscript', *Science and Society*, Vol. 60, No. 4, pp. 452-466.

Heinrich, M. (1999), *Die Wissenschaft vom Wert*, Überarbeitete und erweiterte Neuauflage, Westfälisches Dampfboot, Münster.

Heller, H. (1934), *Staatslehre*, Sijthoff, Leiden.

Hilferding, R. (1981), *Finance Capital*, Routledge, London.

Howard, M. C. and J. E. King (1985), *The Political Economy of Marx*, New York University Press, New York.

Iacono, A. (1992), *Le fétichisme. Histoire d'un concept*, P.U.F., Paris.

Ioakimoglou, E. and J. Milios (1993), 'Capital Accumulation and Over-Accumulation Crisis: The Case of Greece (1960-1989)', *Review of Radical Political Economics*, Vol. 25, No. 2, pp. 81-107.
Itoh, M. (1980), *Value and Crisis*, Pluto Press, London.
Jensen, S. (1994), 'Im Kerngehäuse', in G. Rusch and S. Schmidt (eds.), *Konstruktivismus und Sozialtheorie*, Suhrkamp, Frankfurt/M., pp. 47-69.
Jevons, S. (1866), 'Brief Account of a General Mathematical Theory of Political Economy', [Read in Section F of the British Association, 1862], *Journal of the Royal Statistical Society*, London, XXIX (June), pp. 282-287, in http:/socserv2.socsci.mcmaster.ca/~econ/ugcm/3113/index.html.
Jungnickel, J. (1991), 'Bemerkungen zu den von Engels vorgenommenen Veränderungen am Marxschen Manuskript zum dritten Band des *Kapitals*', *Beiträge zur Marx-Engels-Forschung Neue Folge 1991*, pp. 130-138.
Kalecki, M. (1969), *Theory of Economic Dynamics*, Kelley, New York.
Keynes, J. M. (1993), *The General Theory of Employment Interest and Money*
Kindleberger, Ch. P. (1993), *A Financial History of Western Europe. Second Edition*, Oxford University Press, Oxford.
Klein, D. et al. (1988), *Politische Ökonomie des Kapitalismus*, Dietz, Berlin.
Kliman, A. (1996), 'A value-theoretic critique of the Okishio theorem', in A. Freeman and G. Carchedi (eds.), *Marx and Non-equilibrium Economics*, Edward Elgar, Cheltenham, pp. 206-224.
Kliman, A. (1999), 'Physical quantities, value, and dynamics', in: *The 1999 Value Theory Mini-Conference: Deepening The Dialogues*, http://www.greenwich.ac.uk/~fa03/iwgvt/1999/sessions.html.
Kuhn, R. (2000), 'Preface to the Theory of Economic Crises by H. Grossman', in Zarembka, P. (ed.) (2000), pp. 171-180.
Labica, G. (1985), 'Fétichisme (de la marchandise)', in G. Labica and G. Bensussan (eds.), *Dictionnaire critique du marxisme*, P.U.F., Paris, pp. 464-466.
Laibman, D. (1997), *Capitalist Macrodynamics*, Macmillan, London.
Laibman, D. (1999), 'Okishio and its Critics: Historical cost versus replacement cost', in P. Zarembka, (ed.) (1999), pp. 207-33.
Lapavitsas, C. (1994), 'The Banking School and the monetary thought of Karl Marx', *Cambridge Journal of Economics*, v. 18, pp. 447-461.
La Torre, M. (1999), 'Diritto e potere nella tradizione marxista: un bilancio', *Rivista internazionale di filosofia del diritto*, 76, pp. 387-416.
Lenin V. I. (1977), *Collected Works*, Vols. 1-3, Lawrence and Wishart, London.
Lenin V. I. (1986), *The Agrarian Question and the "Critics of Marx"*, Progress, Moscow.
Lenin, W. I. - internet, 'Three Sources and Three Component parts of Marxism', http://csf.colorado.edu/mirror/marxists.org/archive/lenin/index.htm.
Levine, D. P. (1985), 'What can we do with Money?', *Cahiers d'Économie Politique*, No. 10/11, pp. 115-130.

Lipietz, A. (1985), 'Crise', in G. Labica and G. Bensussan (eds.), *Dictionnaire critique du marxisme*, P.U.F., Paris, pp. 254-259.
Lukács, G. (1988), *Geschichte und Klassenbewußtsein. Studien über marxistische Dialektik*, Luchterhandt, Darmstadt.
Luxemburg, R. (1966), *Die Akkumulation des Kapitals*, Verlag Neue Kritik, Frankfurt/M.
Luxemburg, R. (1971), *The Accumulation of Capital*, Routledge and Kegan Paul, London.
Luxemburg, R. and N. Bukharin (1972), *Imperialism and the Accumulation of Capital*, Allen Lane, The Penguin Press, London.
Mandel, E. (1995), *Long Waves of Capitalist Development*, Verso, London.
Maniatis, T. and Ph. A. O'Hara (1999), 'Commodity Fetishism', in Ph. A. O'Hara (ed.) *Encyclopedia of Political Economy*, Routledge, London, pp. 116-118.
Matsumoto, A. (2001), 'The de facto standard of price and the cost price of gold: estimating the depreciation rate of the Dollar', *The 2001 Value Theory Mini-Conference*, http://www.greenwich.ac.uk/~fa03/iwgvt/2001/sessions.html.
Mattick, P. (1969), *Marx and Keynes*, Porter Sargent Publisher, Boston.
Meek, R. L. (1973), *Studies in the Labour Theory of Value*, Lawrence and Wishart, London.
Meikle, S. (1995), *Aristotle's Economic Thought*, Clarendon Press, Oxford.
Milios, J. (1988), *Kapitalistische Entwicklung, Nationalstaat und Imperialismus*, Kritiki, Athens.
Milios, J. (1989), 'The Problem of Capitalist Development: Theoretical Considerations in View of the Industrial Countries and the New Industrial Countries', in Gottdiener M and N. Komninos (eds.), *Capitalist Development and Crisis Theory*, Macmillan, London.
Milios, J. (1995), 'Marxist Theory and Marxism as a Mass Ideology. The Effects of the Collapse of "Real Existing Socialism" and on West European Marxism', *Rethinking Marxism*, Vol. 8, No. 4, pp. 61-74.
Milios, J. (1999), 'Colonialism and Imperialism: Classic Texts', in Ph. A. O'Hara (ed.), *Encyclopedia of Political Economy*, Routledge, London, pp. 113-116.
Milios, J. (1999-a), 'Preindustrial Capitalist Forms: Lenin's Contribution to a Marxist Theory of Economic Development', *Rethinking Marxism*, Vol. 11, No. 4, pp. 38-56.
Milios, J. (2000), 'Social Classes in Classical and Marxist Political Economy', *The American Journal of Economics and Sociology*, Vol. 59, No. 3, pp. 283-302.
Milios, J. (2001), 'Rudolf Hilferding', Encyclopedia of International Economics, Routledge Publishers, in print.
Mollo, M. L. R. (1999), 'The Endogeneity of Money. Post-Keynesian and Marxian Concepts Compared', in P. Zarembka, (ed.) (1999), pp. 3-26.

Moseley, F. (1993), 'Marx's Logical Method and the "Transformation Problem"', in F. Moseley (ed.), *Marx's Method in Capital: A Reexamination*, Humanities Press, New Jersey, pp. 157-183.
Moseley, F. (1995), 'Capital in General and Marx's Logical Method: A Response to Heinrich's Critique', *Capital and Class*, No. 56, pp. 15-48.
Moseley, F. (1997), 'The Development of Marx's Theory of The Distribution of Surplus-Value', in *New Perspectives on Marx's Method in Capital*, F. Moseley and M. Cambell (eds.), Humanities Press, New Jersey http://home.mtholyoke.edu/~fmoseley/index.htm#papers.
Moseley, F. (2000), 'The "New Solution" to the Transformation Problem: A Sympathetic Critique', *Review of Radical Political Economics*, Vol. 32, No. 2, pp. 282-316.
Moszkowska, N. (1935), *Zur Kritik moderner Krisentheorien*, Paul Kacha Verlag, Prag.
Müller, J. Ch./Reinfeldt, S./Schwarz, R./Tuckfeld, M. (1994), *Der Staat in den Köpfen. Anschlüße an L. Althusser und N. Poulantzas*, Decaton, Mainz.
Müller-Tuckfeld, J. Ch. (1994), 'Gesetz ist Gesetz. Anmerkungen zu einer Theorie der juridischen Anrufung', in H. Böke, J. Ch. Müller and S. Reinfeldt (eds.), *Denk-Prozesse nach Althusser*, Argument, Hamburg, pp. 182-205.
Müller-Tuckfeld, J. Ch. (1997), 'Wahrheitspolitik. Anmerkungen zum Verhältnis von Kontingenz und Kritik in der kritischen Kriminologie', in D. Frehsee, G. Löschper and G. Smaus (eds.), *Konstruktion der Wirklichkeit durch Kriminalität und Strafe*, Nomos, Baden-Baden, pp. 458-493.
Murray, P. (2000), 'Marx's "Truly Social" Labour Theory of Value: Abstract Labour in Marxian Value Theory', Part I, *Historical Materialism*, No. 6, in print.
Murray, P. (2001), 'Marx's "Truly Social" Labour Theory of Value: Abstract Labour in Marxian Value Theory', Part II, *Historical Materialism*, No. 7, in print.
Naves, M. B. (2000), *Marxismo e direito. Um estudo sobre Pachukanis*, Boitempo, São Paulo.
Norrie, A. (1982), 'Pashukanis and the "Commodity Form Theory": a Reply to Warrington', *International Journal of the Sociology of Law*, 10, pp. 419-437.
Norton, B. (1992), 'Radical Theories of Accumulation and Crisis: Developments and Directions', in B. Roberts and S. Feiner (eds.), *Radical Economics*, Kluwer Academic Publishers, Boston, pp. 155-193.
O'Hara, Ph. A. (1999), 'Circuit of social capital', in Ph. A. O'Hara (ed.) *Encyclopedia of Political Economy*, Routledge, London, pp. 84-87.
Okishio, N. (1961), 'Technical Changes and the Rate of Profit', *Kobe University Economic Review* 7, pp. 86-99.
Pareto, V. (1921), 'Introduction to Karl Marx's *Capital*', in *Karl Marx: Capital. A Summary by Paul Lafargue*, Eleftheroudakis, Athens (in Greek), pp. xi-xcvii.

Pareto, V. (1971), *Manual of Political Economy*, Schwier and A. Page, London.
Paschukanis, E. (1929), *Allgemeine Rechtslehre und Marxismus*, Verlag für Literatur und Politik, Wien/Berlin.
Projekt-Ideologie-Theorie (1986), *Theorien über Ideologie*, Argument, Berlin.
Poulantzas, N. (1973), *Political Power and Social Classes*, New Left Books and Seed and Ward, London.
Poulantzas, N. (1973-a), 'On Social Classes', *New Left Review*, No. 78, pp. 27-54.
Ramos-Martínez, A. (2001), 'Preface to the Studies on the Theory and the History of Business Crises in England, Part I: Theory and History of Crises by Tugan-Baranowsky', in Zarembka, P. (ed.) (2000), pp. 43-51.
Ramos-Martínez, A. and A. Rodriguez-Herrera (1996), 'The transformation of values into prices of production: a different reading of Marx's text', in A. Freeman and M. Carchedi (eds.), *Marx and Non-equilibrium Economics*, Edward Elgar, Cheltenham, pp. 49-76.
Rancière, J. (1972), *Der Begriff der Kritik und die Kritik der politischen Ökonomie*, Merve Verlag, Berlin.
Renault, E. (1995), *Marx et l'idée de critique*, P.U.F., Paris.
Resnick, S. and R. Wolff, (1978), 'Marxian Crisis Theory: Structure and Implications', *Review of Radical Political Economics*, Vol. 10, No. 1, pp. 47-57.
Resnick, S. and R. Wolff, (1982), 'Classes in Marxian Theory', *Review of Radical Political Economics*, 13, 4, pp. 1-18.
Reuten, G. (1993), 'The Difficult Labour of a Social Theory of Value', in F. Moseley (ed.), *Marx's Method in Capital*, Humanities Press, New Jersey, pp. 89-113.
Rey, P.-Ph. (1973), *Les alliances de classes*, Maspero, Paris.
Riazanov, D. (1937) *Karl Marx and Frederick Engels. An Introduction to their Lives and Work*, http://www.marx.org/Riazanov.
Ricardo, D. (1810), *On the High Price of Bullion*, http:/socserv2.socsci.mcmaster.ca/~econ/ugcm/3113/index.html.
Ricardo, D. (1992), *The Principles of Political Economy and Taxation*, J. M. Dent and Sons, London.
Robinson, J. (1964), *Economic Philosophy*, Penguin, London.
Robinson, J. (1966), *An Essay on Marxian Economics*, Macmillan, London.
Roll, E. (1989), *A History of Economic Thought*, faber and faber, London.
Rosdolsky, R. (1969), *Zur Entstehungsgeschichte des Marxschen 'Kapital'*, EVA, Frankfurt/M.
Rosdolsky, R. (1977), *The Making of Marx's Capital*, Pluto Press, London.
Rubin I. I. (1972), *Essays on Marx's Theory of Value*, Black and Red, Detroit.
Rubin, I. I. (1978), 'Abstract Labour and Value in Marx's System', *Capital and Class*, No. 5, pp. 109-139.
Rubin I. I. (1989), *A History of Economic Thought*, Pluto Press, London.

Sabadell, A. L. (1999), 'Dalla "donna onesta" alla piena cittadinaza delle donne', *Dei delitti e delle pene*, 1-2, pp. 167-203.
Samuelson, P. (1970), *Economics*, McGraw-Hill, New York.
Say, J. B. (1821), *Letters to Thomas Robert Malthus on Political Economy and Stagnation of Commerce*, translated, London, http://digital.library.upenn.edu/webbin/book/search?author=Say.
Schoer, K. (1976), 'Natalie Moszkowska and the Falling Rate of Profit', *New Left Review*, No. 95, pp. 92-96.
Schumpeter, J. (1952), *Capitalism, Socialism and Democracy*, Allen and Unwin, London.
Schumpeter, J. (1954), *Economic Doctrine and Method. An Historical Sketch*, Allen and Unwin, London.
Schumpeter, J. A. (1994), *History of Economic Analysis*, Routledge, London.
Sismondi, S. de (1815), *Political Economy*, http://socserv2.socsci.mcmaster.ca/~econ/ugcm/3113/sismondi/poliec.
Smith, A. (1981), *An Inquiry into the Nature and Causes of the Wealth of Nations*, 2 vols., Liberty Classics, Indianapolis.
Sohn-Rethel, A. (1990), *Geistige und körperliche Arbeit. Zur Theorie der gesellschaftlichen Synthesis*, Suhrkamp, Frankfurt/M.
Sraffa, P. (1960), *The Production of Commodities by Means of Commodities*, Cambridge University Press, Cambridge.
Stamatis, G. (1977), *Die 'spezifisch kapitalistischen' Produktionsmethoden und der tendenzielle Fall der Profitrate bei Karl Marx*, Berlin.
Stamatis, G. (1984), *Sraffa und sein Verhältnis zu Ricardo und Marx*, Göttinger Beiträge zur Gesellschaftstheorie, Göttingen.
Ste. Croix, G. E. M., de (1984), 'Class in Marx's Conception of History, Ancient and Modern', *New Left Review*, No. 146, pp. 92-111.
Steedman, I. (1975), 'Positive profits with negative surplus value', *The Economic Journal*, Vol. 85, pp. 114-123.
Steedman, I. (1977), *Marx after Sraffa*, New Left Books and Verso, London.
Steedman, I. (1981), *The Value Controversy*, New Left Books and Verso, London.
Sternberg, F. (1971), *Der Imperialismus*, Neue Kritik, Frankfurt/M.
Sweezy, P. M. (1970), *The Theory of Capitalist Development*, Modern Reader, New York.
Tsuru, S. (1951), 'Marx's theory of the falling tendency in the rate of profit', *The Economic Review*, July, pp. 190-199.
Tuckfeld, M. (1997), *Orte des Politischen. Politik, Hegemonie und Ideologie im Marxismus*, Deutscher Universitätsverlag, Wiesbaden.
Tugan-Baranowsky, M. v. (1969), *Studien zur Theorie und Geschichte der Handelskrisen in England*, Scientia Verlag, Aalen.
Tugan-Baranowsky, M. v. (2000), 'Studies on the Theory and the History of Business Crises in England, Part I: Theory and History of Crises', in Zarembka, P. (ed.) (2000), pp. 53-110.

Bibliography 225

Varga, E. (1974), *Die Krise des Kapitalismus und ihre politischen Folgen*, EVA, Frankfurt/M.
Vergopoulos, K. (1975), *The Agrarian Question in Greece - The Social Incorporation of Agriculture*, Exantas, Athens [in Greek].
Vergopoulos, K. (no publication date), 'Deformed Capitalism - The Development of Agriculture in the Modern World', in K. Vergopoulos and S. Amin, *Capitalism and the Agrarian Question: Deformed Capitalism*, Papazisis, Athens [in Greek], pp. 15-241.
Wallerstein, I. (1988), 'Conflits sociaux en Afrique noire indépendante: réexamen des concepts de race et de "status-group"', in E. Balibar and I. Wallerstein, *Race, nation, classe. Les identités ambigües*, La Découverte, Paris, pp. 249-271.
Williams, M. (1998), 'Why Marx neither has nor needs a Commodity Theory of Money', http://www.mk.dmu.ac.uk/~mwilliam.
Wolff, R., A. Callari and B. Roberts (1984), 'A Marxian Alternative to the "Transformation Problem"', *Review of Radical Political Economics*, 16 (2-3), pp. 115-135.
Yaffe, D. (1973), 'The Marxian Theory of Crisis, Capital and the State', *Economy and Society*, Vol. II, No. 2, pp. 186-231.
Zarembka, P. (ed.) (1999), *Research in Political Economy. Vol. 17: Economic Theory of Capitalism and its Crises*, Jai Press, New York.
Zarembka, P. (ed.) (2000), *Research in Political Economy Volume 18. Value, Capitalist Dynamics and Money*, Jai Press, New York.

Index

Abalkin, L. et al 114
abstract labour 17-21, 33n, 77, 105n
Althusser, L. 80-1, 83-5, 86-9, 98, 101-2, 104n, 106n, 107n, 108n, 189n, 191, 203n, 211, 214n
Althusser, L. and Balibar, E. 191
Altvater, E. 25, 116
Aristotle 31n, 32n, 39, 41, 58n
Arthur, C. J. 59n, 60n, 200, 208

Bailey, S. 15-6, 31n, 32n
Balibar, E. 11n, 67, 79, 81-3, 86, 92-3, 98, 99-100, 103, 104n, 106n, 107n, 108n
Baran and Sweezy 175, 188n
barter 23, 28-9
Bauer, O. 160, 170, 175, 188n
Bensch, H.-G. 139
Bentham, J. 12n
Bensussan, G. 209
Berlin, I. 184n
Bettelheim, C. 59n
Bortkiewicz, L. v. 119, 121-2
Brewer, A. 114
Bukharin, N. 148, 160, 175-9, 188n, 189n, 200
Bulgakov, S. 170, 172-3
Bullock, P. and Yaffe, D. 157n

Callinicos, A. 157n
Carchedi, G. 11n
Catefores, G. 59n
cost efficiency 150-6
Clarke, S. 160
class struggle 4-7, 176-9, 199-202
competition 111-7, 207, 212n
composition of capital

value (organic) 145-6, 148-9, 194-9, 157n
technical 145-6, 151
credit 50-56, 91-2, 173, 183
crises 36, 148-9, 158-89, 190-2, 196, 199-202, 203n, 204n, 205n
Cullenberg, S. 157n

Danielson, N. 163-5, 184n, 185n
Dobb, M. 59n, 149
Duménil, G. 130n, 191

Elson, D. 59n
Emsley, S. 139
Engels, F. 59n, 158, 183n, 185n, 186n, 205n, 208-10, 212n, 213n
Engelskirchen, H. 53, 78

fetishism 67-108
Fine, B. 205n
Fine, B. and Harris, L. 201-2, 205n
Foley, D. 130n, 154, 157n
forms of appearance viii, 21-3, 27-9, 36, 42, 113, 119, 122, 128
Freeman, A. 130n, 154
Freud, S. 69, 104n

Giussani, P. 63n
Godelier, M. 88, 92, 107n, 108n
Gandhi, M. 185n
Goux, J.-J. 93, 104n, 195n
Gramsci, A. 30n, 85-6, 101, 107n
Grossmann, H. 148-9, 154, 156n, 157n, 186n, 187n, 188n, 211n

Harvey, D. 138
Hauck, G. 108n

Haug, W. F. 102, 108n
Hecker, R. 58, 59n, 209
Heinrich, M. 21-2, 45, 63n, 92, 123-6, 153-4, 205n, 208, 211n, 212n
Heller, H. 105n
Hilferding, R. 111, 114, 129n, 160, 170, 173, 175, 177, 205n, 214n
hoarding 37, 49-52
Howard, M. C. and King J. E. 20, 59n
Hume, D. 45, 60n

Iacono, A. 69, 70, 93, 104n, 107n, 108n
ideological state apparatuses 97-9
ideology 6, 99-104, 209-11
interest 51-2
Itoh, M. 201

Jensen, S. 108n
Jevons, W.S. 12n, 184n
Jungnickel, J. 205n

Kalecki, M. 118
Kautsky, K. 114, 166-7, 171, 175, 186n
Keynes 47, 51, 58n, 184n, 187n
Kindleberger, C. P. 53
Kliman, A. 154
Kuhn, R. 157n

La Torre, M. 105n
Labica, G. 90, 107n
landowners 132-3, 136, 138-9, 140n, 141n
Laibman, D. 154, 157n
Lapavitsas, K. 59n
Lenin, W. I. 30n, 82, 135, 141n, 160, 170-1, 184n, 185n, 186n, 187n
Levine D. P. 59n
Lipietz, A. 180
Lukács, G. 71-75, 80-1, 87, 93, 98, 101, 104n, 105n
Luxemburg, R. 160, 171, 173-4, 176, 185n, 187n, 188n, 213n

Malthus, T. R. 161-2, 184n, 186n
Mandel, E. 149, 203n
Maniatis, T. 87
Matsumoto, A. 63n

Mattick, P. 107n, 108n
Meek, R. L. 59n
Meikle, S. 31n, 32n, 34n, 58n
mode of production 5, 7, 12n, 98-100, 191-2
    capitalist 5, 6, 18-21, 40, 88-9, 95, 98-100, 131-2, 146, 204n
Mollo, M.L.R. 47, 63n
money 17, 26-30, 36-40, 52-6
money as capital 38-43, 52-6, 57n, 58n
money, quantity theory 44-50
monopoly (accidental, artificial, natural) 116-7, 129n
monopoly of landownership 132-3, 136, 138-9
Moseley, F. 63n, 130n, 211n, 212n
Moszkowska, N. 148-9, 160, 171, 175, 188n
Müller, J. et al 108n
Müller-Tuckfeld, J. Ch. 76, 96-7, 105
Murray, P. 18, 33n, 59n

Narodniks 162-6, 173, 184n, 185n
Naves, M. B. 106n
neoclassical theory 13, 37, 127, 183n, 184n
neoricardian theory 124-8, 130n
Norrie, A., 106n
Norton, B. 205n

O'Hara, P. A. 41, 87, 205n
Okishio, N. 150, 152-5
overaccumulation 158-9, 176, 179, 182-3, 190, 195, 199, 200, 205n

Pareto, V. 16, 31n, 32n, 33n, 35n
Pashukanis, E. 75-81, 99, 105n, 106n
Poulantzas, N. 5, 7, 11n, 12n, 214n
production price 29, 112-7, 127-8, 212n
profit
    average 112-29, 128n, 129n
    extra 114-7
profit rate 114, 146, 190, 192-9
    falling tendency 145-57

Ramos, A. 187n
Ramos, A. and Rodriguez, A. 63n, 130n

Rancière, J. 87, 94, 107n, 108n
Renault, E. 107n
rent 92, 131-140, 207
  absolute 131, 136-40
  differential 131, 133-6, 140
Resnick, S. and Wolff, R. 11n, 201, 205n
Reuten, G. 88
Rey, P.-Ph. 132
Riazanov, D. 185n, 213n, 214n
Ricardo, D. 8, 10, 11n, 14-6, 30n, 31n, 35n, 46-7, 61n, 113, 131, 133-6, 138, 140, 183n, 206-11
Robinson, J. 31n, 118
Rosdolsky, R. 20, 33n, 34n, 75, 171, 185n
Rubin, I.I. 14, 29, 30, 90, 183n, 213n

Sabadell, A. L. 105n
Samuelson, P. 31n, 125
Say's law 36, 161, 183n
Schoer, K. 188n
Schumpeter, J. A., 15
simple commodity production 36-7, 47-8
Sismondi, S. 161-2, 164-5
Smith, A. 11n, 14-5, 29, 30n, 31n, 32n, 34n, 35n, 44, 46, 53, 55-6, 57n, 60n, 61n, 62n, 63n, 64n, 131, 134-5, 140, 141n
social capital 111-3, 207
  circuit of 50-1, 117, 130n
  reproduction of 117-9
Sohn-Rethel, A. 105n
Sraffa, P. 30, 123-6
Stamatis, G. 146, 155
Ste-Croix, G.E.M. 11n
Steedman, I. 125-6

Sternberg, F. 173-4, 187n, 188n
Struve, P. 165, 186n
surplus value vii, 40-43, 145-52
Sweezy, P. 59n, 141n, 188n

Tooke, T. 47-8
Tsuru, S. 157n
Tuckfeld, M. 106n, 107n, 108n
Tugan-Baranowsky, M. 126, 150-2, 154, 156n, 160, 167-71, 176-9, 182-3, 186n, 187n, 188n, 214n

underconsumption 159-73, 179, 182, 187n, 188n, 201

value vii, 9, 10
  Classical viii, 8, 9, 13-6, 37, 55-6, 119-20, 127-8
  Marxian viii, 10, 17-21, 206-11
  of exchange 15-7
  transformation into production prices 119-27, 130n, 206, 209, 212n, 213n
value form 23-30
Varga, E. 116
Vergopoulos, K. 138-9
Vorontsov, V. 163-5, 185n

Wallerstein, I. 11n
Williams, M. 63n
Wolff, R. et al 130n

Yaffe, D. 157n

Zarembka, P. 154